Understanding Children's Books

Understanding Children's Books

A Guide for Education Professionals

Prue Goodwin

Los Angeles • London • New Delhi • Singapore

First published 2008

SAGE Publications Ltd
1 Oliver's Yard
55 City Road
London EC1Y 1SP

SAGE Publications Inc.
2455 Teller Road
Thousand Oaks, California 91320

SAGE Publications India Pvt Ltd
B 1/I 1 Mohan Cooperative Industrial Area
Mathura Road
New Delhi 110 044

SAGE Publications Asia-Pacific Pte Ltd
33 Pekin Street #02–01
Far East Square
Singapore 048763

Library of Congress Control Number: 2007942662

British Library Cataloguing in Publication data

A catalogue record for this book is available from the British Library

ISBN 978–1–84787–031–5
ISBN 978–1–84787–032–2 (pbk)

Typeset by Dorwyn, Wells, Somerset
Printed in Great Britain by the Cromwell Press, Trowbridge, Wiltshire
Printed on paper from sustainable resources

For Bill and all the children, students and colleagues with whom I have ever shared children's books.

Contents

About the Author

Prue Goodwin is a freelance lecturer in literacy and children's books and works part-time with trainee teachers at the University of Reading. In 2005, Prue edited the second edition of *The Literate Classroom*, a collection of articles by leading teacher educators published by David Fulton. *The Articulate Classroom*, on speaking and listening, was published in 2001 and *Literacy through Creativity* in 2004. Prue regularly returns to the classroom to introduce children to a range of literature and to encourage wide, voracious reading.

About the Contributors

Liz Attenborough manages 'Talk to Your Baby', the early language campaign of the National Literacy Trust, encouraging parents and carers to talk more to children from birth to 3. Liz was a children's book publisher for 24 years, including 12 years as Publisher of Puffin Books. From January 1998 to September 1999 she was Director of the National Year of Reading, a government campaign to encourage reading for pleasure across the community. The following year she studied for an MA in Child Studies at King's College, London.

Nikki Gamble is an education consultant specializing in children's literature, drama and arts education. She is Director of Write Away, an organization that seeks to promote literature and the arts in education. Nikki was formerly a primary and secondary school teacher and subsequently taught students on primary teacher training programmes. She continues to work with children, young people, teachers and families in both formal and informal educational contexts. Recent publications include *Family Fictions* (2001), with Nick Tucker, *Exploring Children's Literature* (2008) (2nd edition forthcoming, Paul Chapman Publishing), with Sally Yates and *Guiding Reading* (2006) (2nd edition), with Angela Hobsbaum and David Reedy.

Dr Mel Gibson has run training and promotional events about comics, picturebooks, manga and graphic novels for libraries, schools and other organizations since 1993 when she contributed to *Graphic Account* on developing graphic novels collections for 16–25-year-olds, published by the Youth Libraries Group (YLG). She is also a Senior Lecturer at the University of Northumbria. Her doctoral thesis was on British women's memories of their girlhood comics reading. She is a National Teaching Fellow and is also Carnegie and Kate Greenaway Award judge for Northern YLG. She teaches modules in both 'Children's Literature in Context' and 'Picture Books and Comics for the Developing Reader'.

Judith Graham, although officially retired (and enjoying grandmother-hood), still works occasionally at Roehampton University and in the Faculty of Education in Cambridge. Her interests are in all areas of literacy and children's literature. She is the author of *Pictures on the Page* and *Cracking Good Books* (NATE, 1990 and 1997), co-editor, with Alison Kelly, of *Reading under Control* and *Writing Under Control* (David Fulton, 2007 and 2003) and co-author, with Fiona Collins, of *Historical Fiction: Capturing the Past* (David Fulton, 2001), an edited collection of pieces on historical fiction for children.

Dr Gillian Lathey is Reader in Children's Literature at Roehampton University and Director of the National Centre for Research in Children's Literature. She began her career as an infant teacher in north London and joined the staff at Roehampton as a teacher trainer. Combining interests in languages, childhood and literature, she now teaches children's literature at undergraduate and Master's levels, supervises PhD students undertaking children's literature projects, and researches the practices and history of translating for children. She also administers the biennial Marsh Award for Children's Literature in Translation.

Ann Lazim has been Librarian at the Centre for Literacy in Primary Education (CLPE) in London for 15 years having previously worked in school and public libraries. She is Chair of the British Section of International Board on Books for Young People (IBBY) and is currently serving on IBBY's international Executive Committee. Ann completed her MA in Children's Literature at Roehampton University. She has a long-standing interest in traditional stories and how they are retold and illustrated in different countries and cultures.

Dr Michael Lockwood taught in schools in Oxford before becoming Lecturer in English and Education at the University of Reading, where he is course leader for the BAEd English programme. His research and teaching interests are in the areas of knowledge about language for primary school pupils, teachers and ITT students, and children's literature, especially poetry. Publications include *Opportunities for English in the Primary School* (Trentham, 1996), *Poetry In and Out of the Literacy Hour* (RALIC, 1999), contributions to *The Articulate Classroom* (David Fulton, 2001) and *Literacy through Creativity* (David Fulton 2004), as well as classroom literacy resources and poems for children.

Catriona Nicholson was a teacher in primary and special schools before becoming a Lecturer in English and Education at the University of Reading. She has been a co-director of CIRCL and was a tutor on the MA in Children's Literature. Recent publications include contributions to: *The Cambridge Guide to Children's Books in English* (2001); *Children in War: The International Journal of Evacuee and War Child Studies* (2004); *Literacy Through Creativity* (David Fulton, 2004); *Twentieth Century Literary Criticism* (Thomson Gale, 2006)

Dr Margaret Perkins has worked in initial teaching training for many years in different institutions. She has taught across the whole primary age range, although is predominantly an early years teacher. Her research has been into teachers as readers and the teaching of reading. She has a keen interest in children's ideas about and response to popular culture. In 1998 she co-authored, with Diane Godwin, *Teaching Language and Literacy in the Early Years*, published by David Fulton.

Dr Vivienne Smith was a primary teacher in Suffolk before completing a doctorate and moving into higher education. She now works as a lecturer in the department of Childhood and Primary Studies at the University of Strathclyde, where she teaches in the language team and pursues research interests in children's literature, critical literacy and the development of children as readers. She has been a passionate reader of children's books for many years, and, for some time, has been particularly interested in how the best picturebooks and lift-the-flap books orientate children towards becoming engaged and active readers of all sorts of texts.

Acknowledgements

Many thanks to the children, parents and staff of St. Joseph's RC Primary School, Guildford, and St. John's CE Primary School, Reading, for the cover photographs and so much more.

Thank you to David Higham Associates for permission to reproduce two pages from Child, L., *My Uncle is a Hunkle, Says Clarice Bean* and to Palgrave Macmillan for permission to reproduce extracts from Reynolds, K. *Modern Children's Literature: an Introduction*.

I am very grateful to my friends and colleagues who have contributed chapters to this book.

1

A World of Children's Books

Prue Goodwin

This chapter looks at:

> Why enthusiasm for and enjoyment of children's books is so vital for every-
one working with children and young people

> The business of publishing

> Ways to develop professional knowledge of children's books

I have spent a lifetime enjoying, collecting and sharing children's books. Some of my earliest memories include my parents reading aloud to me and, now, one of my greatest pleasures is sharing books with others – children, colleagues and anyone else who is interested. Fortunately for me, introducing books to people – especially those who have chosen to work with children – is a professional responsibility. Throughout my career in education I have remained convinced that my knowledge of and delight in children's books has been central to any success I may have had in enabling young learners to become readers.

I hope that this book can be an introduction to the pleasures and power of writing and illustration for children. It aims to provide information about children's books for anyone who shares books with children and young people. It is particularly for those who are professionally involved in helping children to become confident, lifelong readers – for example, teachers, librarians, teaching assistants, foundation stage professionals, childminders and youth workers. It is essential that professionals who work with children are:

> informed about the world of children's books
> familiar with writers, illustrators and publishers for children
> knowledgeable about the essential role that books play in children's intellectual, spiritual and moral development.

The most influential people in helping children to become readers are families and friends, so this book is also for them.

If, as education professionals, we are to fully comprehend the world of children's books, it will help to be aware of all the different points of view represented by people associated with that world. For example, educators and librarians are concerned with the creation of competent, confident readers; academics consider a range of theoretical perspectives that can offer alternative interpretations of a text; publishers, always hoping to discover a bestseller, work to produce popular titles; and authors and illustrators, absorbed in their creative art, endeavour to convey something of that enthusiasm to their readers. This introductory chapter will touch briefly on aspects and issues concerning the production of children's books under the subheadings of publishing, becoming a reader, and the development of a professional knowledge of children's books.

What are children's books?

A simple answer to the question 'What are children's books?' could be, books intended for readers under the age of 18. However, when you start to explore that statement it becomes clear that it is impossible to define children's books in such a straightforward way. There are as many different sorts of books for children as there are for adults – novels, information, poetry, dictionaries, short stories, travelogues, plays, biographies, annuals, and so on – in fact, there are multiple versions of each genre because, as a child of 6 is obviously not going to want to read the same books as a teenager, there are novels, information, poetry, and so on for each stage of childhood from infancy to the verge of adulthood. There is also variety within each genre; for example, the range of children's fiction includes contemporary and historical novels, science fiction, detective stories, fantasy adventure, horror and romance. When we describe a book as a story for children we must remember that most children's literature is concerned with storytelling. When we talk about Margery Williams's story about a lost toy, *The Velveteen Rabbit*, being a children's book we must remember that the same term is applied to *Doing It* by Melvyn Burgess (2003), a tale of the sexual experiences of three boys in their late adolescence. In other words, to refer to children's books as a homogeneous group is incorrect and confusing: the range of subject matter, genres, literary quality, illustrative style is diverse and the impact of this diversity as significant as that associated with adult publishing.

Publishing children's books

Another similarity between children's and adult publishing is the vast quantity of books produced every year. Relatively few of the hundreds of titles will be considered of any literary value and fewer still will become 'bestsellers'. There may be one or two exceptionally well-written and engaging books which will continue to be read and reread until they acquire 'classic' status. The thousands of children's books published annually are a testament to a very healthy children's book trade in the United Kingdom. With the coming of Harry Potter in 1997, writing for children became 'big business'. Currently, some children's books are supported by marketing teams with large promotion budgets, and a few successful authors become famous – one or two gaining the status of media stars. If books become very popular, film, television and theatre adaptations bring them to the attention of an even wider audience; as a result, spin-off products (such as computer games, toys, and so on) and lucrative advertising deals are always a possibility. However, for every 'star' children's author there must be a hundred who struggle to publish at all. Not many children's authors are wealthy, nor are the artists who illustrate children's books and create the brilliant visual genre, picturebook.

Trade and education

There are two sectors of publishing associated with child readers; trade and education. Trade publishers are the child equivalent of adult publishing; their market is the book-buying public, which includes specialists who buy for libraries and schools. Educational publishers produce textbooks, reading schemes and teaching resources; their market is schools and a few educationally aspirational parents. Debates about the teaching of reading have led to all sorts of misguided opinions and arguments about the differences between trade (sometimes termed 'real') books and educational materials. Most of the time, the arguments are pointless. The products from trade and education publishing serve completely different purposes.

Educational publishers provide functional 'tools' for teachers to use when teaching reading. There is a role for materials that provide attractive texts at appropriate times in a child's journey to becoming a competent reader but no one expects a riveting literary experience from *Here We Go* (Janet and John Book 1). Encounters with educational materials might promote in young readers personal pride in developing skills but those readers are unlikely to experience the deeply felt emotional responses that engagement with great literature can offer.

Books which deserve to be described as literature are provided by trade publishers. Although not intended to have any didactic purpose, there is no doubt that well-written and beautifully illustrated trade books can provide a most effective learning and enriching reading experience for young readers: not simply as a means by which they learn to read, but the stimulus and motivation for continuing to doing so.

All publishers are businesses, they exist in order to sell books, but that does not mean that money is the only motivation in publishing. The majority of both children's and educational publishers want to produce books for children that meet the highest standards of writing, illustration and book production. However, a word of caution: all publishers' marketing departments recognize the value of sales to schools but they seldom understand how children learn to read. In the past, this has led to some misleading marketing techniques, notably the flagging up of suggested ages and curriculum levels on the backs of books. It is also important to realize that the multinational media corporations that wield a lot of power in the marketplace, have both education and trade sectors. Teachers, librarians and carers looking for certain sorts of books may not be aware of titles from smaller, independent publishers. It is a good idea to subscribe to the children's books journal such as *Carousel*, *Books for Keeps* or *School Librarian* (also see references for websites).

Learning to read

Proficient readers are seldom conscious of what cognitive processes they go through as they encounter a new text. However, if required to make explicit how they create meaning from a series of symbols strung together into words and organized into sentences, paragraphs and chapters, it is possible to identify three layers of understanding. All readers, to differing degrees, understand:

> at the literal level – seeing and translating symbols into speech sounds and literal meanings
> beyond the literal – applying knowledge, judgement and experience to the literal information

> at a personal level – an emotional response to the impact of the text (interest, boredom, delight, fear, anger, amusement, inspiration, annoyance, indifference) which, arguably, informs our understanding more deeply than any other aspect of reading.

The first engages the eye, the second the mind and the third the heart. Engagement of the heart distinguishes a reader from someone who is merely able to read. A good teacher of reading ensures that, right from the start, children learn not only how to read but about being a reader.

There are many books on the market which explore how to read, how to teach reading and how children become readers (for example, Appleyard, 1990; Jennings, 2003; Meek, 1991) a common factor in such texts is the recognition that good children's books have an essential role to play. It follows that anyone engaged in teaching children to read needs to be a reader themselves, and in particular, a reader of children's books. At the earliest stages of learning to read, a book's capacity to assist an inexperienced reader will often go hand in hand with its potential to engage the imagination. Once children can read to themselves, the quality of the books they read will have a direct influence over their motivation to read and an impact upon their future as readers. Having said that, adult involvement and enthusiasm is the key to developing young readers, and the value of adults reading aloud to children cannot be overestimated.

Reading aloud engages imaginations and inspires youngsters to pick up books for themselves. What better way can there be to teach the purposes of literacy than to demonstrate how it provides us all with enlightenment, comfort and delight?

There is research evidence (Medwell et al., 1998) that successful teachers of literacy engage their pupils in the pleasures of reading, ensuring that learning to read never becomes a chore and that, every day, books are shared for sheer enjoyment. Many other influential educationalists have indicated the importance of reading aloud to children (Graham, 2005; Meek, 1991; Perera, 1984) not just to enhance reading development but also to support writing and encourage thinking and debate. This simple truth about reading aloud to children has been understood by good teachers for years but it has not always been given sufficient focus in the literacy curriculum. However, since 2006, primary teachers in English schools are required to provide their classes with a 'read aloud programme' (DfES and PNS, 2006) which will require practitioners to keep up to date with children's books. As Aidan Chambers pointed out in 1993, all teachers of reading need a 'store' of at least 500 books that they can rely on at to support youngsters in becoming enthusiastic readers.

Providing the right books

It is not possible to categorize books according to the age or ability of a reader. Books are not related to stages of reading development, nor are they a means of measuring growing literacy skills. Terms such as 'easy' and 'difficult' are of little value when selecting books. Being able to read a book with ease should be encouraged. On the other hand, books can be too difficult for some inexperienced readers and enjoyment of both their burgeoning skills and the content of a book will be impeded by a text which is too demanding for them to read confidently. However, it is quite common for children to tackle linguistically challenging texts, and to gain pleasure from doing so, if the subject matter engages them. In contrast, many children have been put off reading because some well-intentioned adult has deemed their chosen reading materials to be too easy or too hard. Decisions on behalf of a child reader can only be made by someone who knows both the child and the book very well. With so many different opinions about books, how are teachers supposed to select suitable materials for the young readers in their care? Although there is plenty of advice available, nothing is as effective as a secure knowledge of books when helping children to make selections for themselves.

Developing a professional knowledge of children's books

As with many art forms, there can be a certain snobbishness in some people's opinions about 'good' books. This can lead to a lack of confidence in personal responses and a misconception about the difference between literary appreciation and personal enjoyment. There are many children's books which, in the words of the old cliché, have 'stood the test of time'. Referred to as classics, these books are outstanding for the time in which they were written; they are often engrossing narratives, even though the content and language are remote from the world inhabited by the modern reader. The tendency by some to refer to 'good' or 'significant' books can lead inexperienced readers to believe there are fixed views with which all readers agree. However, being a reader is not dependent on having read a prescribed list of books. All readers are entitled to have subjective opinions about what they read and no one person, or group of people, can determine the value of a piece of literature. It is impossible to decide the quality of a children's book without reading it – and even then personal opinion and taste will have a great deal to do with any judgement.

Some books which have even achieved 'classic' status are the cause of the greatest disagreements between established readers of children's books.

Take, for example, the work of Arthur Ransome. Many adults remember being totally absorbed by the sailing exploits of his child characters, while others find them irritating. Another example is the work of Tolkien, whose writing inspires some people to become passionate devotees, while others find such high fantasy uninteresting. There is no question that both Ransome and Tolkien are deserving of their reputations as authors but that does not mean that everyone will enjoy reading their work. It is possible to appreciate literary quality without emotional engagement. Describing books as 'good' or 'significant' should always prompt the further questions: 'Who has decided it is good?' and 'To whom is it significant?'

Suitable material for children

Opinions differ about what topics are suitable as the focus of a children's book. Some people argue that life is not always pleasant and that children's books should reflect reality. Others feel that young people should be protected from the disagreeable side of life, and have their innocence left unsullied for as long as possible. Both these views are to some degree didactic and neither take into account young readers' right to make their own decisions about what they read, to make choices about what interests them and to seek out books that will help them make sense of their worlds. That said, however, the majority of children will have their books selected for them, which is another reason why the adults who make the selections should read the books rather than be at the mercy of others' opinions. It is easy to be persuaded to think well or poorly of a book if you have not read it. Here, for example, is a synopsis of a story published for young children.

> Peter, whose father has been killed whilst taking part in a robbery, is determined to get involved in similar criminal activity despite the pleas of his mother. The story starts as the lad sets out with the deliberate intention of stealing from an elderly neighbour. He breaks into the old man's property and steals some food. The rest of the story recounts the consequences of Peter's delinquency.

What is your initial response to this synopsis? Would it be appropriate for a 3-year-old? Most people would agree that the tales of Beatrix Potter, especially Peter Rabbit (for it is he) is a classic piece of literature for the very young. Here is another synopsis of the opening of another story:

> A little girl is left in the care of a teenager who falls asleep. The little girl wanders away, down an unknown passageway where she finds and eats some tempting foodstuff which causes her to hallucinate.

The little girl is Alice, at the start of her Adventures in Wonderland. It is fun to play this game with famous books but it also serves to point out how deceptive one person's opinion on a book can be. Reviewers and commentators on children's books can sometimes mislead. Although all sources of information and opinion are worth consulting, reading a book yourself is the only way of discovering whether or not it is 'good' or 'significant' for you. Once you have started to read, the decisive factor on which to base your judgement of a book is whether you want to finish it or not. What is it about the book that keeps you engaged or causes you abandon it? Why do we respond to some books and not others? Whatever the answer, we know that how we, as adult readers, respond has a direct bearing on how we convey that response to younger readers. A confident knowledge of children's books will enable you to make informed, critical judgements and to pass on to those with whom you work, not only your personal enthusiasms but an appropriate language for talking about literature. This book offers a starting point for enriching that knowledge.

What will you find in *Understanding Children's Books?*

This book is concerned with books for the whole span of childhood and is founded on the belief that there is writing of literary worth for children of all ages. Chapters consider books for babies, for children who are still learning to read and for young readers up to and beyond the age of 15. Children learning to read and becoming readers are themes which inevitably run through each chapter, however, the authors are concerned principally with the quality of the books that youngsters will meet rather than how texts are used as teaching resources. Colleagues from the worlds of education, libraries and publishing have been invited to contribute chapters on areas of personal interest and expertise.

All the contributors to *Understanding Children's Books* have two things in common; they are involved with young readers and they are passionate about children's books. Their different professional circumstances are reflected in their points of view but, no matter what field they represent, they all aspire to ensure that the adults who teach reading, introduce children to books and share the great stories of the world with young people are enthusiastic readers themselves, who know about children's books.

Most chapters contain book lists that make good starting points for anyone wanting to develop their knowledge of children's books. Inevitably, as the lists represent some of the best children's books available, there are several titles that appear on more than one list. Also, because there simply is not enough space, there are hundreds of titles that go unmentioned. Agreeing these lists has proved one of the most difficult things to do and it has been approached with much thought and considerable frustration about what has had to be left out, and the titles offered may be out of print. However, you need only go to a library or good children's book shop to be offered more advice and below are listed some other useful sources of recommended titles.

Learning how to read and about being a reader begins as soon as we share books with children, no matter how young they are. Liz Attenborough (Chapter 2), Margaret Perkins (Chapter 3) and Vivienne Smith (Chapter 4) look at books which will support the very young through their earliest childhood and first few years of schooling. Learning to read can be hard work, but it is a lot harder if you never encounter the sort of literature and non-fiction that will engage you and motivate you to see the whole learning process as worthwhile.

Writing about traditional tales (Chapter 5), Ann Lazim opens our eyes to the vast range of stories from across the world that have inspired both readers and writers for centuries. These tales are the heritage of every child; they also provide the foundations of all great literature and, as such, an essential element of literary experience for us all.

Fiction forms the heart of children's literature and it is novels written for children that Catriona Nicholson considers in Chapter 6. Since the late nineteenth century, a wealth of literature for young audiences has been produced across the English-speaking world. Nicholson reflects on the classics of the past and the 'state of the art' in the twenty-first century, when new media dominates our lives.

In Chapter 7, Gillian Lathey highlights how books in translation can open young minds to both the similarities and the differences of children's lives across the world. At the time when we are more globally aware, it is important to 'hear' voices from as many cultures as we can. Although in recent years – thanks in large part to the Marsh Award – more children's books are being translated into English, there is much to be done in opening up the world of literature for young readers.

In her chapter on non-fiction (Chapter 8), Nikki Gamble points out the high quality and distinction of many current information texts, which is made possible by the work of writers, artists and photographers engaged in illuminating the world for young readers. There is a wealth of books to appeal to the curious, the studious and to those who just prefer to read non-fiction.

Michael Lockwood (Chapter 9) considers the role of poetry in young lives and its power to encapsulate ideas, stories and feelings. He traces the history of poetry for children and comments on current views about the use of poetry with youngsters. Judith Graham (Chapter 10) opens our eyes to the potential of a relatively new genre of literature, the picturebook, and Mel Gibson (Chapter 11) continues the visual literacy with her exploration of graphic texts.

This introduction ends with a personal choice of books. They are books that I love; what makes them more precious is the knowledge that by sharing them with hundreds of children and colleagues, their potential to create and support new readers has been realized. I hope these books will also inspire the readers of *Understanding Children's Books* to share the magic of literature with all the aspiring young readers in their care.

Further reading

Prue's personal choice
Allan Ahlberg, *Burglar Bill*, Puffin
Anthony Browne, *The Tunnel*, Walker Books
Quentin Blake, *The Story of the Dancing Frog*, Red Fox
Carol Ann Duffy, *The Stolen Childhood*, London: Puffin
Russell Hoban and Quentin Blake, *How Tom beat Captain Najork and his Hired Sportsmen*, Jonathan Cape
Margaret Mahy, *The Great Piratical Rumbustification* and *The Librarian and the Robbers*, Puffin
Jon Scieszka and Lane Smith, *The Stinky Cheese Man*, Puffin
Morag Styles and Helen Cook, *Ink-Slinger*, A & C Black
Martin Waddell, *Farmer Duck*, Walker Books
Marcia Williams, *Archie's War*, Walker Books

Useful websites

Websites to find out more about children's books
www.achuka.co.uk
www.booksforkeeps.co.uk
www.booktrusted.org.uk
www.carouselguide.co.uk
www.fcbg.org.uk
www.readingzone.com
www.sla.org.uk
www.writeaway.org.uk

2

Babies Really Do Need Books

Liz Attenborough

This chapter looks at:

> The development of children's books

> Ways to share books with babies

> Some great books to use with babies

It was in 1980 that New Zealand bookseller Dorothy Butler published her book *Babies Need Books*. Others may have used those words before, but the passion in the book, and all that it said, made a powerful case for everyone to remember that from their earliest days the very youngest children should be included in the wonderful world of books and stories. It is never too soon to start learning how to become a reader, for all that it teaches about the world around us, and teaches about the books themselves.

The development of books for the very young

Colour illustrations have been used in books for children since Victorian times, with text far outweighing the illustrative content in the majority of cases beyond alphabet primers. During the Second World War, Puffin Books introduced paperback picturebooks covering non-fiction topics, with illustrations making up the bulk of the content. It was in the early 1960s that the UK benefited from improved printing techniques that allowed full colour to be printed on both sides of one large sheet of paper that could be folded and cut before being bound. There followed a steady stream of the now familiar format of high-quality, full-colour, 32 page picturebooks, inspiring new writers and artists to create for the youngest child. Usually these books were put together by an author/artist who would write and illustrate the whole book themselves, author/illustrators such as Brian Wildsmith, John Burningham and Pat Hutchins. Gradually more texts were produced that illustrators were separately commissioned to illustrate.

Skilful illustrators who can also write magical texts, like Maurice Sendak, Lauren Child and Mick Inkpen, have the particular advantage of working out right from the start which part of the story will be told in text, and which can be better shown through illustration. Today there are many writers, such as Martin Waddell, whose skill is to create excellent picture-book texts, and they are then matched with different illustrators to suit particular stories. There are also author/illustrator teams that have been successfully brought together by publishers – Julia Donaldson and Axel Scheffler, for example – to create a whole range or series of books. In rare examples, some teams have the particularly special advantage of being a married couple, like Allan and Janet Ahlberg, who can work closely together so that the reader really does not see the join between text and illustration in the telling of the tale.

As printing and paper technologies have developed, so too have creators' imaginations. Books for babies now include touch and feel books, using different fabrics and textures, books with holes (first used to great effect in 1969 by Eric Carle in *The Very Hungry Caterpillar*), lift-the-flap books (a genre created in 1980 by Eric Hill's *Where's Spot?*), and books with all manner of sounds. Books with pop-ups introduced a whole new range of novelty, as well as the new profession of paper engineer. It was in 1977 that Robert Crowther first updated the Victorian pop-up style with his multi-faceted *Most Amazing Hide-and-Seek Alphabet Book*. Some board books, too, have the sophistication and attention that shows that only the best quality should be put before our youngest readers, with Helen Oxenbury's series for babies in 1981 showing the way.

These differently formatted books tell stories, show pictures, and have the added benefit of helping small fingers and hands become more dexterous and co-ordinated, adding to the many skills acquired through making friends with books. Not all illustrated picturebooks are suitable for babies, though, as some are sophisticated in style, content and story, and those books take a mature reading brain to truly decipher. A single story strand works best, with one voice leading the narrative at this very young age.

Stories are important

We all know how much we as adults need stories in our lives. In fiction and non-fiction, the stories we read and hear help us to make sense of our own lives. And so it is for babies. Language is at the root of human communication, something we need to master not only for our learning but also for our social and emotional well-being. We need language in order to think. What better way to learn language than through books and stories, shared lovingly with a trusted adult?

Sharing a story is a simple way to talk to a baby before they have any spoken language of their own. Through the rhythms of a short story with its accompanying pictures, and the repetition of that story and pictures, words with meaning begin to emerge, and a new young mind grows. Babies love to communicate. They are born sociable and come into the world with a willingness to communicate and learn. Their experiences in their early years shape their future social, communication and learning skills, and books can be a great way of helping babies and their carers during this period of discovery. Storytelling and book-reading are an easy way to have regular, additional talking time, and storytelling introduces structure and language patterns that help to form the building blocks for later reading and writing skills.

Our understanding of the development of babies' brains has expanded enormously in recent years. Studies by developmental psychologists have shown the importance of early engagement for later learning. The neural pathways at birth need to be connected through stimulation and activity, through affection and warmth and through a young child's attachment to an adult and the world around them. For new parents who will be having a wealth of new experiences as they learn about the health and growth of their baby, communication may not be at the forefront of their thinking. But it should be. A baby's mind needs feeding if it is to grow and develop. For any parent who thinks that they do not know what to say to their baby, or who thinks that their young child will not understand, books can provide an easy way to start communicating. Books use the power of words to connect adult to child, and to powerfully make associations between what happens on the page and what is happening all around.

Babies and young children do understand when they are being read to and they respond in many ways, by cooing, babbling and smiling. Those coos, babbles and smiles are the early signs of communication, and will turn into words when the mouth and tongue are ready to copy the words that have been heard. Books introduce children to the exciting world of words, and in time help them learn to express their own thoughts and emotions. Reading aloud combines the benefits of talking, listening and storytelling within a single activity, and helps to build the foundation for language development.

Learn and play with books

Alongside toys in the toy box there need to be plenty of books, for no amount of 'educational' toys can compete with books for the skills they encourage through looking at the pictures, listening to the words and thinking about the meaning. A short time sharing a book each day will be time well spent and gradually, as the book-sharing habit begins to grow, time will be spent looking at books without adult involvement. Physically books are immensely practical 'toys' as they can be slipped into bags when going out, for those journeys and waiting times that are so taxing for a restless toddler. They really can be read anywhere, and no qualifications are needed on the part of the reader. Adults do not necessarily need to bring great reading skills of their own to the endeavour; the pictures will tell much of the story, and act as a prompt for telling any stories. Everyone in the family, older siblings and visiting relatives, can take their turn at sharing books with babies.

Sharing books with babies is not teaching them to read, but it is teaching them in the broadest sense about the interpretation of print, the way that a book 'works' from left to right, that text conveys the story, that stories have structures and that a story can be told through words and pictures. Visual literacy comes easily to young children who are presented with high-quality picturebooks when they are given time to pore over the illustrations by themselves or talk about them with an adult. When sharing a book which is familiar to them both, it is not unusual for a young child to notice details about the pictures that adults may have missed, for example, that there is a small dog following through the narrative of the pictures which is not mentioned in the text. This kind of active participation and engagement with the book helps to nurture later literacy skills.

Familiarity with the physical aspects of a book is the best possible start for young children to become ready for reading, to know the conventions of handling books and following stories. Some words, particularly as titles, will be 'learnt' with little effort. In time the proud adult will be 'read' the book, as the young reader remembers and replicates the words on the pages, the intonation of the adult voice and even the sound effects that are usually used. As recent research has highlighted, engaging young children in pre-reading activities makes for a better start for the majority of five year olds when they come to start school. Speaking, listening, reading and writing are described as the 'four interdependent strands of language' (Rose, 2006: 1, Interim Report).

Reading aloud

Reading aloud with a young child has many benefits, not least in encouraging the vital ability to listen. In order to become a reader it is important to be able to learn to distinguish different sounds, and to concentrate for sustained amounts of time. If you are listening to books regularly, new words are constantly introduced and the context of the words in the story allows for a gradual understanding.

On reading a new book together for the first time, do either of you feel as you get to the end that you immediately want to start at the beginning again? If the answer is yes, you have found a book with the quality to become a favourite. Illustrations that go beyond a straightforward retelling of the text, which add depth to our understanding of and interest in what is going on, will certainly last through many, many readings. Add a quality text that never tires on rereading, that sings with rhythm and style, and a lifelong friendship has begun.

Take more time to talk about the pictures, encouraging pointing as you go. For the very youngest children, you will be looking for clear, uncluttered illustrations that might even be presented photographically. Photographs of other babies and familiar items from around the house or the park will be well received: connections will be made by the youngest children when they see their own experiences reflected in books.

In no time, you will be looking for texts that rhyme, as that is a wonderful way for an emerging talker to hear how words work, and to remember them. You will need texts and pictures that will allow you both to enter a new world together, a world of make-believe that you can share. Books with numbers are often excitingly cumulative, reaching towards a magnificent climax, and along the way the joys of counting can be absorbed. Humour is always a treat, and when you are learning about life and language you can never hear a good joke too often. Books with surprises, perhaps under flaps, will take years to tire of, too, as the excitement builds in anticipation as the familiar page comes along.

The recognition that a pre-verbal child is anticipating something in a picturebook can take even the most alert parent by surprise. Here is clear evidence that this little person with a developing mind has understood what is going on, has remembered from the last time, and is pleased that you have introduced the book and the characters again. The word 'again' will be an early one, allowing for real affection for the characters and the story to grow during those important repeated reads. A book that has been asked for again and again may be left for a while. On a later reading the depth of understanding may be greater, as new aspects of the book begin to take on more meaning as the growing child has experienced much more in their own life.

Books of nursery rhymes and books of fairy tales have survived for so long because they both fulfil useful functions. Although any song sung by a most treasured adult will bring pleasure to a young mind, a nursery rhyme has special qualities of playing with language, and rhyming in a playful way, that help the young mind with a growing facility with words. Fairy tales explore universal truths, and the conventions in those stories – from the opening 'Once upon a time' – will recur with great familiarity through the canon of children's literature. Besides, if you have never heard the original rhymes or fairy tales, you will find it hard to laugh at the parodies.

Time to share a book

It is no coincidence that a tradition has grown up of reading a book at bedtime or at the end of a nursery session. It is a really effective way to bring the tempo down, after a frenetic day of play and excitement. Young children who finish the day by being read a favourite story about a loved character, in a familiar comforting voice, are much more likely to fall into restful sleep than those who have watched screen-based entertainment before going to bed. Believing in magic and suspending disbelief can be a powerful motivator for imagination, with stories supplying the launch pad for entertaining personal flights of fancy.

Active reading

Of course, the adult will not be able to resist making appropriate noises as the book requires, or stroking the page when a cat appears, and they should never feel any inhibition in doing so. The only danger is having to repeat the noise and actions at every reading, so if you think a book has a particularly annoying but oft repeated chorus, perhaps it is wise to leave that one on the library shelf. There may be books loved by the adult that the child does not, for some reason, take to: no one has to like every book they are shown.

Do the voices and sound effects

Be slow and clear when you read and do not be afraid to use sing-song or funny voices for characters, or for words or phrases that are repeated throughout the book. Go at a pace the child can manage, and only turn the page when they are ready. Add to the text as you go along, but always read the actual printed text, too, so that it is the same the next time. After reading a book several times, the young child will anticipate hearing the change in tone and may well show this with a smile, widening of the eyes or a wiggle. Give your child time to respond to your chatter. This could be with a babble, arm-waving or gentler finger movement. Listening shows how interested you are in hearing a response, and is an encouragement in a natural discovery of communication. When language emerges, encourage joining in with both noises and words.

Embrace the emotions

Picturebooks can be especially useful as a way of exploring and managing emotions, as well as introducing issues that need to be absorbed gently. Being scared, just a little, through reading a book about a monster, is an experience that will end in relief when the drama is resolved, and the book can be put away. The closeness of the reader, the soothing interjections if fear is observed, all point to an individual support structure of immense importance. Rereading the same scary book will offer useful reassurance that the problems are surmountable, that they are under control, that they will go away. They offer a wonderful opportunity to talk about what might appear to be frightening.

Learn about life

The right book can provide ways to talk about tricky subjects, too, like moving house or the imminent arrival of a new sibling. Seeing a picturebook character coping will gently allow the child to work through their own anxieties, and prepare their own response to whatever comes along. The book allows the adult to expand on the topic, to personalize what is going on, and for a verbal child to be prompted to ask about anything worrying.

Being read stories allows young children to experience things beyond their current personal understanding, and opens windows into the experiences of other people, in other places. The seeds of empathy are born as a reader shares good and bad activity, shares the frightening bits and the happy moments, and wonders how it would really feel to be doing that thing on their own. Social skills, too, can be learnt through a range of high-quality books, as the reader sees how to behave, or what might happen if you misbehave. They will want to ask questions as the story unfolds, and reading aloud one-to-one allows answers to come immediately.

Talk about words

Through books, vocabulary can grow in unexpected ways. A child with very few words can seem to get their tongue around 'Diplodocus' once the dinosaur has been introduced in a fun and dramatic way. It can be a surprise to see how strongly book-sharing can influence and enrich a toddler's vocabulary. There are not many monkeys or lions wandering around our towns or countryside, but there are plenty to meet in books. Books can be the starting point for imaginative play, as characters met on the page can be included in games and activities, and dogs met out walking can be linked to the dogs already met in a story.

Books right from the start

In the UK there is such a strong belief that being introduced to books in babyhood will bring lifelong advantages that we have the world's first universal book-gifting scheme, Bookstart. This imaginative and inspirational programme involves a free book pack being given by health visitors to every parent when their child is around 8 months old. At around 18 months, a further Bookstart + pack is given, and a Bookstart Treasure Chest is gifted at 3 years old. There is a Booktouch scheme for blind and partially-sighted children, using books with different textures and sounds, and Bookshine, with specific materials to help the deaf or hearing-impaired child.

Bookstart, which comes with information on books and reading, is inextricably linked to the public library system. Regular activities such as 'Baby Rhyme Times' encourage parents and carers to join in simple rhyming games and songs, modelling ways to recite or sing with extravagant gestures. At a later stage, library story times will be enjoyed, providing ongoing support and encouragement to parents to ensure that book-sharing is adopted as custom and practice in the home. Being read stories aloud shows pre-readers how fluent readers read books. There is growing recognition within the library profession that proficiency in early years librarianship is a particular skill, and one that can have a lasting impact on young readers and their families if delivered with understanding and flair.

Bookstart and library sessions are just some of the ways to establish key early literacy practices in the home, sowing the foundations for later literacy learning, which have been shown to have such an impact on later educational achievement (Collins et al., 2005).

Further reading

'Read it again!'

Any picturebook suggestions can only be a personal choice, but I list below some titles that have never let me down with any child, so you might want to take a look at them to see what you think. Each has brought a smile to a very young face, with the implied or spoken word 'Again'.

Recommendations to share with babies and toddlers

These books will continue to be favourites and should be shared long after children have left very early childhood behind. They will be especially supportive of children as they start to learn to read.

Rod Campbell, *Dear Zoo*, Campbell Books

Janet and Allan Ahlberg, *Each Peach Pear Plum*, Puffin

Lynley Dodd, *Hairy Maclary from Donaldson's Dairy*, Puffin

Quentin Blake, *Mr Magnolia*, Red Fox

Nick Butterworth, *One Snowy Night*, HarperCollins Children's Books

Martin Waddell and Patrick Benson, *Owl Babies*, Walker Books

Pat Hutchins, *Rosie's Walk*, Red Fox

Judith Kerr, *The Tiger Who Came to Tea*, HarperCollins Children's Books

Eric Carle, *The Very Hungry Caterpillar*, Puffin

Eric Hill, *Where's Spot?*, Puffin

A bookshelf for babies and toddlers should include:

Collections of nursery rhymes and simple traditional tales from a range of cultures: for example, *First Fairy Tales* by Margaret Mayo (Orchard) and *Pudding and Pie: Favourite Nursery Rhymes* by Sarah Williams and Ian Beck (Oxford).

Picture story books with stories about other babies, animals and imaginary creatures: for example, *Calm Down Boris* by Sam Lloyd (Templar).

Poetry written for the very young, for example, counting rhymes and lullabies: for example, *The Usborne Book of Lullabies* by Nickey Butler (Usborne).

Action rhymes, games and songs that involve lots of joining in with actions, singing, clapping, and so on. For example, *Hippety Hop, Hippety Hay* by Opal Dunn (Frances Lincoln).

Books that invite the reader to lift a flap or pull a lever: for example, *Cluck, Cluck Who's There?* by James Mayhew (Chicken House) and *Maisy's Big Flap Book* by Lucy Cousins (Walker).

Books with textured pictures to touch and feel.

Books made from a variety of materials – cloth, card and soft plastic: *Play with Me* by Satoshi Kitamura (Andersen) and *Quack said the Duck* by Ana Martin-Larranga (Treehouse).

Stories and songs on CD and DVD: for example, *Whole World* by Fred Penner and Christopher Corr (Barefoot).

Useful websites

Bookstart, a national programme which aims to encourage parents to share books with children from as early an age as possible, administered by Booktrust: www.bookstart.org.uk

3

Literature for the Very Young

Margaret Perkins

This chapter looks at:

> Ways to share great texts with young children

> How to select good books to share

There is a tendency to think of 'literature' as being something rather elitist. I prefer not to tell people about the fat book with a gold-embossed cover which I read on the beach this summer but am happy to discuss my views on the shortlist for the latest book prize. Why do we have these distinctions? What do we mean when we discuss 'literature'?

Young babies often see books as artefacts. As with all experiences, they react with every sense and their reactions are large scale and unrefined. A baby will laugh at the colours and shapes, will chew, wave, throw, suck and smell a book. A baby's own interaction with a book is wholehearted, all encompassing and generally physical. However, as soon as they are read to, even very young children focus on the details of the story (in both words and the pictures) and enjoy the rhythms of the language. Anyone who has read a well-loved story to a toddler will know that skipping a few pages is not allowed; children know and love each word. What is it that some books offer to the very young child?

The joy of literature for all ages is that it allows us to reflect on our own lives. As I read about the experiences of someone in a novel I realize that I am not alone in reacting as I do and I begin to see how I might understand myself and those around me. The same is true for the very young child. As children read or hear about Alfie going off to his very first birthday party (Hughes, 1997) feeling rather shy and timid, they will know that it is all right to feel like that and things will work out in the end. Literature gives us the opportunity for reflection, empathy and catharsis. It allows for a response which is both cognitive and affective, and develops understanding of life and living.

In this chapter I look at different types of books for children at the age when they start learning about reading and try to identify what it is in the books that encourages and enables children to make those valuable responses. What are the characteristics of a book that allow the very young child to engage with them in a critically reflective way? It is important to realize at the outset that many of these books are not ones which very young children will be able to read independently; they will need to be mediated by a more experienced reader who will read them to the child or talk about the illustrations with the child. It is the quality of these interactions which are vital; the experienced co-learner within the zone of proximal development (Vygotsky, 1986) will scaffold the meaning-making process.

Wordless picturebooks

It is often assumed that a picturebook without any printed words must be for very young children who are not yet able to decode for themselves. This is a misconception. There are many picturebooks which are highly challenging and sophisticated reads and are suitable only for older children, for example, *Clown* by Quentin Blake (1995). However, there are also many wordless books which are a delight to share with very young children and which offer both opportunities to empathize and to reflect on experience.

Going Shopping by Sarah Garland (1985) is such a text. It tells of a mum and her young children going off to the shops. They depart down the garden path and the two small children are loaded into the car by a very harassed looking mum. At the supermarket the children are pointing out what they would like and occasionally slipping it, unbeknown to their mother, into the trolley. The mum does not smile once through the book and there is a strong sense that the children are seeing the shopping trip in one way while the mother is having a completely different experience.

It is almost inevitable that reading such a book will cause comparisons to be made between the experience of shopping as portrayed in the book and the experience of shopping as known by the young reader. The book is deeply embedded within white middle-class cultural practices and invites comparison with other ways of shopping.

We can see that reading a text such as this offers many opportunities for very young readers:

> It extends their experiences and shows other ways of doing something. Thus, reading the book broadens horizons and opens doors. 'Why is the mummy buying so many potatoes? Why do they drive to the shop?'
> It invites critical reflection on their own experiences and ways of living and being. 'We don't go shopping like that. Why is she doing that? What sort of shop is it? Why aren't they talking to each other? Why did they take the dog shopping?'
> It develops awareness of story structure and of the sequencing of ideas. There is a clear structure to the story, with a start, an event and a resolution. The journey to the shop and home again provides the journey of the story.
> It helps children to see things from other points of view. 'Why doesn't the mummy smile? What is the shopping trip like for her?' Readers can stand back from well-known experiences and look at them through different eyes.
> It enables children to see the patterns and relationships in life and to stand back from events to look at the big picture. The little girl is trying to help – she puts things in the trolley, tries to find a box at the till, brings the dog back to the car and carries the baby. 'Is she really helping? Is it fair to her to do all that? Do I help my mum?'
> It shows readers that they can use their own experiences and understanding to comprehend a book. 'Why isn't the mum going straight inside? Has she lost the door key or is she just tired?'

The wordless picturebook allows children to become storytellers. Often the story told will be different and richer each time because more and more is seen in the pictures. Children are learning the benefits of re-reading well-known texts and that books do not have one meaning for all readers. Reading is a powerful and enabling experience.

Repeating texts

Young children's developing language involves not just an ever-increasing vocabulary, learning the labels for objects, actions, feelings and events but also a growing understanding of how language can be used to express oneself. *We're going on a bear hunt* by Michael Rosen (1989) is a book which provides a framework for understanding how language works within a fun and exciting story. A group of people are off on a bear hunt and to find the bear have to go through different terrains. At the end they find their bear but the experience is so frightening that they run back home to the safety of their bed. The bear is left to wander along the beach alone.

There are many themes to this book which make it very accessible to very young children. The idea of an ordinary and everyday experience like a walk turning into the excitement of a bear hunt is an integral part of childhood. The joy of this book is the uncertainty about the bear. He seems real – but surely not? The book helps very young readers to take part in this great adventure, to confront their fears, to go outside the boundaries of safety, to explore the mud and cold river but before the cover is closed to return to the safety of being under the quilt on my bed.

Who are the people going on this hunt? There's a baby – so it won't be too dangerous. Is that a dad or a big brother with the children? Whoever he is, he's bigger than us so he'll look after us. There's a big girl too and she helps with getting shoes on and off and carrying the baby. And of course the dog comes too. It looks like a normal day out and yet this lurking sense of danger and anticipation is just below the surface. Each new obstacle is more difficult to cross and more scary. Finally, the bear is found and as the dog faces the great beast we see that both the bear and the dog look as surprised and worried as each other!

The great joy of this book for the very young reader is the way in which the language mirrors the experiences of the story. The repetition means that I can, and indeed feel compelled, to join in. The rhythm of the first refrain reflects the optimism and confidence of the hunters:

> We're going to catch a big one.
> We're not scared.

The 'uh-uh' which signals each obstacle slows the tempo right down and acknowledges the problem and the need for thought. Each option is considered and the final assertion, 'We've got to go through it!' has to be read with a sureness in the voice which might belie true feelings. The onomatopoeia, for example 'Squishy, squashy' and 'squelch, squerch' show how the sound of the words used emphasize the meaning, and it is difficult to read these words without accompanying them with actions. The final race home is reflected in the structure of the language used and it is impossible to read these last pages slowly. The pace gradually slows down,

> Into bed.
> Under the covers.
> We're not going on a bear hunt again.

They are finally safe, although the faces peering out from under the quilt do not look so convinced. From the safety of the bed, readers may begin to think that the bear was all a figment of the imagination but then we turn the page and find a bear looking rather sad as he walks away along the beach. The young readers are forced to think again. Was I wrong? Was he really there? Did he just want to play? Was there no danger at all?

The repeating text with the strong rhythm of the story forces very young readers to become involved and to share in the experiences of the story. Not only do young children experience all the emotions and doubts of the story, but they are able to 'read' the book alone with fluency and expression. The book is allowing and enabling children to experience the richness of being readers.

Literary language

Part of the joy of reading literature is revelling in the language that authors use. This language is carefully chosen to reflect and convey the meaning of the text. It is not the casual language of everyday spoken language but provides a depth of feeling and experience which goes beyond the everyday. Written language in literature is not spoken language written down; the words, the structure and the style are carefully chosen by the author to give the required effect. *Peace at Last* by Jill Murphy (1980) is an example of this richness of language. 'The hour was late.' What impression does that give to the reader? It implies a significance that the ordinary words, 'It was getting late' do not convey. With those opening words we know that something is going to happen. It conveys to the reader that we are about to enter another world which is different from but similar to the ordinary. The hour is late ... and anything might happen.

Another book which uses language in a very special way is *Lullabyhullaballoo!* by Mick Inkpen (1993). With this book a very different impression is given by the language used. Even the title requires reading with a crescendo of volume and pace, and hints at the ensuing chaos. The first page opens with a juxtaposition which mirrors the contrast between the quietness of the Little Princess's sleep inside the castle and the noise made by those outside the castle.

> The sun is down.
> The moon is up.

The rhythm of the language conveys the growing sense of panic. There is clanking, rattling, clunking, stamping, galumphing, stomping, howling, hooting, croaking, squeaking, flapping, growling, guzzling, gobbling, slurping and even burping! What joyful anarchy! As the moon rises so does the noise. But it is not a threatening noise; it is fun to say these wonderful words and they reflect the activity and playfulness of those making the sounds. The despair of the Little Princess is reflected in the oft repeated question which slows the pace of reading right down – 'What shall we do?'

The response reflects the lack of malice and the innocence of the noise-makers – 'Who me?' This is a response that most young children will have often made themselves to the request to be quiet. They understand and they will empathize with both the princess and the noise-makers. The author's choice of words, syntax, rhythm and rhyme emphasize and support the very young child in understanding this story and entering into the experience of others.

Rhyme and rhythm

Try and read the book *Tanka Tanka Skunk* by Steve Webb (2003) sitting down quietly. It will be impossible. Tanka and Skunk bang their drums and together with their other friends – llamas, lemurs, kangaroos, badgers – they dance and sing across the pages. This book is one where the strong rhythmic pattern of the text leads the reader to respond with dance, movement and song. The rhythm of the language carries readers along and draws them into the world of fun and movement. It is texts like this which introduce children to the 'tune' of literature. This book cannot be read word by word; it has to be seen as a whole. It has to be felt and experienced rather than analysed. Literature can often go beyond the cognitive and this book is one which does just that for young children.

Different books have different rhythms and it is important that children are introduced to a variety of tunes within the texts they hear. *Tickle Tickle* by Dakari Hru (2002) is a similar type of book but the 'tune' of the language is not that of standard English.

> he tickle me tummy, me chest, me arm,
> his fingers fly so wild,
> he say, 'Come here, little man.
> You my ticklin' chile.'

For many young children this will be the rhythm and pattern of language with which they are familiar and so they immediately become the expert. For many others enjoying texts like these enable them to see language as something which can be played with, enjoyed and changed according to purpose.

It is true that books like *Tickle Tickle* are superb for beginner readers in helping them to recognize syllables and word structures and so develop their word recognition skills. They have so much more to offer. They are the introduction to poetry, the celebration of language and the expression of deeply felt feelings and emotions. If literature serves to allow us to reflect on our own lives then *Tanka Tanka Skunk* allows us to play with the language we use. We know that play is a vital part of children's learning and development and play with language is no exception.

Concept books

Literature allows us to reflect on our own experiences and to makes sense of them in the light of the new experiences we encounter every day. We learn by exploring the unknown and questioning the unknown. Significant learning experiences for very young children come when their understandings are challenged and they are introduced to new perspectives on life. If you go into any bookshop you will see lots of books which purport to 'teach' children about how life 'is'. They portray a world of certainty where all bananas are bright yellow and all summer days are warm, bright and sunny. Even very young children know that life is just not like that. Bananas become bruised and brown; summer days are sometimes cold, dull and wet. Children are much more capable of understanding subtleties and uncertainties than we often give them credit for, and books need to reflect the variety and uncertainty of life.

There are some books which do just that. They explore concepts such as colour, shape, size and sound but do it in a way which invites question and reflection. *Alfie's Weather* by Shirley Hughes (2002) is such a book. The language is simple and rhythmic and, together with the brilliantly detailed and evocative illustrations, introduces children to different kinds of weather. Along with Alfie the children can splash in puddles and walk in crisp snow. In some instances they will be able to compare their experiences with Alfie's and in others they will use their imagination to explore. If you have never seen crisp new snow you will understand much more about what it is like by sharing in the excitement of walking through it with a well-known character than reading an impersonal description of it which is detached from your own emotions. It is that emotive response which is so crucial to the experience of reading literature and which distinguishes the reader from the person who just decodes the symbols.

Traditional stories

When we hear the words 'Once upon a time' we immediately know what is to follow and settle down to hear a good story. At the end of the story when we hear 'and they all lived happily ever after' we breathe a sigh of relief and enjoy the satisfaction of a happy ending. What makes these words have such strong connotations for so many people? It is because so many traditional stories begin and end in this way and we have heard these stories from when we were very young. They have a recognizable pattern to them – there will be the goodies and the baddies; there will be a problem or a crisis; the hero will win through and everybody will receive their just rewards. Often these stories challenge accepted notions of good and evil, of family structure and of relationships. The three little pigs will outwit the big bad wolf; Cinderella will go to the ball and marry the handsome prince; Sleeping Beauty will be woken by a kiss; the Billy Goats Gruff will eat the grass on the other side of the bridge. So it continues – good wins in the end, evil is conquered and riches restored to their rightful owner.

It is through stories like this that young children learn about their social and cultural heritage. The values, beliefs and practices are passed on, challenged and revised. It is also through these stories that young children become part of history and understand how and why things come to them.

It is also a way in which the values, beliefs and practices of other cultures can be made familiar and understood. Often it is found that the basic story is the same. *Jamil's Clever Cat* by Fiona French (1998) is a version of a Bengali folk tale and those who know it will recognize links with the story of Puss in Boots. Literature identifies the common humanity which links different cultural groups and helps the reader to empathize and understand different ways of being.

Familiarity with well-known stories allows children to explore how stories work. They see that each story has a similar pattern – introduction, events, problems, resolution – and so are supported when they come to write and tell their own. They identify the characteristics of typical stereotypical characters and see how these characters are created through language and plot. Their own first stories will imitate the way in which these traditional stories work. They can then play with these stories and change some elements of them. As they innovate they will begin to understand more of the elements of story, and reading some published innovations helps them do this. For example, *The True Story of the 3 Little Pigs* by Jon Scieszka (1991) tells the familiar story from a different perspective. Alternative versions of stories will not be appreciated without a strong knowledge of the original tale.

Literature allows us to know ourselves, our world and other people better, and literature for the very young is no exception to that. So how do we choose when we are selecting books for the very young? The principles of teaching early reading identified by the Primary National Strategy (DfES, 2003) (which is followed by primary schools in the UK) are guided by the 'simple' view of reading (Gough and Tumner, 1986) which considers word identification and language comprehension as the two processes central to reading. It is recommended that young readers are given books containing simple phonically consistent words which they are able to identify for themselves. But there is much more to choosing books for young children than that, as we have seen in this chapter.

Selecting books

What do we look for in a book for very young children? Let us use the book *Owl Babies* by Martin Waddell (1992) to illustrate the answer.

First, we need a book with which children can identify and emotionally engage. All young children have been in a situation where they have worried if their mother would ever return. They know the feeling that the baby owls, Sarah, Percy and Bill, are experiencing and they can identify with their responses. A good book for young children is one with which they can make an emotional link.

Second, a book should invite involvement. This might be through:

> identification – 'When I first went to nursery I didn't think my mummy was going to come back.'
> investigation – 'I wonder why she left when they were asleep? Can you see the pattern of feathers on the page?'
> innovation – 'What would happen if she didn't come back?'
> critical reflection – 'Why does Bill always say the same thing?'
> becoming involved in the text. The relationship between the text and the illustrations is crucial – they work as one in helping the child to create meaning.

Third, the language supports the child in reading and understanding the book. In *Owl Babies* there is repetition – 'I want my mummy'. The children will join in with this because of the repetition and because it is something they themselves will have said many times and they will have shared in the emotion behind it. There is a pattern to the language; each time the owl babies speak in the same order and there is a similarity to the things each says. We begin to get to know the characters and to be able to predict their reactions. The language is literary; it introduces the young reader to the language of books.

AND SHE CAME. Soft and silent, she swooped through the trees to Sarah and Percy and Bill.

How much more powerful and emotionally satisfying is that than the simple but phonically consistent, 'Mum came back'.

Sharing books

Having chosen a book on the basis of personal engagement, active involvement and powerful language, how can we share that book with a very young child in a way which will enable him or her to enjoy the richness that literature will offer.

In reading books aloud to children we act as mediator between the text and the book. We talk with them about the book, allowing them to relate their own experiences and understanding to the book. We read fluently and with expression allowing the power of the language to be heard and felt. We allow responses to be made. These responses may not always be made with words. The young child might respond to the return of the mother by running around the room arms wide, swooping through the air. Children might respond to the fear of the three babies by snuggling up close to their co-readers. They might join in with Bill's cry. They might well answer Sarah's surmises and Percy's answers. It is important to remember that every response is valid; the power of literature works its magic differently in every reader.

We began by distinguishing between books as artefacts and books as literature. For the very young child it is important that they are given every opportunity to experience the joys and challenges of literature. As they learn to read independently, they need experiences which remind them that all that hard work of learning to decode those strange marks on the page is worthwhile and that reading meets those indefinable inner needs as well as being an essential skill for day-to-day living.

Further reading

A bookshelf for beginning readers should include:

A wide range of engaging stories including traditional, contemporary and fantasy tales: for example, *Anacy and Mr Drybone* by Fiona French (Frances Lincoln), *Tatty Ratty* by Helen Cooper (Red Fox) and *Q Pootle 5* by Nick Butterworth (Harper Collins).

Stories and nursery rhymes from their own culture and the wider cultural heritage: for example, *Sing Me A Story* by Grace Hallworth and John Clementson (Frances Lincoln) and *Hairy Toes and Scary Bones* by Rose Impey (Orchard).

Stories with lots of repetition, alliteration, rhyme and language play: for example, *In the Dark, Dark Wood* by Jessica Souhami (Frances Lincoln).

Poems, games and songs that encourage everyone to join in with words and actions: *The Barefoot Book of Classic Poems* edited by Jackie Morris and Carol Ann Duffy (Barefoot).

Books that invite readers to marvel at pop-up pages, to lift flaps or to pull levers: for example, *The Animals Went in Two by Two* by Jan Pienkowski (Walker Books).

Alphabets and counting books: for example, *Many hands counting book* by Brita Branstrom (Walker Books) and *South African Animals* by Lindiwe Mabuza and Alan Baker (Tamarind).

Stories in languages other than English and in dual language: for example, *Farmer Duck* by Martin Waddell and Helen Oxenbury in Bengali and English (MantraLingua,UK).

Information books about the immediate environment and further afield: for example, *Think of an Eel* by Karen Wallace (Walker Books)

Books that tie in with popular television programmes and films: for example, *But I am an Alligator* by Lauren Child (Puffin).

Stories and songs in books with accompanying story boxes, related toys, CDs or DVDs: for example, *Creepy Crawly Calypso* by Tony Langham and Debbie Harter (Barefoot).

Learning to be a Reader: Promoting Good Textual Health

Vivienne Smith

This chapter looks at:

> The pedagogy of reading

> Developing active readers

> Good books to foster healthy reading habits

What matters? Learning to read, or learning to be a reader? How does the way we teach reading in school and the books we encourage children to read help them achieve one or the other? This chapter looks at the pedagogy of reading and the significant part that books themselves have to play in the important business of learning what it is that readers do when they read. It argues that the best books promote strong, healthy reading habits in the readers who engage with them.

The teaching of reading

Universal schooling made an enormous difference in the way most people learned to read. Historically, it seems, learning to read was a domestic process. It happened, on the whole, in middle-class homes, *before* the children (mostly boys!) went to school. Mothers or governesses did the job. They worked with boys and girls, probably individually, teaching them to recognize letters and then finding and adapting short stories and familiar passages for the children to read. We have proof of this. Styles and Arizpe's (2006) work with the Johnson collection shows us how one mother, Jane Johnson, in the mid-eighteenth century, painstakingly and lovingly developed the materials to teach her own children to read. She made alphabets and found sentences, poems, fables and stories and items of local interest for her children. All these she meticulously mounted on small cards to fit the children's hands. They were beautifully decorated and illustrated to please.

Learning to read for the Johnson children must have been an intimate and individual business, wrapped up with their emerging personalities and their relationship with their mother. The texts they read matched the contexts and interests of their lives, and carried them forward towards the purposeful and satisfying literacy they saw modelled by their parents every day at home. There was no gap between learning to read and being a reader.

But what can be achieved with two or three children at their mother's knee is not the same as a class teacher can do with 25, or 30, or even more children in her charge, all of whom need to be taught to read if they are to cope with the demands of the school curriculum. I know teachers who remember class sizes of over 40; bigger classes still were common in the early years of the twentieth century. How could any teacher with a class of 50 or more create individual resources and reading programmes for each child as Jane Johnson had done? It was partly in response to large numbers and the constraints of time they occasioned that the commercial reading scheme came about. Here at last was a standard, reliable and foolproof system, with built in progression that would kick-start the majority of children into reading, and which would save overworked teachers from having to reinvent the wheel for each one of the many children that passed through their hands.

So successful and so widely used were reading schemes in the mid-twentieth century that they became part of the national psyche in the UK. Janet and John and Peter and Jane became cultural referents to the extent that advertisers and poets could parody both the assumptions that govern the social worlds of the texts and the distinctive reading scheme language they are cast in (for example, Cope, 1986). Schemes were so generally accepted that seemed to represent a natural way to learn to read.

But there were detractors. Criticisms were levelled against commercial reading schemes for all sorts of reasons (Meek, 1982; Waterland, 1988; Williams, 2001). This is not the place to rehearse those arguments, but we should note that publishers took the criticisms seriously and responded to them magnificently. These days, the best schemes are more inclusive and less sexist. They use recognizable language (rather than the 'reading-scheme-ese' that Cope sends up in her poem), are well and generously illustrated, and tell worthwhile, sometimes funny, stories. Many children genuinely like them, and are as interested in reading the stories as they are in getting on to the next book in the scheme.

But for all the improvements, some things about reading schemes have remained constant. They continue to be designed to get large numbers of children to learn to read print as quickly and efficiently as possible. Because of this, they cannot take into account the differing needs, interests and dispositions of the children who read them. More important still, they continue to assume that reading is a neutral skill that can be learnt on practice texts (such as they provide) and that this skill can later be transferred to any text the reader meets. I argue here that reading is more complex than this.

Why texts matter

Twenty years ago, Margaret Meek in her book *How Texts Teach What Readers Learn* (1988) made a significant contribution to our understanding of how readers are made. She showed beyond doubt that although decoding and sight vocabulary matter and good teachers help, texts themselves play an important role in teaching children (and older people too) to be readers, rather than merely people who can read. Meek showed us how rich, allusive texts such as Allan and Janet Ahlberg's *Each Peach Pear Plum* (1978) introduce children to the intertextual thinking that is a great part of what successful readers do, how *Rosie's Walk* (Hutchins, 1968) shows that a text can mean more than the words themselves say and that irony is worth looking for. She showed how, for older children, *The Silver Sword* (Serraillier, 1960) and other powerful texts teach children the satisfaction of becoming completely absorbed in the emotional intensity of a story.

These are lessons in reading that *could* be taught by a teacher or parent, but are better left to texts themselves. No amount of explaining irony is as funny as the joke in *Rosie's Walk*. No amount of telling children that good readers make use of what they already know about text is as effective as the delight of discovering that The Three Bears from one story have walked confidently into another and that Cinderella and all sorts of other characters are there too. Children learn that they and the writer share a common range of referents, and that recognizing those referents makes reading a richer and more entertaining game. These lessons matter. The adult reader who has never learned to spot irony misses the sharp wit of Jane Austen. The viewer who cannot think intertextually misses most of the jokes in the Simpsons, and the reader who cannot get involved in the emotions of a story might as well not, and probably does not, bother to read much at all.

Meek showed us how very good texts teach the very best lessons. What she inferred, but did not make explicit, is that there is a corollary to this: less good texts teach less useful lessons. While the best texts encourage the reader to think, connect, wonder, imagine and engage, others encourage lazier, less healthy reading habits, for example, to accept without question, to be easily satisfied and that getting to the end of the book matters more than the journey through it.

The understanding that Meek made accessible to us is that *all* texts matter. Even the texts we read at the very beginning are important because they inculcate the habits of thinking we will use as readers all through our reading lives. For teachers of young children, this understanding is crucially important. They need to be able to recognize the sort of lessons in reading, beyond reading the words, which the texts they use in their classrooms teach. They need to know which texts encourage the best reading habits and which do not, because, as we all know, bad habits learned young are very hard to break in later life!

In the next part of this chapter, I look at two examples of text that a child of about 7 might be encouraged to read at school. I want to consider the sort of lessons in reading these texts offer to the child and what that child needs to know about reading in order to make the most of them.

Example 1: *Lost in the Mist*

The first text I discuss is *Lost in the Mist* by Jill Atkins and Shelagh McNicholas (1997), a story from level 8 of Heinemann's Storyworld Reading scheme. It is a typical text of its sort: narrative, straightforward and supportive of an inexperienced reader. It is published as a little pamphlet, like all the other books in the series, about 8 inches long and 6 inches wide. I want to look particularly carefully at the double spread that opens the story.

Here is the text, spread over two pages:

> In the summer Alison went to stay with her gran and grandad in Scotland. A boy named Jamie lived next door to them. One day Alison and Gran were going for a walk in the hills.
> 'Do you want to come with us?' Alison asked Jamie.
> 'Yes please.' said Jamie. (p. 2)
>
> Alison, Gran and Jamie set off.
> Alison put her hand in her pocket and took out a whistle. Alison blew on the whistle. It made a very loud noise.
> 'Stop that noise!' said Gran.
> So Alison put the whistle back in her pocket. (p. 3)

These words cover about half of the white space of the double spread, with continuous linear prose. A wide gutter separates the pages. There is a picture above the text on page 2, and another below it, on page 3. The first picture shows an image of a street. There are two whitewashed cottages. In the foreground, a small girl and an older woman are coming out of one cottage, closing the door behind them. Both are wearing coats, hats and sturdy shoes. In the background, a boy emerges from the second cottage. The second picture shows Gran and the children walking in the hills. Jamie and Gran are both looking at Alison, and she looks up at Gran. Gran seems to be alarmed and Alison appears to be in the act of taking the whistle from her mouth. All coats are buttoned up. Gran has a rucksack on her back and the sky is overcast.

What might a reader make of this?

Some things are immediately clear. First is that it is the words that matter, not the pictures. We can tell this from the way they are centrally placed on the page, uncluttered, and taking up most of the prime space. These are words that have been designed to make confusion unlikely. The prose is bald and repetitive: the emphasis on consolidating vocabulary rather than building atmosphere or character. Because of an assumed need to keep vocabulary simple and the plot moving on, the pace of this text is fast and functional. The reader is not encouraged to wonder about the walk or the characters or even the whistle.

Conversely, the pictures, pushed to the edges, are less important. Their position, at the top and at the bottom, suggests what they are for: to orientate the reader into the story and to reinforce what she has read. As such, the pictures give very little information that is not in the words as well. They show key features, Alison, Gran, Jamie-next-door, hills and the whistle. Those things which are not explicitly mentioned but are illustrated, for example, the warm clothes, strong boots and grey sky, are there to help to position the story in the reader's mind, and with the help of the title, hint a little at how the plot is likely to unfold. But these pictures, like the text, give up their secrets easily. Readers who go back and examine the pictures after they have read the words will not find much to think about. These illustrations give their clues in order and, metaphorically, lie down and die. They don't have a 'life' without the words.

Lost in the Mist is a perfectly acceptable story: it is interesting, accessible and well produced. It is typical of the vast majority of stories in the vast majority of reading schemes. It provides a number of affordances for learning that a young reader might take up. Some of them are very important lessons in reading indeed. One is that reading is achievable: with a limited sight vocabulary, some decoding skills and a supportive atmosphere, many children could read this text competently at a relatively early stage in their reading lives. We are foolish if we underestimate the importance of this. Developing confidence in young readers is the teacher's first priority. Texts like this, which minimize the likelihood of error, do a lot to make emerging readers believe in themselves at a time when they are vulnerable.

Another plus is that this text teaches children about the layout and form of conventional fiction. Illustrations of any sort are rare in adult novels. Learning to focus on continuous prose is what readers of fiction have to learn to do.

More than that, this text teaches about narrative. Two things are important. Both concern narrative voice. First, who is telling the story? We are not told. Readers who make sense of *Lost in the Mist* have to learn to accommodate a hidden, omniscient third-person narrator: a teller they cannot see, and who does not address them directly. As Gregory (1992) suggests, some readers find this hard to learn, yet without it, much of the fiction of western civilization is inaccessible. Second, this text teaches readers to comply with narrative direction. This is a narrator that brooks no argument. The relentless and determined pace of this narrative, the lack of ambiguity in the prose and the directive nature of the illustrations mean that the reader is carried along on a strong current of purposefulness. The narrative voice controls the reader, ensures that he or she sees and thinks in the way the author wants. Strong narrative direction like this is present in many well regarded texts. Look, for example, at how J.K. Rowling directs and positions the reader's attention at the start of *Harry Potter and the Philosopher's Stone* (1997), or how George Eliot brings the reader's attention down, close and closer, in the first paragraphs of *Adam Bede* (1859). *Lost in the Mist* helps readers to go along with a writer's purposes in a way that much literature appears to demand.

These are valuable lessons. But are they *enough*?

Example 2: *My Uncle is a Hunkle, Says Clarice Bean*

This spread (Figure 4.1) from *My Uncle is a Hunkle, Says Clarice Bean* (Child, 2000), also comes from the very beginning of the book, though it is difficult here, as with most of Lauren Child's work, to make clear distinctions between endpapers, title pages and story proper. It is clear after even a cursory glance that this text makes quite different demands on the reader from *Lost in the Mist*.

Most obvious, the balance between picture and word is different. There is no separation that makes one element more important than the other. Image dominates, but there are words here, in fact only 20 or so, fewer than in the first text. Words are integrated into the image and wander, perhaps alarmingly, across the page. Several fonts are used.

Figure 4.1 Pages from *My Uncle is a Hunkle, Says Clarice Bean*
© Lauren Child, *My Uncle is a Hunkle, Says Clarice Bean* (Orchard Books, 2000)

The two images that comprise this spread are connected by the words of the nurse who is speaking on the telephone. They meander across the gutter, suggesting to the reader that events are concurrent rather than sequential, and encouraging the eye and the mind to wander, rather than proceed in an ordered linear way. The images themselves compound this effect: collage creates a slightly chaotic effect and cut-out drawings contrast with the realism of the cityscape through the window. All of this encourages playful and divergent thinking in the reader, quite unlike the earnest, purposeful direction of *Lost in the Mist*.

Here it is image that carries the story, not words. The reader sees Uncle Ernie with his legs in the air, and notices Minal Cricket making life difficult for mum. Some words confirm what the pictures show, but they provide very little 'connective tissue' to direct and orientate the reader. To make sense of this text, the reader must be able to read what the words *do not* say, as well as what they *do*.

What the words do say is not the stuff of reading schemes. There is no controlled vocabulary here and word choices are unexpected. No reader, I suggest, would predict 'doughnut' in the first line from the semantic information already given, and there is no picture clue to help. The tone is colloquial and jokey. 'Life's ups and downs', for example, works on several levels, and there is ambiguity in what Mum says. Why, the reader wonders is this time particularly inconvenient for eating doughnuts?

The narrative voice, too, affords challenges. In this text, the narrator is explicit. It is Clarice Bean. One might expect this clarity to make everything easier, but it does not. There are two reasons for this. First, Clarice is not omniscient and neutral, like the narrator of *Lost in the Mist*; she is positioned *in* the story, and so can only tell what she sees and hears and thinks, and that, of course, might not be the whole story. Second, she does not provide a single, straightforward narrative. She includes others' words both directly, when she quotes mum and the nurse, and indirectly, when she imports the phrases of adults into her own telling (for example, life's 'ups and downs'). Because of this, the reader can glimpse versions of the story as others might tell it and guess at the connected stories that have informed what those speakers say. The effect of all this is twofold. There is a diminution of the authority of the narrative voice, and a widening of the positioning of text in the reader's head. The reader might deduce that this is one telling of a story that is part of a vast, interconnected web of narrative. It is not a single, complete event. *Lost in the Mist* is presented as though it were.

Does this ambiguity mean that *My Uncle is a Hunkle, Says Clarice Bean* is less suitable for inexperienced readers than *Lost in the Mist* and a thousand other scheme books? My argument is that it does not. Instead, I argue that it is the ambiguity of this text and the work the reader has to do to make sense of it that teaches young readers the good habits of reading that they will need to take them confidently into the literate world of the twenty-first century.

Good habits of reading

> Good readers know that reading is an active process. They know that the more they put in to making a text mean, the more they get out of it, and texts that make the reader work are inherently more satisfying than ones which do not. This is because, as reading theorists have shown us (see Chambers, 1992), the business of making texts mean has more to do with what goes on in readers' heads than what the words on the page say. Books such as *My Uncle is a Hunkle, Says Clarice Bean* are important because it is impossible to read them without thinking widely and divergently, and using the results of that thinking to fill in the gaps the text leaves. Children who learn to do this find that reading is entertaining and satisfying. There is a danger that children who only read directive texts like *Lost in the Mist*, which require relatively little input, never learn to think in this way, and so only engage with texts at a superficial level.
> Good readers bring all they can to their reading. They know to look widely in the text, and beyond the text, to make reading mean. In *My Uncle is a*

Hunkle, Says Clarice Bean, the need to make sense of the quirky pictures and the hint that there are stories here, beyond stories, encourages children to do this. This ability to think beyond the words in a text and juxtapose one text with another is a vital reading habit that children need to learn if they are to cope with the complex demands of the literacy in the twenty-first century. Texts like *Lost in the Mist* encourage children to believe that words and texts exist in a vacuum.

> Good readers learn to read against the grain. They learn to recognize tone and narrative voice, and they know that writers use both for effect. They recognize when writers are playing with them, and when narrators are unreliable. These understandings are important in fiction, because readers can gain enormous pleasure from 'reading beyond the words'. But it is even more important in non-fiction where readers need to be alert to narrative intent and propaganda in media, advertising and political texts. Readers who learn early on, through playful texts like *My Uncle is a Hunkle, Says Clarice Bean*, that narrative is positioned and slippery, and that narrators might not always be reliable, are in a better position than those who have become used to trusting everything a strong narrator tells them. Learning to mistrust directive prose is an important political understanding.

> Good readers are flexible. Unusual texts, such as *My Uncle is a Hunkle, Says Clarice Bean*, are good for readers, because they challenge expectations. Readers have to work out, for each new text, *how* it needs to be read. Where does the reading start? What does one *do* with the pictures? How does one make sense of the wriggly writing? Learning to negotiate all sorts of texts makes readers adaptable and flexible. Flexible readers can cope with all sorts of text, however innovative or whacky these might seem. Readers who are used only to traditional narrative and traditional layout are not so lucky. They often struggle when texts do not immediately meet their expectations. Readers like this are not well equipped to cope in times of rapid literacy change, such as our own.

Promoting good textual health is something we should take seriously for young readers. As society continues to change, and as the uses to which society puts literacy continue to develop, our job will be to produce readers who can cope with those changes. We will need readers who are active, engaged, astute and flexible, and we need to find texts that nurture the habits of thinking that enable them to be so. Literature is a good place to look for those texts. Books produced by creative people for creative purposes are likely to encourage creative thinking. Books that tease, charm and challenge will produce readers that are alert and responsive.

Classrooms need to be full of good books that encourage good reading habits and teachers need to promote them. They cannot risk leaving the job of teaching reading to schemes that equip children with a limited understanding of what reading is and what readers do. Reading is too important for that.

Further reading

Some useful books for children of this age:

Allan Ahlberg, *Ten in a Bed* and *Jeremiah in the Dark Woods.* Two short, funny, easy-to-read books that encourage intertextual thinking.

Anthony Browne, *Changes.* Anthony Browne's books always encourage readers to explore the pictures and make sense beyond the words. This early text is one of Browne's most innovative and thought provoking.

Lauren Child, All the Clarice Bean stories, for example, *What Planet are you on, Clarice Bean?* Lauren Child is a really exciting new author–illustrator. Her books stretch the reader in many useful ways. Clarice Bean is an engaging character whose narrative voice affords the reader with a number of important lessons (see above).

Penny Dolan, *The Tale of Highover Hill.* The second of a quirky and witty series of very readable stories. There is a sense of gothic here that will delight young readers who are becoming aware of narrative form, and a rollicking good plot to draw in the others.

Anne Fine, *Diary of a Killer Cat.* A rather more difficult read – but this will teach children that not all narrators are to be trusted, and help them understand irony.

Paul Stewart and Chris Riddell, *Fergus Crane.* An illustrated story of high adventure and pirates that will keep young readers on the edge of their seats.

Philip Pullman, *I Was A Rat.* An unusual take on the Cinderella story. Pullman plays games with texts and readers that children who are becoming aware of literary conventions will enjoy.

5

Traditional Tales: The Bedrock of Storytelling

Ann Lazim

> **This chapter looks at:**
>
> > Traditional stories and a wide range of narrative
>
> > Tales from many cultures
>
> > Modern versions of old stories

When traditional stories are mentioned, fairy tales such as 'Cinderella', 'Sleeping Beauty' and 'Snow White' are often what first spring to mind. Way beyond this small but significant clutch of well-known stories, the term 'traditional stories' encompasses a culturally diverse range of tale types and themes which stretch around the world. However, beyond the diversity, many of the same patterns and plots emerge in stories from community to community, from culture to culture. Across the world we also share story language and understandings such as the term 'a fairy-tale ending' to denote a happy resolution, usually a marriage between two attractive protagonists (the global reach of Walt Disney films has a lot to answer for here). Even celebrated and well-known stories, such as 'Sleeping Beauty', are not always all they seem. For example, Charles Perrault's version does not end with the princess waking up with the prince's kiss. There is a much darker coda to this story, involving a child-eating mother-in-law. All in all, traditional stories are not the simple, comforting tales we are sometimes led to expect. It is important to be aware that traditional stories were generally not originally told specifically with an audience of children in mind.

The patterns and journeys of traditional stories are the bedrock of story-telling, whether in oral or written form. They may be retold in the time-honoured way, allowing for embellishments and the personal touches of the teller, or form the basic structure of a narrative, sometimes overtly, sometimes in more subtle ways. It is occasionally possible to trace the lineage of a story, but often stories appear in different cultures without this 'hierarchy' of evolution. The appearance of similar stories throughout the world can be partly explained by humankind's universal need to understand their surroundings and by common human characteristics. However, stories have also spread as humans have travelled the world, passing on stories – orally at first – and shaping them to suit a new environment and culture. As prolific commentator on fairy tales, Jack Zipes, has said: 'The fairy tale is a polygenetic cultural artefact that has spread throughout the world through human contact and technologies invented to bring about effective communication' (Zipes, 2006b: xiv).

Among those technologies, pride of place can still be given to printing and books which have enabled stories to be recorded and spread more widely, although to these must be added more recent and rapidly-developing media – films, audio-recordings and the Internet. Setting a story into a fixed format may preserve it and give it a wider audience. However, it can sometimes have an adverse effect leading to a tale being 'set in stone' so that many people believe there is one 'correct' version of a story.

Traditional stories include a wide range of narratives – myths and legends, fables, folk and fairy tales – and there is only space to discuss these briefly here, highlighting some well-known examples and drawing in stories from a wide range of cultures where possible. However, I have focused on books which are reasonably accessible in libraries and bookshops, and inevitably this will lead to some gaps.

Myths

Myths were first invented to explain the world's mysteries and reflect a human need to explain how things came to be. As part of a desire to explain natural phenomena, such as why there is day and night or the reason for the seasons, people have invented a whole variety of gods and supernatural beings. Most well known in Western cultures are the gods of Mount Olympus who people the Greek myths. Many books retelling these stories for children have been produced, with far fewer featuring their Roman counterparts. As with Bible stories, some knowledge of Greek mythology is necessary to fully appreciate much Western literature which is pervaded by overt and underlying references to these classical stories.

Stories from religion and mythology are intimately entwined, as they are both linked to humankind's beliefs and a quest to understand our existence. The great Indian epics the Mahabharata and the Ramayana tell the stories of the gods and goddesses of Hinduism. These stirring stories are passed on orally and sung and danced in live performance as well as being recorded in literature. Examples of retellings for children include Madhur Jaffrey's *Seasons of Splendour* (Puffin) and Jessica Souhami's picturebook *Rama and the Demon King* (Frances Lincoln) which tells the famous story from the Ramayana, of how Prince Rama rescues his wife Sita and destroys Ravanna, the ten-headed king of all the demons, with the help of Hanuman and the monkey army. The dramatic illustrations are adapted from the author/illustrator's own shadow puppets.

In addition to the Indian epics, other myths and legends predate the Greek myths. Retellings of stories from Sumer and Babylon, both parts of Ancient Mesopotamia, now modern Iraq, are not plentiful. This is partly because some were only rediscovered comparatively recently. The story *Lugalbanda: The Boy Who Was Caught Up in a War* (Walker) has been retold by Kathy Henderson with Jane Ray's distinctive and carefully researched illustrations, and marks an interest in the region caused by current conflicts. Christina Balit draws on influences from her Middle Eastern childhood in her artwork for the Babylonian myth of the seasons *Ishtar and Tammuz* (Frances Lincoln), retold by Christopher Moore. The Greek myth of Demeter and Persephone has many parallels with this story.

In addition to the Greek myths, the Scandinavian stories of the Norse gods and giants are strongly present today in the English language, where their names form the basis of most days of the week, and in their influence on literature such as J.R.R. Tolkien's *Lord of the Rings*.

The cycles of Irish myths have also frequently been retold for children. The story of Oisìn and the land of Tír na nÓg in which a man travels to a magic land and, when he returns, finds that many hundreds of years have passed, finds parallels in many other cultures, such as the Japanese story of Urashima, a fisherman who spends many years in an underwater world.

Legends

Legends usually tell of heroes and brave deeds and are often based on characters who may have really existed around whom a web of myths and stories have been woven. One of the most enduring of these is King Arthur. Thought to have a leader of the Britons against the Saxons, early stories about him appear in Geoffrey of Monmouth's 1136 Celtic 'history' of

Britain. Further stories about him, the Knights of the Round Table, the search for the Holy Grail, and the sorcerer Merlin were added from a variety of sources, particularly French and Welsh (*The Mabinogion*). The stories were gathered together by Sir Thomas Malory in *Le Morte d'Arthur* (1485) and have been retold in myriad ways since.

The legends surrounding King Arthur continue to seize the imaginations of writers and filmmakers. The first part of T.H. White's *The Once and Future King* took on a different guise as the Disney animation, *The Sword in the Stone*. Historical novelist Rosemary Sutcliff produced a beautifully written trilogy. Arthurian legends underpin Susan Cooper's fantasy quintet *The Dark is Rising* (Puffin). Interesting recent examples include Kevin Crossley-Holland's *Arthur* trilogy (Orion) which juxtaposes the legend with the life of a young man during the Crusades allowing for subtle commentary on parallels with modern-day war and politics. In *Here Lies Arthur* (Scholastic) Philip Reeve demonstrates how the legends about Arthur could have emanated from rumours perpetrated by spin doctor Merlin.

The adventures of Robin Hood and his band of outlaws in Sherwood Forest who rob from the rich to give to the poor have also been much filmed and the subject of at least three television series in addition to many retellings in print.

Folk and fairy tales

Most of the popular folk and fairy tales retold today are in the books of stories recorded and written by the Brothers Grimm in Germany and, prior to this, Charles Perrault in France. Ladies of the French court in the seventeenth century told stories for their own amusement in literary salons. Perrault's stories were published in 1697 as *Histoires ou contes du temps passé* and included new literary versions of 'Sleeping Beauty', 'Cinderella', 'Little Red Riding Hood' and 'Puss in Boots'. There being no literature specifically published for children at that time, these stories were not told directly for them, although there is no doubt that they have subsequently become classics in France and far beyond, and have influenced subsequent retellers of tales. The names of Grimm and Perrault are well known. However, many of the stories they retold can be traced further back to sixteenth-century Italian writers Giovan Francesco Straparola who authored *Le piacevoli notti* and Giambattista Basile and his *Pentamerone*.

Jacob and Wilhelm Grimm were folklorists and philologists who collected over 200 folk tales from friends and neighbours. Their collection was not originally intended for children but the popularity of many of the tales with young people led to subsequent reshaping and editing of these stories, which include 'Little Red Cap', 'Hansel and Gretel', 'Rumpelstiltskin' and 'Rapunzel'. It was previously thought that the stories were collected direct from the peasants of Germany but later research showed that their informants were from more educated backgrounds and that many of the tales may have come from written sources, including Perrault. However, this does not diminish the Grimms' achievement as these have become some of the best loved folk tales in Europe and beyond.

The Grimm brothers collected and published tales they felt to be representative of their national culture, and collections of folk tales were made in other countries or regions during the nineteenth century. These included Peter Christen Asbjørnsen and Jørgen Moe in Norway (their collection included 'The Three Billy Goats Gruff' and 'East o' the Sun, West o' the Moon'), Aleksandr Afanasyev in Russia, and later Joseph Jacobs who collected English and Celtic stories.

Scottish folklorist Andrew Lang started his series of colour Fairy Books in 1889 with *The Blue Fairy Book* and ended with *The Lilac Fairy Book* in 1910. He began by using only European sources but in the later books he included stories from many other parts of the world. The series was very popular, reviving an interest in fairy tales, and is still in print today.

Hans Christian Andersen was from Denmark and is one of the most famous names associated with fairy tales for children. The most significant international children's literature award given biennially to an author and an illustrator for lifetime achievement is named after him (see www.ibby.org). Andersen differed from the Grimm brothers and other nineteenth-century collectors of folk tales. While some of his stories are based on folklore, many were written from his own imagination and addressed children directly in a colloquial style. He did not always think it necessary to provide a happy ending to his tales. Readers who have only come across 'The Steadfast Tin Soldier' sequence in *Fantasia 2* or *The Little Mermaid*, both Disney films, will be in for a shock if they read the original tales. His most well-known stories include 'The Snow Queen', 'The Ugly Duckling' and 'The Emperor's New Clothes'.

Many cultures, many traditions, one world

Many of the folk tales familiar to children in the UK are from Europe and have been available in book form for many years. However, in many societies in Africa and Asia, the oral tradition is still highly significant and some of these stories have been set down in written form, which means they can be shared with children elsewhere. Often this has been done by people who have come from a Western tradition, although they may have a close affinity with the local people, and this works most successfully when the co-operation of local storytellers has been sought to ensure that traditions are respected. Some early collections were made due to the colonial presence of Europeans in other parts of the world. Later collectors have been concerned with preserving tales that might otherwise be lost owing to changes in society which erode the passing on of traditional stories. Peggy Appiah was married to a Ghanaian and immersed herself in the culture of her adopted country. Among the collections of folk tales she published was *The Pineapple Child and Other Tales from Ashanti* (1969) which became available at a time when there was a shortage of published stories for children from Africa.

More recently Elizabeth Laird collected stories from around Ethiopia and published them as *When the World Began* (Oxford University Press), and storyteller Sally Pomme Clayton travelled in Central Asia and has related the stories she heard there in *Tales Told in Tents* (Frances Lincoln).

However, there are some cultural and ethnic groups who are deeply unhappy about what they see as others appropriating their tales – for example, some Native Americans and Australian Aboriginals. Another potential barrier to the free flow of tales may be the increase in copyrighting material, mainly in the USA. It is important not to dismiss a collection or story retold by someone not from that place but to be aware that his or her perceptions may vary.

In the 1960s and 1970s many collections of tales from particular regions and countries were published in the UK as there was a growing concern with an emerging multicultural society and this led to a search for stories from a variety of cultures. There were also multi-country collections, such as thematic anthologies by Ruth Manning-Sanders (*A Book of Ghosts and Goblins*, *A Book of Enchantments and Curses*, and so on) and age-related short story collections by Sara and Stephen Corrin. Modern publishing tends towards the glossy gift book, recycling the same set of stories. Honourable exceptions come from Barefoot Books and Frances Lincoln who both publish very attractive books but spread a wider net around the world. A *Folk and Fairy Tales* book guide published by Booktrust in 2004 (Hallford and Zaghini, 2004) appears to be quite Eurocentric. However, this is not the fault of the editors – it is a valuable summary of what is available and reflects what publishers believe will sell.

The Thousand and One Nights have had a tremendous global influence on storytelling. The stories travelled to Europe from the Middle East via translations into French by Antoine Galland, and were added to and embellished. Some of the most often retold tales are 'Aladdin' (a popular pan-tomime as well as a controversial Disney film and, it is thought, not one of the original tales), 'Sindbad the Sailor' and 'Ali Baba and the Forty Thieves'. The stories are set in the context of a framework of nightly stories told by Scherezade to the King who she has married and who is having his brides daily executed because of his anger at the unfaithfulness of his first wife. Scherezade is able to stave off death by leaving her stories at an enticing point each night so that the King will desire to hear the rest. Only a few of the stories are generally well known. This is partly because the sensuous nature of some of the stories is considered unsuitable for children who, after all, were not their original intended audience.

Many cultures have a trickster character, often portrayed as a 'wise fool'. They may take human form such as the Turkish Nasruddin Hodja (also known in other Middle Eastern countries; he is Joha in Arabic) or the German Til Eulenspiegel. They may be animals – Coyote, Raven and Rabbit all appear as trickster characters in Native American folk tales, while Tortoise and Hare appear in some parts of Africa. One of the best known of all tricksters is half man and half spider – Anancy – a character who has travelled from Africa to the Caribbean and America due to slavery. Brer Rabbit also has a place in African American folklore. Trickster tales are spread around many collections and there are some stories in picturebook form. Many oral storytellers include Hodja and Anancy tales in their repertoire.

Illustration

In his influential psychoanalytic study of the meaning and importance of fairy tales *The Uses of Enchantment*, Bruno Bettelheim (1991) declares against illustrating traditional stories, stating that 'a fairy tale loses much of its personal meaning when its figures and events are given substance not by the child's imagination, but by that of an illustrator'. However, the trend has been towards publishing elaborately illustrated and designed collections of traditional stories and picturebooks of individual tales. While in some respects this does draw away from the oral origins of the stories when people built up their own mental pictures, there are positive aspects too, in our visual age.

Some illustrators draw out underlying meanings that readers may not have discovered themselves. Angela Barrett has illustrated several well-known stories, including 'The Emperor's New Clothes' and 'Beauty and the Beast'. Her interpretation of 'Snow White', in particular, repays close examination. In Anthony Browne's 'Hansel and Gretel', the likeness between the children's stepmother and the witch, the two characters framed in similar poses, is suggestive.

Some stories are chosen for picturebook treatment much more often than others and it is interesting to speculate about the reasons for this. However, this also provides an opportunity as it makes it possible to compare many different variants of a story in terms of illustration as well as the text. There are numerous picturebook versions of 'Cinderella' which place her in a variety of settings. They include the Chinese *Wishbones* illustrated by Meilo So and *Yeh-shen* illustrated by Chinese American Ed Young and an Irish variant *Fair, Brown and Trembling* by South African illustrator Jude Daly. There are not so many illustrated versions of 'Little Red Riding Hood' in English but this could provide an opportunity to explore picturebooks in other languages even if the written text is not fully understood, as many illustrators from France, Italy and Belgium have produced interesting versions of this story.

Modern manifestations

Knowledge of traditional stories is important in enjoying much modern literature. Many novels for both children and adults rework fairy tale stories and themes. Traditional tales frequently form the basis for modern retellings, sometimes explicitly, such as in Robin McKinley's novels *Beauty* and *Spindle's End* (both Corgi) which expand on the tales of 'Beauty and the Beast' and 'Sleeping Beauty' respectively. These novels maintain the timeless feel of fantasy. In her 'Happy Ever After' trilogy (Red Fox Definitions) set in a girls' boarding school, Adele Geras uses the fairy tales 'Rapunzel', 'Sleeping Beauty' and 'Snow White' as the basis for the novels. In the third novel, *Pictures in the Night*, a band with seven members are the seven dwarfs in disguise, an idea also used by Fiona French in her stunning art deco style picturebook *Snow White in New York* (Oxford University Press).

In the 1970s, there was a move to rediscover stories with strong female protagonists as it was thought that heroines such as Snow White and Sleeping Beauty were too passive. Sometimes these stories were retold to give them a feminist slant. It was also realized that many stories did contain more interesting female characters but these had been sidelined, and several anthologies demonstrating these were compiled, including Alison Lurie's *Clever Gretchen and Other Forgotten Folk Tales*.

Many accomplished writers have turned their hands to original stories written in the style of fairy tales. Notable examples include *Fairy Tales* by Terry Jones (Puffin), illustrated by Michael Foreman, and Carol Ann Duffy's *The Stolen Childhood and Other Dark Fairy Tales*, illustrated by Jane Ray (Puffin).

The scope for parody and intertextual links seems ever increasing but getting the most enjoyment from subversive texts like these does, of course, rely on knowing the original stories. Roald Dahl and Quentin Blake's *Revolting Rhymes* (Puffin), Jon Scieszka and Lane Smith's *The True Story of the 3 Little Pigs by A. Wolf* (Puffin) and *The Stinky Cheese Man* (Puffin), Janet and Allan Ahlberg's *The Jolly Postman* (Puffin) and its sequels, and Lauren Child's postmodern picturebooks *Beware of the Storybook Wolves* and *Who's afraid of the big bad book?* (both Hodder) are just some of more exceptional examples, not to mention films such as *Shrek*.

Building a collection of traditional stories to share with children or for your own interest, or a mixture of both, can be joyful and rewarding. It is not usually possible to put together a culturally diverse collection by relying on the output of mainstream UK publishers. Other sources include imported titles which can be obtained from independent booksellers who seek out multicultural books, and via the Internet. There are many interesting collections that are now out of print but may be available secondhand.

There follows an annotated list of books, beginning with collections which include simple tales such as 'The Gingerbread Man', 'The Three Little Pigs', 'Goldilocks and the Three Bears' and 'The Three Billy Goats Gruff' which support children learning to read, because of their repetitive refrains and strong patterns. I then go on to suggest collections which represent the myths and legends, folk and fairy tales mentioned in this chapter.

Finally, traditional stories originated in an oral tradition and there has been a revival of oral storytelling for children and adults over the past 20 or so years. Listeners young and old can hear stories from around the world and tell stories themselves in many settings. Two established annual storytelling festivals in particular can be mentioned: Beyond the Border in South Wales (www.beyondtheborder.com) and Festival at the Edge in Shropshire (www.festivalattheedge.org).

Further reading

Recommended traditional story collections

Orchard Book of Nursery Stories by Sophie Windham (Orchard Books).
Includes the well-known tales that are particularly suitable to read to very young children.

The Story Tree by Hugh Lupton, illustrated by Sophie Fatus (Barefoot Books). A culturally diverse collection for young children which includes familiar European tales as well as African, American, Indian and Jewish stories. Also see this storyteller's collection for older children *Tales of Wisdom and Wonder* illustrated by Niamh Sharkey (Barefoot Books). Both books are accompanied by audio CDs.

Tales of Hans Christian Andersen, translated and introduced by Naomi Lewis, illustrated by Joel Stewart (Walker Books).

Rumpelstiltskin and other Grimm Tales by Carol Ann Duffy and illustrated by Marketa Prachatika (Faber and Faber). Spare prose retellings including 'Hansel and Gretel', 'Ashputtel' (Cinderella), 'Snow White' and 'Little Red Cap' which originated in the adaptations Duffy developed for the Young Vic Theatre's two productions of *Grimm Tales*.

Golden Myths and Legends of the World and *Silver Myths and Legends of the World* by Geraldine McCaughrean (Orion). Two terrific compendia of myths and legends from all around the world. These dramatic retellings are in versions short enough to read aloud in one sitting.

The Thousand Nights and One Night by David Walser and illustrated by Jan Pienkowski (Puffin). The best known stories form the basis of this stunningly illustrated volume.

Greek Myths by Marcia Williams (Walker Books). Comic strip style pictures illustrate some of the best known Greek myths. Other stories retold in this format and published by Walker Books include *The Adventures of Robin Hood* and *King Arthur and the Knights of the Round Table*.

The Names Upon the Harp by Marie Heaney and illustrated by P.J. Lynch (Faber and Faber). Stories from the traditional Irish storytelling cycles.

The Orchard Book of Stories from Ancient Egypt by Robert Swindells and illustrated by Stephen Lambert (Orchard Books). The author uses an accessible colloquial style accompanied by modern illustrations which still manage to suggest that the people are from ancient times. Robert Swindells has also explored Norse myths in *The Orchard Book of Viking Stories*.

The King Arthur Trilogy by Rosemary Sutcliff (Red Fox). Magical retellings of the legends.

The Magic Lands: Folk Tales of Britain and Ireland by Kevin Crossley-Holland (Orion). Spirited retellings of a variety of tales, written in a manner which reflects the oral tradition. Kevin Crossley-Holland is an expert translator of stories from Northern Europe.

Tales Told in Tents by Sally Pomme Clayton and illustrated by Sophie Herxheimer (Frances Lincoln). Sally Pomme Clayton travelled through the countries of Central Asia collecting stories from local people.

South and North, East and West edited by Michael Rosen (Walker Books). A compilation of stories from around the world, many collected from London schoolchildren.

Sing me a Story by Grace Hallworth and illustrated by John Clementson (Frances Lincoln). Stories from the Caribbean, illustrated with bright pictures and incorporating songs with words and music provided.

Hidden Tales from Eastern Europe by Antonia Barber and illustrated by Paul Hess (Frances Lincoln).

Fairy Tales by Berlie Doherty and illustrated by Jane Ray (Walker Books). Stories mostly taken from Western European tradition, Jane Ray's sumptuous illustrations portray the characters with a variety of skin hues.

A Bag of Moonshine by Alan Garner and illustrated by Patrick Lynch (CollinsVoyager). Alan Garner mines the rich seam of British folk tales for this collection.

Seasons of Splendour: Tales, Myths and Legends of India by Madhur Jaffrey and illustrated by Michael Foreman (Puffin). The author recalls the rich storytelling traditions of her own childhood in Delhi.

Unwitting Wisdom. An Anthology of Aesop's Animal Fables by Helen Ward (Templar). A beautifully illustrated selection of Aesop's fables.

Favorite Folktales from Around the World by Jane Yolen published in New York by Pantheon. Not for children, this book is for anyone seeking an international collection of stories suitable for retelling.

Useful websites

Society for Storytelling (www.sfs.org.uk) formed in 1993 to bring together all those interested in the oral tradition. An invaluable source of information about many aspects of fairy tales is the website www.surlalunefairytales.com.

Centre for Literacy in Primary Education, Webber Street, London SE1 8QW (www.clpe.co.uk). The library has a collection of folk and fairy tales, myths and legends from all over the world. There is also an array of folk tale collections arranged according to their country of origin and compilations with stories from a variety of countries.

Fiction for Children and Young People: The State of the Art

Catriona Nicholson

This chapter looks at:

> How children's literature has developed over the centuries

> Contemporary children's literature

It is a truth universally acknowledged that fiction for children is enjoying a profile unprecedented in the history of the genre. Twenty years ago Roald Dahl held a unique position as a children's writer. In his lifetime the success of his books made him the world's most successful living author and his name established a publishing phenomenon. The blend of humour, subversion and violence that characterizes his stories captured, and continues to capture, the imaginations of children. However, since the turn of this century, that enduring popularity has been eclipsed by the gathering momentum of J.K. Rowling's prodigiously successful Harry Potter series which, over the course of seven novels, has generated a global fan club of addicted readers both young and old, from Beijing to Brighton. The final book has smashed records in the UK and a mere three months after publication achieved sales nearing 4 million.

There is no doubt that Rowling will take her place among the greats who have written fiction for children. Amanda Craig (2007a), writing in the *Times*, suggests that 'Rowling's imagination has changed the perception of an entire generation.' While agreeing with this appraisal one might suggest that, additionally, Rowling's books have helped change adult perceptions about children's books: the universal appeal of the Harry Potter series has led to a blurring of the formerly distinct boundaries that differentiated readers of adult and children's fiction. It is now commonplace to see readers of all ages in repose, or travelling, immersed in a Harry Potter novel. There is a shared addiction for the books and many adult readers enjoy the frisson of youthful pleasure offered by that complicity.

Although one would not want to see the series being used as a benchmark for assessing the quality of contemporary writing for children, it has undoubtedly promoted the 'status' of children's literature and has spawned new and 'serious' media and public interest in the genre. Declaring one's 'academic' interest in children's literature nowadays prompts comments such as, 'Oh, like Harry Potter. I've read them all. I'm a big fan.' When one proffers the suggestion that books by other contemporary children's writers might appeal in similar or different ways there is often an earnest request for personal recommendations. As a result of the present surge of interest in children's books, experienced (or enthusiastic) readers of the genre are in a singular position to promote, recommend and inspire. And the current catalogue of children's writers and book titles is extensive. Adults and children who have been captivated by the Potter phenomenon can be encouraged to extend boundaries of what Aidan Chambers (2001: 13) refers to as 'flat earth' reading and be introduced to the challenges and rewards of books that, unlike Potter, more deeply reflect the complexities of our times and explore aspects of the human condition. Adult and child readers alike, once 'hooked' and anticipating pleasurable experiences from the genre, will willingly invest in the contagious enthusiasm of another reader and want to share the delights of nominated texts.

Brief historical overview

The eighteenth century saw the beginnings of literature written specifically for children. These publications were chap books, religious tracts, educational pamphlets and folk tales that were written more for the guidance and instruction they offered than for a child's entertainment and delight. By the time of the Romantic Movement of the nineteenth century, which idealized childhood, the child had become 'an important figure in the English literary imagination' (Carpenter, 1987: 10). Accordingly, '[t]he real change in writing for children' (Hunt, 1994: 10), referred to by scholars as the Golden Age of children's literature, came about. Familiar titles such as Charles Kingsley's *The Water Babies* (1863), Lewis Carroll's *Alice's Adventures in Wonderland* (1866), Louisa Alcott's *Little Women* (1868), R.L. Stevenson's *Treasure Island* (1883), L.M. Baum's *The Wizard of Oz* (1900), J.M. Barrie's *Peter Pan* (1904) and Kenneth Grahame's *The Wind in the Willows* (1908) were published to pleasing critical acclaim. These fantasies, school and adventure stories (for boys), domestic stories (for girls) abandoned the pretence of instruction and offered children simply entertainment and enjoyment. By the beginning of the twentieth century, some libraries had set aside designated rooms for children's books, and fiction encompassed a greater diversity of style and theme. Alongside the emerging interest in science and psychology, writers like Edith Nesbit and Frances Hodgson Burnett were exploring emotional and psychological states of being in their young protagonists. Literary quality in children's books was beginning to be recognized and by 1936 the Library Association, in memory of the Scottish-born philanthropist and champion of libraries, Andrew Carnegie, had established the Carnegie Medal award for children's literature. Its first recipient was Arthur Ransome for *Pigeon Post*, a story about middle-class children, but interestingly, its second recipient, Eve Garnett, chose to focus attention on the plight of London's poor and wrote *The Family from One End Street* as a result of her own experiences of working there.

Over the past 60 years the publishing of literature for children has had significant commercial impact. The enduring popularity of classic writers mentioned above, and the exciting wave of 'new' children's writers (like Lucy Boston, Mary Norton, Leon Garfield, Alan Garner, William Mayne, Philippa Pearce, Catherine Storr and Rosemary Sutcliff) who emerged, after the barren war years, in the late 1950s and early 1960s marked a kind of new beginning in children's literature. Fantasy was the common mode of storytelling. Kimberley Reynolds (1994: 41) suggests that such use of a fantasy world enabled a writer to 'make comments about the present state of civilisation', adding that through this medium writers could 'explore the potential of fantasy to deal with the kinds of problems children faced as part of the process of growing up: fear of separation, loss, sexuality, death, anger and so on'.

Although fantasy as a sub-genre of children's literature continued to prevail in the 1970s and 1980s with writers like Susan Cooper, Penelope Lively, Jill Paton Walsh and Helen Cresswell, social realism was the predominant theme. Writers such as Bernard Ashley, Jan Mark, Robert Westall and Robert Swindells were exploring in their novels, perhaps in a more 'gritty' and overt way than the fantasists, personal and general issues of sexism, racism, war, death, physical disability, domestic upheaval, adolescent angst, psychological disturbance, and so on. In short, writers were exploring tough contemporary issues that, one could argue, might seem more suitable content for adult novels. But children's novels have *always* reflected something of the age in which they are written and children, like adults, read not only to find reflections of their own lives but also to better understand the lives of others. Michael Morpurgo (1997), Children's Laureate from 2003 to 2005, commented a decade ago that 'children need difficult experiences. When I am writing, if I feel that the end should be tragic, then it is. That's what life is like.'

The times they are always a-changing and as Jan Mark (1993: xix) wisely commented 'the boundaries between childhood and adolescence and adolescence and adulthood constantly shift'. From its beginnings, fiction for children can be said to have served as a cultural barometer reflecting, through the physical, psychological and cultural worlds of fictional characters, the concerns, beliefs and values of a particular time.

Now, as the first decade of the new millennium nears its end, it seems that children's writers, at least those whose texts appeal to readers in the upper primary stages and beyond, are preoccupied with ambitious and increasingly uncompromising themes. Therefore, the vexed question of what constitutes the definition 'children's literature' is frequently debated within the academy and through the media. It has to be accepted that children's literature is no longer the domain of the very young. The genre has redefined its literary classifications and extended boundaries beyond the former categories of 'for younger' and 'for older' readers. Books for 'young adults', now account for a significant corner of the market and, with their 'mature' content and sophisticated narrative techniques, they constitute that much referred to 'crossover' territory between adult and children's fiction. Their focus is primarily on the individual and the 'inner' journey he or she undertakes towards a better understanding of the self, and of the self in relation to the world's complexities. Northrop Frye (1957) defined the 'one great story of literature' as being the 'loss and regaining of identity'. Indeed, a trawl through the list of recent Carnegie winners reveals how that preoccupation characterizes much contemporary literature for older children and young adults.

Contemporary children's literature

Rowling's phenomenal success is not the sole reason for the present intensity of interest in children's books. Philip Pullman's winning of the prestigious Book of the Year Whitbread Award in 2001 with *The Amber Spyglass* (the third book in the *His Dark Materials* trilogy) was, for most of us concerned with children's literature, not only a cause for celebration and congratulation but a timely recognition by the literary establishment that excellence in books for young people has long deserved wider publicity and explicit endorsement. Pullman, a former teacher, believes in the power of stories and the ways in which they can teach us about the world we create and the morality by which we live. He considers that 'grand ' or 'overarching narratives' can be used to offer certainties and liberating possibilities for the child (and adult) reader. Drawing his themes for the trilogy (comprising *Northern Lights*, *The Subtle Knife* and *The Amber Spyglass*) from Milton's *Paradise Lost*, he exemplifies his belief that a single story can encompass issues that seem to transcend time and place. The books have sold more than 15 million copies around the world; the themes and issues that weave through the trilogy have generated passionate and provocative debate in literary circles, reading groups, classrooms and university seminar rooms around the globe. Shortly, we understand, a sequel to the trilogy will be published. To be called *The Book of Dust*, it will be, says Pullman (2007) 'a big, big book on a big subject'.

Another indication that children's fiction is being held in high regard is demonstrated by the many and varied ways it has been represented in film and on stage. From the 1960s onwards, classic and 'modern' classic novels like Lewis Carroll's *Alice in Wonderland*, Frances Hodgson Burnett's *The Secret Garden,* Mary Norton's *The Borrowers*, E. Nesbit's *The Railway Children*, J.M. Barrie's *Peter Pan*, C.S. Lewis's *Narnia* series, Kenneth Grahame's *The Wind in the Willows*, E.B. White's *Charlotte's Web*, Arthur Ransome's *Swallows and Amazons*, Nina Bawden's *Carrie's War*, Roald Dahl's *The BFG* and *Danny the Champion of the World*, have been adapted for television serialization or as full-length feature films. More recently adaptations of J.R.R. Tolkien's *The Lord of the Rings*, Dahl's *Charlie and the Chocolate Factory* and *Matilda*, Anne Fine's *Madame Doubtfire,* E.B. White's *Charlotte's Web* and several Harry Potter novels have become cinema box-office successes. The ambitious film version of Pullman's epic trilogy, released as *The Golden Compass*, will surely promote the cause of children's fiction.

And now, more than ever before, the 'cross-over' nature and appeal of many books published for children and young people has been recognized and exploited in positive and exemplary ways through theatrical productions. A quick survey of these would highlight The National Theatre's stage adaptation of Pullman's *His Dark Materials* which played to capacity houses for two Christmas seasons in successive years. The National similarly adapted Jamila Gavin's *Coram Boy* which also ran for two seasons and most recently Michael Morpurgo's *War Horse* has been its central long-running Christmas production. In Stratford-upon-Avon, The Royal Shakespeare Company have performed Malorie Blackman's *Noughts and Crosses*. Morpurgo's *Kensuke's Kingdom* and *Private Peaceful* have played to London theatres and toured theatres in Britain. Philippa Pearce's *Tom's Midnight Garden*, Melvin Burgess's *Junk*, Jacqueline Wilson's *The Suitcase Kid*, Maurice Gleitzman's *Two Weeks with the Queen* and David Almond's *Skellig*, Catherine Storr's *Marianne Dreams* and Anne Cassidy's *Looking for JJ* have similarly delighted London audiences.

Books by Philip Pullman and a slew of other contemporary writers bear out the little maxim printed on the purchase bags given out by my local bookshop that '[t]he book to read is not the one which thinks for you but the one which makes you think' (James McCosh). Indeed, a visit to any high street bookshop or independent bookseller will confront a buying reader with a diverse and engaging choice of texts that 'make you think'. Sharing shelves with reissues of the classic writers mentioned above will be the books of well established writers whose work has been delighting child and young adult readers, sometimes for as long as four decades: names such as David Almond, Lynne Reid Banks, Nina Bawden, Malorie Blackman, Judy Blume, Melvyn Burgess, Betsy Byars, Aidan Chambers, Eoin Colfer, Susan Cooper, Sharon Creech, Gillian Cross, Kevin Crossley-Holland, Roald Dahl, Berlie Doherty, Anne Fine, Paula Fox, Alan Garner, Jamila Gavin, Maurice Gleitzman, Sonya Hartnett, Janni Howker, Ted Hughes, Elizabeth Laird, Lois Lowry, Geraldine McCaughrean, Michelle Magorian, Margaret Mahy, Jan Mark, Michael Morpurgo, Beverley Naidoo, Linda Newbery, Katherine Paterson, Philippa Pearce, Terry Pratchett, Philip Pullman, Celia Rees, Catherine Storr, Robert Swindells, Cynthia Voigt, Jill Paton Walsh, Robert Westall and Jacqueline Wilson. In addition there will be the less familiar names whose books have received recent critical acclaim, like Anne Cassidy, Jennifer Donnelly, Anthony Horowitz, Hilary McKay, Mal Peet, Meg Rosoff and Philip Reeve.

Other popular authors on offer will have captured niche markets of reader appeal with their formulaic structures and here names like Meg Cabot, Cornelia Funke, Caroline Lawrence, Robin Jarvis, Andy McNab, J.K. Rowling, Louis Sachar, Francesca Simon and Lemony Snicket come to mind.

What qualities to look for in the book

So with such a wealth of texts on offer, how can we as students, teachers or simply enthusiastic readers make good choices? How can we choose the best in fantasy writing, contemporary realism, science fiction, historical fiction, time travel, trilogies, novellas and short stories? How can we select those books that will make us think beyond the page-turning appeal of the story and deepen our understanding of the world in which we live? Why do some books impact on our imagination and senses to such a degree that the reading experience resonates and sometimes haunts us long after the narrative ends? Why do so many of us find such consolation and private satisfaction in books written for children?

Children's writers have much to tell us about their aims and their craft and, by way of answering the questions posed above it is helpful to call on three who share the common belief that a good novel can help readers towards a better understanding of themselves and of the human condition: thus through sensing some affinity with character, circumstance or setting in a fictional world, readers can feel more attuned to the world in which they themselves live.

Katherine Paterson (1989: 44) refers to the novelist's task as 'shaping human experience so that a reader might be able to find not only order but meaning in the story'.

Nina Bawden (1980) echoes this by commenting that the books she read as a child helped her towards some sort of understanding of her growing self. She writes that they 'were not myths or magic or fantasy but books that seemed ... to be about real people – that is people I could recognize as real, even if they sometimes had rather unlikely adventures ... they were books that for some reason I could live inside' (ibid.: 27).

Bawden's sure conviction is that young readers need realism in the narratives they read and she believes that 'the most important realism that children need ... is the emotional landscape in which the book is set, a landscape that a child can recognise whether he is rich or poor, whether he lives in a tenement or a palace' (ibid.: 28–9).

Philippa Pearce (1969) is clear about what constitutes a good novel for children. She makes the point that all young readers are 'facing toward maturity and taking steps towards it'. Developing this truth she offers her crucial criterion for measuring a book's worth by proposing that 'in a good children's book ... the child-characters, although not actually growing up, always appear capable of it'. She explains that in writing a children's novel a writer has to make the connection between present maturity and past childhood. She goes on to suggest that:

> He does the same for his child-characters in reverse – makes the connection between their present childhood and their future maturity ... there will be the certainty that the child character [will] grow up after the end of the book. Such a character is a fit companion for the imagination of an actual child who is actually growing up. (ibid.: 53)

Bawden, referring to the 'darker' side of contemporary novels, contends that 'if a writer presents his characters honestly ... he is giving his readers "a means to gain a hold on fate", by showing them they can trust their thoughts and their feelings, that they can have faith in themselves' (1980: 33). She believes that a good writer for young people can 'show [readers] a bit of the world, the beginning of the path they have to tread; but the most important thing he has to offer is a little hope and courage for the journey' (ibid.: 33).

This 'journey' metaphor defines much contemporary writing for children and young people and it reiterates well Northrop Frye's contention (1957: 2) that serious literature is concerned with the search for identity: protagonists in contemporary fiction are engaged in struggles for emotional, cultural or familial survival and understanding. Amanda Craig (2003), questioning why adult readers are drawn to characters in children's stories, suggests that it is because these characters 'enact a journey in which ordinary people discover their own potential for heroism against seemingly hopeless odds in a vast and terrifying world'.

This journey motif has linked writers of fiction for children, from Ian Serrallier's *The Silver Sword* (1956), through Ann Holm's classic *I am David* (1963), Cynthia Voigt's *Homecoming* (1981), Ann Pilling's *Stan* (1988), Robert Westall's *The Kingdom by the Sea* (1990), Sharon Creech's *Walk Two Moons* (1994) to Meg Rosoff's *How I live Now* (2004). In the course of a novel, young protagonists whose narratives begin in confusion, adversity or with a sense of loss, can be seen to have acquired a new understanding of themselves, and of others. Victor Watson (2003: 1), echoing Pearce's view, comments tellingly that, '[m]ost of the main characters in children's fiction are wiser at the end of their narratives than they were at the beginning'. He suggests that 'maturation is a theme not a genre' and that the process 'saturates children's stories and colours narratives of every kind'.

Notwithstanding that premise, it has to be noted that the implicit 'hope and courage for the journey' of children's novels has been thinly stretched in recent novels for young people, the most notable example perhaps being John Boyne's *The Boy in the Striped Pyjamas* (2006). Although the jacket blurb informs the reader that 'if you start to read this book you will go on a journey with a nine year old boy called Bruno ...', this is not a novel about consolation or the gaining of wisdom, it is a novel about the Holocaust. Recalling something of the irrevocable darkness of Robert Cormier's nihilistic writing (in such novels as *I am the Cheese* and *After the First Death*), Boyne's disingenuous title and narrative convey all too starkly the 'ironies of innocence' (Kellaway, 2006).

Book prizes and prize winners

Despite what Kevin Crossley-Holland (2007) describes as 'the rise and rise' of children's book awards, in the UK (notably, the Smarties, the Whitbread, now known as the Costa, the *Guardian*), the award of the Carnegie Medal is the most coveted of prizes for children's literature, referred to as 'the Booker of the playground', and recognizing 'quality and quality fullgrown, not in the bud'. Over the past two decades, the question of what *kind* of writing should be recognized and honoured has been much discussed and debated. Award winning novels such as Melvin Burgess's *Junk*, Robert Swindells' *Stone Cold*, Aidan Chambers' *Postcards from No-Man's Land*, Berlie Doherty's *Dear Nobody* address the worlds of young people and the painful social problems confronting them. These titles reveal and reflect how times have changed and themes and concerns have grown 'darker'. Nevertheless, there is clearly a need to acknowledge that, in the vulnerable hinterland before adulthood, adolescents need 'an intermediate form of literature that addresses their feelings of confusion, ambition and hostility' (Craig, 2007b). Many would propose, along with Crossley-Holland, that two discrete awards should be established: one for books whose content and style appeals to primary school-aged children and one for those that explore more explicit, adult themes.

Further reading

Ten 'must read' novels for children and young people

Alice's Adventures in Wonderland by Lewis Carroll (1866). Continuously in print since its first publication with various illustrators, this was one of the first books written for the amusement and delight of children rather than for their instruction and improvement.

The Secret Garden by Frances Hodgson Burnett (1911). Set in rural Yorkshire, this story of two lonely children whose physical and emotional lives are enriched through the transforming power of the natural world, has become well loved by children and adults.

Swallows and Amazons by Arthur Ransome (1930). Comprising 12 books of which this is the first, the series falls into the 'camping, tramping' genre of fiction for children. Strong on 'real' descriptions of land and seascapes and on children's impulses for make-believe the books clearly influenced writers like Enid Blyton.

Charlotte's Web by E.B. White (1952). Fifty years after publication White's tale of farm-yard friendship remains a classic. Multi-layered, allusive and lyrical the text remains a source for scholarly comment and interpretation.

Tom's Midnight Garden by Philippa Pearce (1958). Winner of the Carnegie Medal, the book has been described as 'one of the tiny handful of masterpieces of English children's Literature'. A time-slip fantasy, it is threaded with a strong and celebratory sense of place. Connections between past and present and their reconciliation are central issues.

Dear Nobody by Berlie Doherty (1991). Probably Doherty's best-known novel and win-ner of the Carnegie Medal in 1992. The story of sixth-former Helen's pregnancy, told in a heartfelt way through letters to her unborn child, broke new ground in terms of what was considered suitable content for children's stories

Junk by Melvin Burgess (1996). Based on first-hand research and set in inner-city Bristol in the 1980s, this novel won the Carnegie Medal and the *Guardian* Award for Children's Fiction. Successive monologues sustain the narrative drive which documents the view-points of teenage characters caught up in the downward spiral of drug addiction.

His Dark Materials trilogy by Philip Pullman (1995–2000). The three books, in epic style, examine and address the great themes of good, evil, the nature of the human soul and the afterlife. This trilogy is regarded as one of the most distinguished literary achieve-ments of the twentieth century.

Harry Potter and the Philosopher's Stone by J.K. Rowling (1997). First of the series of seven that chart the years the eponymous hero spends at Hogwart's School of Witchcraft and Wizardry. Something of a landmark in children's publishing and there-fore a must-read!

Noughts and Crosses by Malorie Blackman (2001). The first novel of a much acclaimed trilogy set in a racist dystopia. Described by the author as a modern day *Romeo and Juliet* story, the narrative makes for tragic and compelling reading.

Personal recommendations

Carrie's War by Nina Bawden (1973). Set in rural Wales during the Second World war, Bawden's novel concerns Carrie's moral dilemmas and inner struggles. Quiet resolution of conflict pervades the conclusion making it one of the most memorable of children's books.

The Eighteenth Emergency by Betsy Byars (1973). Preoccupied with fears of all kinds, 'Mouse', who has offended the school bully, awaits the ultimate fear – that of his impending punishment. An outstanding novel in terms of exploring this dynamic and ever-present issue.

Thunder and Lightnings by Jan Mark (1976). Jan Mark's sensitive ear for dialogue, her acerbic wit, evocative descriptions of place and her gently sensitive portrayal of a child with particular learning difficulties, made this a worthy Carnegie Medal winner.

The Stone Book by Alan Garner (1976). First book of a quartet that has been described as 'one as the great originals of children's literature'.

Bridge to Terabithia by Katherine Paterson (1977). Paterson drew on real life in order to authenticate the events of this award-winning novel. Set in rural Virginia, her story documents the growing friendship between a young boy and girl from different social backgrounds.

Sarah Plain and Tall by Patricia MacLachlan (1985). McLachlan's small gem of a novel is set in the Midwest of America in the late nineteenth century. Its haunting themes articulate the grief of loss and the intensity of longing.

Kit's Wilderness by David Almond (1999). Set in the North East mining country of England, emotionally involving and told with economical brilliance, Almond's narrative skills balance the real with the magical.

The Other Side of Truth by Beverley Naidoo (2000). A Carnegie Medal winner, Naidoo's fourth novel, set in Lagos and London, challenges and informs the issue of racism.

How I Live Now by Meg Rosoff (2004). Told through the voice of her American protagonist, Daisy, Rosoff's novel conveys the pain and strength of adolescence in an unforgettable way, offsetting scenes of horror and brutality with those of tenderness and caring.

The Silver Donkey by Cynthia Hartnett (2006). Told with eloquent economy Hartnett's novel carries lightly its themes of great complexity. Set during the First World War, the overarching story provides a layered framework for four embedded tales.

Into New Worlds: Children's Books in Translation

Gillian Lathey

> **This chapter looks at:**
>
> > The history of, and new directions in, translations of children's books
>
> > Different trends in writing for young people
>
> > Ways to access translated books for young readers

Just imagine British children's literature without Aesop's fables, Cinderella, Little Red Riding Hood, Hansel and Gretel, the tales of Hans Christian Andersen, the Moomins, Heidi, Babar, Aladdin, Mrs. Pepperpot, Astérix or Pinocchio ... All of these stories and characters, originating in German, French, Italian, Swedish, Danish, Greek and Arabic, have become familiar to English-speaking children thanks to those invisible and often unacknowledged storytellers, the translators. Children's literature benefits to this day from the new directions represented by translations despite a long-term imbalance between translations into and out of English: in the past 30 years up to 40 per cent of French and German children's books have been translations compared to less than 3 per cent of British publications. Fortunately, there has been a welcome upturn in the quality and quantity of translations for children in the past decade. German author Cornelia Funke's compelling fantasy novels *The Thief Lord* (2002) and *Inkheart* (2003), for example, have overcome all obstacles to enter the bestseller lists in the English-language market. Children are entitled to read the work of the best writers from across the world and, through translated literature, to appreciate unique voices and cultural difference.

Historical overview

When looking back at the history of English-language children's literature, it soon becomes clear that translations, some of them of tales originally written for adults, have had a significant impact on the development of a separate literature for children. From William Caxton's translations of Aesop's fables and *The History of Reynard the Fox* in the late fifteenth century to the *Arabian Nights* in the eighteenth, and from the influx of French fairy tales in the early eighteenth century to the translation of tales by the Grimm Brothers (1823) from German and Hans Christian Andersen from Danish (1846), British children's literature has been enriched and changed by stories from Europe and beyond. European fairy tales played their part in promoting imaginative writing in the age of the sober moral tale before 1900 and resonate to this day in countless retellings and multimedia adaptations. Motifs from the Arabian Nights, too, run through children's literature, surfacing in the work of E. Nesbit (*Five Children and It*, 1902) or, more recently, in retellings by Geraldine McCaughrean (1982), Robert Leeson (*My Sister Shahrazad*, 2001) and Theresa Breslin (2004). Carlo Collodi's *Pinocchio*, translated from Italian in 1891, and Johanna Spyri's *Heidi* from Swiss-German in 1880, quickly became children's classics. In the same period children also appropriated the novels of Alexandre Dumas, *The Three Musketeers* (1846a) and *The Count of Monte Cristo* (1846b), as well as the early science fiction of Jules Verne – all translated from French. Then, in the early part of the last century, German writer Erich Kästner's *Emil and the Detectives* (2001, first published 1931) startled the conservative world of British children's literature with a modern, urban tale of unaccompanied child detectives that paved the way for the child adventurers and sleuths of British authors Enid Blyton and Malcolm Saville, and of French writer Paul Berna: a translation of his *A Hundred Million Francs* (1957) enthralled young readers in the 1950s and 1960s. Further twentieth-century landmarks are the eccentric, playful and angst-ridden Moomins of Finnish author Tove Jansson (2001), the work of Swedish author Astrid Lindgren that touches both the joys and troubling undercurrents of children's lives in her own blend of fairy tale and fantasy, and the clever, amusing antics of Alf Prøysen's (2000) Mrs. Pepperpot from Norway. Since its inception in 1996, submissions for the Marsh Award for Children's Literature in Translation reflect the twin poles of fantasy and social realism of late twentieth-century translations for children.

What qualities to look for in translations

All these translated stories have stood the test of time because of their narrative suspense or the uniqueness of their imagined worlds. But what can a

translated book offer children by way of *difference*? First, there is the opportunity for insights into other places and cultures. When presenting the first
Marsh Award for Children's Literature in Translation in 1997, Penelope
Lively asserted that she always turns to fiction if she wants to get to know a
country, while the 1999 presenter, children's author Michael Morpurgo,
spoke of the political necessity of an engagement with international literature: 'What we have to do surely in this ever shrinking, ever more interdependent world is to keep learning, keep our hearts open, and our ability to
empathise alive so that understanding between peoples and cultures can
grow' (1999: 61). Philip Pullman expressed a child's view of encountering
new worlds through literature in his 2001 presentation speech, recalling his
reading of the Moomin books and *Emil and the Detectives*. Fictional characters from these stories became his friends: 'I felt at home in their households
and their cities and I got to know the valleys and forests and coastlines that
they knew. I was European before I'd discovered whether I was English or
British' (2001: 6). Such is the potential of children's books to introduce children to new ways of thinking and imagining, whether in the setting of the
Finnish midwinter or the dynamic Berlin of the 1920s.

Second, translations introduce the unfamiliar through an artful use of language by both the author and indeed by the translator, since translating
for children is a very particular craft, requiring an understanding of the
rhythms and modes of address best suited to child readers. A translation
should, of course, read well in English, without the awkwardness of expression that indicates either too close an adherence to the source text, or the
work of a translator unused to writing for children. Yet there should still
be some linguistic indications that the book was first written in another
language, perhaps in the names of characters, food or places, so that children keep in mind that they are reading a translation and enjoy and reflect
on the flavour of the original writing. Wholesale cultural adaptation
diminishes the experience of reading a book set in another country, and is
unnecessary. As David Almond, Marsh Award presenter in 2003, commented: 'One of the things I love about writing for children is that they
don't know the categories yet. They don't know that they're supposed to
think something is "foreign", something is difficult' (2003: 12). As authors
of nonsense verse or Beatrix Potter with her use of 'galoshes' and 'soporific'
have always known, strange names, unusual sounds and combinations of
letters intrigue children rather than alienate them.

Translations, too, introduce different traditions of writing for children. In
contemporary continental European prose fiction for older children, for
example, there is a degree of experimentation with narrative form that can
only be compared to the work of Aidan Chambers or Janni Howker. Guus
Kuijer's protagonist in *The Book of Everything*, a surprisingly successful translation from Dutch published in 2006, tells his story in elliptical and at times

uncomfortable prose with an opening that throws the whole narrative into question with finesse and humour. Nor do a number of European writers shy away from intellectually challenging readers. There is a philosophical strand to their writing that is lacking in English-language children's literature. It is no accident that the Norwegian Jostein Gaarder's best-selling narrative survey of the history of philosophy, *Sophie's World* (1995) was written and marketed for children throughout Scandinavia and in Germany, but targeted at adults by British publishers. In Hans Magnus Enzensberger's *Where Were You Robert?* (2001), the hero discusses mathematics, astronomy and the origins of the universe with eminent thinkers of the past in scenarios unlikely to appear in a British children's book.

Visual texts of all kinds also present British readers with new artistic developments, genres and formats in translations where, as Anthea Bell has commented, the delicate balance or counterpoint between text and image must be maintained. Bell's translation, together with her colleague Derek Hockridge, of the Astérix books and Leslie Lonsdale Cooper's translations of the Tintin series made many a young reader into a lifelong fan of the comic strip and graphic novel, a form that is currently gaining new ground thanks to Japanese manga. Marjane Satrapi's two autobiographical graphic novels *Persepolis: The Story of a Childhood* (2003) and *Persepolis 2: The Story of a Return* (2004), translations from French that depict a childhood in Iran during the Islamic Revolution and the war with Iraq, offer young adult readers first-hand insights into a young girl's life in those turbulent times. As for the modern picturebook, French author-illustrator Jean de Brunhoff's *The Story of Babar*, drawing on contemporary trends in European illustration in the 1930s, inspired Kathleen Hale to use the same large format for her books about Marmalade the cat, just as Dutch artist Dick Bruna's little square Miffy books, his bold use of opaque colour and black outlines introduced a new and distinctive style in the mid-twentieth century. In terms of content, too, European picturebooks break new boundaries: Werner Holzwarth and Wolf Erlbruch's popular *The Story of the Little Mole Who Knew It Was None of His Business* (1994), translated from German, brought a touch of northern European directness in dealing with bodily functions into the picturebook world of the 1990s.

Finally, children can read about historical events or social developments from different and sometimes unexpected points of view through translations. Teachers have long been aware that including Anne Frank's *The Diary of a Young Girl* (1997) and Hans Peter Richter's *Friedrich* (1987), the semi-autobiographical story of a German boy and his Jewish friend, in a unit of work on the Second World War will introduce children to other sides of that particular story. The war continues to be one of the most popular subjects for translations into English, so there are plenty more titles to choose from, including German author Gudrun Pausewang's *Traitor*

(2004), the story of a German girl who hides a fleeing Russian soldier, and Anne Holm's allegorical *I Am David*, translated from Danish and reissued by Egmont in 2000. Similar cross-cultural insights into more recent social issues can be surprisingly complex. Henning Mankell, best known as an author of adult crime fiction, lives half the year in his native Sweden and half in Mozambique, where he runs a theatre for local performers. His novels on the life-shattering consequences for a young Mozambiquan girl of stepping on a landmine in *Secrets in the Fire* (2000), and of AIDS in its sequel *Playing With Fire* (2002), arise from years of engagement with the country and culture, whereas his recent autobiographical novel *A Bridge to the Stars* (2005) and its sequel *Shadows in the Twilight* (2007), take the reader into the pain and joyful, eccentric friendships of a motherless 8-year-old boy growing up in the Sweden of the 1950s.

A translated book for children should, therefore, offer at least some of the following:

> a good story well told in a fluent translation into English
> different settings and ways of life
> an intriguing use of the original language in names and other cultural markers
> new ways of writing for children and new illustrative styles
> alternative insights into historical events or social issues.

Accessing translated books for young readers

Luckily, information on translated books for children is now far more readily accessible thanks to *Outside In: Children's Books in Translation*, edited by Deborah Hallford and Ed Zaghini and published in 2005 by Milet with support from the Arts Council. This informative booklist with accompanying essays is divided into age-related sections on books for children under 5; from 5 to 8; 9 to 11 and 12+ and 14+, with additional sections on the graphic novel, non-fiction and dual-language texts. Illustrated with full-colour photographs of book covers, annotations give a brief plot summary and an indication of each book's qualities and audience. Biographies of contributors, authors, illustrators and translators, as well as a resources list, make this an indispensable guide for anyone wishing to introduce translated books into a school library or classroom.

It is always worth looking out for translated books in review sections in the *Times Educational Supplement* (*TES*) or the national press, and the *School Librarian*, in addition to publishing regular reviews of translated books, also reprints the full text of the biennial Marsh Award presentation speech and the shortlist. A glance at the websites or catalogues of children's publishers who do regularly publish translated books is worthwhile for information on new publications. North-South Books issue a series of sturdy, illustrated hardback editions of translated stories ideal for the 7- to 8-year-old, while Andersen Press, Walker Books, Bloomsbury, The Chicken House, Egmont (in the Mammoth World Literature Series), Hodder, Dolphin (Orion Children's Books), Macmillan, HarperCollins, Puffin and Frances Lincoln have all published or distributed a number of translations in recent years.

There is advice, too, on introducing translated books into the classroom in the Qualifications and Curriculum Authority's (QCA's) 'Reading Differences' project designed to fulfil the National Curriculum requirement for reading across different cultures. Materials published jointly by the QCA and Centre for Literacy in Primary Education (CLPE) include teaching sequences for Years 5 to 6 on a Norwegian fairy tale, *East o' the Sun and West o' the Moon* (Dasent and Lynch, 2004), on Daniel Pennac's *Eye of the Wolf* (2002), Geraldine McCaughrean's *One Thousand and One Arabian Nights* (1982), and a collection of East European poetry, *Sheep Don't Go to School*, edited by Andrew Fusek Peters (1999). All materials can be downloaded from the QCA website. For teachers who wish to introduce children to a wider range of picturebooks than those on the British market, the website of the European Picture Book Project (www.ncrcl.ac.uk/epbc) has information on how to obtain sets of picturebooks from across Europe with accompanying materials in the form of translations, CDs, teachers' notes and a video of the collection in use in the classroom.

An obvious and important starting point when introducing a translated book is to find out what children already know about the country, language and culture of the original. Once they are hooked on the story, children can engage in a whole range of comparative projects from discovering the meanings and origins of characters' names to looking at representations of family life in different countries. And at the micro level, a comparison of different versions of a particular passage or incident from a classic children's story that has been retranslated a number of times gives the practice of working with extracts from texts a real purpose in line with strands seven and eight of the Primary National Strategy. A reading of the gruesome shoe-fitting episode in the first translation by Edgar Taylor of the Grimm Brothers' Cinderella ('Aschenputtel' in the current Puffin edition) is quite a shock to readers familiar with censored translations. When compared with one or two other versions of the same passage, it raises questions about how stories change and develop both in translation and in retellings within the same language.

Aidan Chambers made further suggestions for raising the profile of translated books in his 2005 Marsh Award presentation speech where he argued that: 'Teachers, school and public children's librarians should be encouraged to mount displays of books in translation – themed perhaps by language of origin, or connecting themes, or an author, and so on. Translators should be invited much more often than they are to speak to pupils' : 12. Translators can be contacted via the publisher of the book, and many are willing to talk to children about their craft or to read from their translations. Sarah Adams, for example, the translator of Pennac's *Eye of the Wolf* (2002), has spoken in secondary schools about her dialogue with young people in Brixton in an attempt to find an equivalent for the street language used on a run-down housing project in urban France for the Golem series she translated from French (see her article in *Outside In*). Many bilingual children in British class-rooms will recognize the processes translators describe of transferring mean-ing and trying to match words and concepts between languages, while monolingual children will learn valuable lessons about how languages work.

Further reading

Ten 'must-reads'

In compiling a list of currently available books that are great reads and reflect the variety translations can offer, I have not included Perrault's tales ('Cinderella', 'Little Red Riding Hood', 'Puss in Boots' and 'Sleeping Beauty') or editions of Grimms' tales because they are already recognized as essential reading for children, and because there are so many anthologies and editions of individual tales on the market. It is, however, important to have a collected edition of Grimms' tales by a reputable translator. Edgar Taylor's 1823 translation, still published by Puffin, is a lively, close rendering of the original German, although Ralph Manheim, Jack Zipes and Maria Tatar have all issued new translations in the last 30 years. Picturebook editions of single tales should be chosen with care, both for the quality of the illustrations and because some retellings are heavily abridged.

Starting with books for younger children, Alf Prøysen's Mrs. Pepperpot stories are a delight to read aloud in Marianne Helweg's translation, both for their humour and humanity, and for the representation of life in rural Scandinavia in the mid-twentieth century. Mrs. Pepperpot (Mrs. Teaspoon in Norwegian) has the habit of shrinking at the most inopportune moments, much to the irritation of her husband and amusement of young readers or listeners. There's a forest setting with spruce, pine and larch, as well as a midsummer bonfire to celebrate 24 hours of daylight. Prøysen's linguistic humour enlivens every tale: the toddler who finds a 'talkin' tato' after Mrs. Pepperpot falls into a pail of potatoes is a memorable moment. Astrid Lindgren's *Pippi Longstocking* (2002), a twentieth-century classic, has the same joyful and creative treatment of language, with Pippi inventing or mispronouncing words at the drop of a hat, from 'turnupstuffer' as a name for someone who always finds things, to 'pluttification' for multiplication. The anarchic Pippi, who upset many Scandinavian educators when she first appeared on the scene in 1945, spends half a day at school but finds it sorely wanting. She debunks both phonics and mathematics lessons before returning to her daredevil ways, enjoyed vicariously by the conformist children living next door. A second twentieth-cen-tury landmark, Erich Kästner's *Emil and the Detectives* (2001), still engages children because, like Lindgren, Kästner understood young readers' underlying anxieties and could integrate them into an entertaining and well-paced adventure where children gain autonomy and outwit adults at every turn.

Two recently reissued picturebooks by Tove Jansson, *The Book about Moomin, Mymble and Little My* (2001) and *Who Will Comfort Toffle?* (2003) draw younger children into her quirky neck of the Scandinavian woods as expressed through handwritten text, striking graphic techniques and unusual colour combinations. Jansson, a great artist and writer, transforms the landscape of the Gulf of Finland into an imagined world that, once encountered, is never forgotten. Children of all ages should also get to know the stories of another great Nordic writer, Hans Christian Andersen, particularly 'The Emperor's New Clothes', 'The Snow Queen', 'The Little Match Girl' and 'The Steadfast Tin Soldier'. Several handsome new editions and translations were published on the occasion of the bicentenary of Andersen's birth in 2005, so now is the time to acquire one. Without a knowledge of these stories or Perrault's and Grimms' tales many an intertextual reference will be lost to young readers.

For older children, two books set in the era of the Second World War remain essential reading, the already mentioned *Friedrich* (Richter, 1987) and Roberto Innocenti's picturebook *Rose Blanche* (1985). Rose is a young German girl who discovers a concentration camp on the edge of her town towards the end of the war. Innocenti's stark photo-realism provokes questions, reflection and an emotional response that requires careful handling and guidance on the part of the teacher, but promotes an understanding of the human toll of that terrible era. With the exception of novels set in the war and Henning Mankell's autobiographical novels, fantasy – often in the form of quartets or trilogies – is the dominant mode in recent translations, probably in the wake of the Harry Potter effect. Two books that stand out from the rest in the integration of magical or supernatural elements into a realistic setting are Daniel Pennac's *Eye of the Wolf* (2002) and Cornelia Funke's *Inkheart* (2003), translated from French and German respectively. Pennac's tale of telepathic communication between an African child and an Alaskan wolf, both of them driven from their homes, is told with delicacy and simplicity. *Inkheart* is reminiscent of Michael Ende's *The Neverending Story* in that the boundary between real and imaginary worlds is that of the book. Meggie reads voraciously, but her bookbinder father is cautious about reading aloud because he has the ability to bring fictional characters to life. This is, of course, exactly what happens, giving rise to a sequence of frightening and challenging adventures as Meggie searches for her lost mother.

Two novels to challenge experienced readers of 11 and over are Bjarne Reuter's *The Ring of the Slave Prince* (2004) and Enzensberger's *Where Were You Robert?* (2001). Reuter is Danish, but his is not a book that displays Scandinavian culture; it is, rather, a rollicking tale of Caribbean piracy in the seventeenth century that will delight fans of the recent films on this theme. Spirited, half-Irish Tom O'Connor embarks on a series of wild adventures in a novel of high adventure that verges on parody at times, but also conveys a strong anti-slavery message. Enzensberger, an intellectual colossus in his native Germany, has written a time-slip novel that compels its readers to think about ideological, artistic and ethical issues in a cleverly constructed series of historical scenarios as Robert travels back through European history. This is a book from which British readers can learn a great deal about the intellectual and artistic history of their European neighbours.

While it is marvellous for English-speaking children to have access to the work of a wealth of authors from a variety of cultural backgrounds who write in English, the increasing domination of the global market by English-language children's books leads to a paucity of books that require publishers to undertake the effort and expense of commissioning a translation. It is therefore all the more important that teachers and children should be on the lookout for translated books that add a different dimension to their discussions of literature. Without translations, how are British children to gain access to new, different voices and pioneering children's writers who don't happen to write in English?

8

More than Information: Engaging Hearts and Minds with Non-fiction

Nikki Gamble

This chapter looks at:

> **Non-fiction books that can have a great impact on young readers**

> **Making sure that reading for pleasure is part of the plan**

> **Developments in the production and design of children's non-fiction books**

> NOW, what I want is, Facts. Teach these boys and girls nothing but Facts. Facts alone are wanted in life. Plant nothing else, and root out everything else. You can only form the minds of reasoning animals upon Facts: nothing else will ever be of any service to them. (Charles Dickens, 2007, *Hard Times*)

Prior to reading this chapter, you may find it useful to reflect on these questions, which will be addressed in the following discussion. If possible, discuss your thoughts with a colleague:

> Identify a non-fiction book which has had a great impact on you either as an adult or child. What was it about the book that affected you?
> Are there any differences in the way in which non-fiction for adults and for children is written, produced, promoted and read?
> In what ways have you observed non-fiction being introduced to children in school?

First, a definition: what is non-fiction? Well, the label implies anything that is not fiction. Perhaps it strikes you as strange that books are categorized according to what they are not. This notion demands some consideration. Recently the term 'knowledge books' has been proposed as an alternative label as it avoids the negative prefix. The label 'non-fiction' invites us to define it in relation to fiction. Indeed, juxtaposing fiction against non-fiction and thinking about the ways in which they relate to each other can be illuminating. A search for definitions throws up some interesting issues. For instance, one Internet source states that fiction is untrue, while non-fiction is true; and another that non-fiction is concerned with reality. Is it that straightforward? You do not have to delve far into the range of texts classified as either fiction or non-fiction to find flaws in these simplistic definitions. It is the attempt to define non-fiction by delimiting it rather than reflecting on what the books themselves actually reveal about the characteristics of non-fiction writing that is problematic. However, we can proffer the working definition that non-fiction is an account of a subject which is presented as fact.

If non-fiction embraces all texts except fiction – and poetry – it is unsurprising that the range is vast both in content and form, encompassing biography and autobiography, diary, essay, travelogue, cookery book, dictionary, encyclopedia, photograph, diagram, scientific report and many other text types including school information texts. I do not intend to attempt a pedestrian classification or discuss examples of each type. Principally, my focus is non-fiction books for pleasurable reading rather than research and study, though of course both purposes can be fulfilled at the same time. For an excellent account of young researchers see Margaret Mallett (1999).

Recently attention has been drawn to 'hybrid genres' that encompass more than one information text type. This recognition that non-fiction texts are sophisticated is important, though 'hybrid' is not my preferred term as it implies an amalgam of text types from *different origins*. While books Like Dugald Steer's imaginatively conceived *Mythology* (2007) and *Egyptology* (2004) consciously incorporate a range of non-fiction genres, others implicitly embrace a range of discourse types, simply because non-fiction books are more complex than simple categorization can account for. Al Gore's *An Inconvenient Truth* (2007, children's version) contains a range of 'information genres' explanation moving into report via description and at the same time has an overarching persuasive aim. While explicitly examining the constituents of the different discourse modes (persuasion, report and so on) might usefully help children become more proficient at recognizing and using them, this is not the same process as reading a non-fiction book, though it may be misconceived as the same activity.

A direct consequence of a school curriculum dominated by objectives that require children to master reading and writing in the six 'information genres', is the flurry of educational texts written to formula and removing nonconformity in order that organizational and grammatical features can be examined. While these books may have merits and can be very well written and researched, their objective is to fulfil a curricular purpose. On the other hand, literary or creative non-fiction emanates from the writer's desire to examine the world in order to better understand it. Well-written creative non-fiction will contain accurate information that has been properly researched and verified, but it is far more than a text to be used to locate snippets of information. Creative non-fiction engages the reader often by using elements that are familiar in fiction texts, drama, tension, narrative, dialogue, character development, description and may even include poetry. When speaking at a conference on non-fiction in 2005, Philip Ardagh, an author and advocate for creative non-fiction, expressed these qualities as the three Cs – character, context and close-up.

Unlike good quality fiction, non-fiction quickly shows its age and most of it is transitory. The non-fiction that transcends its original time tends to be viewed as either exceptionally well made or perfectly embodying the ideas, manners and attitudes of the time it was produced. One recent example is the reissue of Clarke Hutton's *A Picture History of Britain* (2007). First published in 1945 this chronological account from the early history to the end of the Second World War is celebrated for the quality and charm of the four-colour illustrations that animate the pages. But this is more a collector's piece or a nostalgia purchase for adults who recall the book from childhood. As Nicolette Jones observed in her review for the *Sunday Times*, 'the text protects children from the unsavoury or horrific by calling Nell Gwynn Charles II's 'great friend', by omitting to mention Mrs Simpson when discussing Edward VIII's abdication, and by talking about the Nazis' 'special hate' for the Jews, without making any reference to the death camps' (3 June 2007). The construction of the child audience and the writer's relationship towards the reader has signalled one of the most dramatic changes in non-fiction writing since Hutton's book was published in the 1940s.

Voice in non-fiction

To turn our attention to one of those opening questions, were you able to identify a non-fiction book that made an impact on you as a child or adult reader? When I ask my students this question, the titles that currently crop up most frequently are Bill Bryson *A Short History of Nearly Everything* (to be published in a children's edition towards the end of 2008), Simon Sebag Montefiore *Young Stalin* and Al Gore's *An Inconvenient Truth* (2007, available in a children's edition). After considering the reasons why these titles had the most mentions we reached the conclusion that they were connected by the compelling voice of the writer. Students described this as feeling as though the writer was talking directly to them. Children also respond to 'voice' in non-fiction texts but its importance is often overlooked in selection criteria which usually offer guidance on accuracy, currency, inclusion of structural guiders and linguistic accessibility but omit comment on literary style. Non-fiction books that seek to impart knowledge but fail to pay attention to authorial voice can lack the context that supports young children in accessing these worlds that lie outside their direct experience (Arnold, 1992; Meek,1996).

Imagine that you have in your hand a biography of Mozart. What is the first chapter about? What information is included in the first paragraph? And how do you expect the first sentence to read? Most biographies written for children present their subject chronologically, so the first chapter is likely to detail the circumstances of the subject's birth and the opening sentence stereotypically will be something along these lines: Wolfgang Amadeus Mozart, baptized Joannes Chrysostomus Wolfgangus Theophilus Mozart, was born in Salzburg on 27 January 1756. Compare this to the opening of Gill Hornby's *Wolfgang Amadeus Mozart: The boy who made music*:

> On a crisp, clear, winter's morning, with no warning at all, a terrible earthquake ripped a giant hole through the city of Lisbon. As the people ran, screaming for their lives, a giant tsunami rose up over the coast and swept right over them. One hundred thousand people were killed. Many of them, and much of their city, had vanished without trace: flushed down into the bowels of the earth. Lisbon was completely destroyed.
>   As the new year of 1756 dawned, all of Europe was in a state of shock. There was a sense of change – a whiff of danger – in the air. (2006: 7)

Into this momentous period when knowledge was in flux, Mozart is born – the composer who took music into the Enlightenment. Hornby's brilliant introduction does several things that set it apart from the run-of-the-mill. First, she knows that she has to engage her readers from the outset. But this is not merely a hollow attention-grabbing strategy; her analysis of Mozart's significance in history is related to the zeitgeist and she suggests that the course of events is determined to some extent by chance – being in the right place at the right time.

Conventionally, we associate biography with the life story of a person but a recent trend in adult non-fiction is the biography of objects and places such as Peter Ackroyd's *London: The Biography* (2001). Vivian French captures the story of chocolate in her beautifully produced book *Chocolate: The Bean that Conquered the World* (2007). Care has been lavished on this book; it looks good enough to eat but it is the quality of the writing that makes it worthy of mention here. The book is well researched, but what is particularly pleasing is the way French provides windows into this process of discovery: she quotes from primary sources, explains archaeological findings, and makes it clear where hard evidence gives way to speculation. All this, without sacrificing pace or clarity. The result is a text which not only informs, but also inducts young readers into the excitement of historical research itself.

A voice frequently employed in children's non-fiction today is the first person, present tense, perhaps in the form of a diary, so that the reader is guided through a historical period or geographical location. This approach is a particular feature of non-fiction writing for children with no real counterpart in writing for adults. Adele Geras's *Cleopatra* (2007) uses this device; her first person narrator, Nefret, tells of events between 41 and 40 BCE and refers back to earlier dates. Of course these dates would not have been known to Nefret and as the author's note states: 'Like most ordinary people in Egypt, Nefret did not use a calendar or give names to months' so the diary has headings like 'Before Sunset, third month. Five days before the full moon'. Writing about history in the first person present tense creates challenges, so when occasion demands it Nefret's account switches to the past tense to provide context for current events, and for a more knowing understanding an adult comment is interwoven with her own account: 'Here's what else I know. The queen's family was from Macedonia, but she was born in Egypt and wants to make us as powerful as the Romans. My mother says she had a great struggle to become queen, overcoming many enemies to do so.' The diary ends as Nefret prepares to marry. Geras continues to write about Cleopatra's death in a third person narrative.

The fictionalized diary as a vehicle for conveying factual information is just one way in which fact and fiction are interwoven. In the Walker Books 'Read and Wonder' series, aimed broadly at children from 4+ years, a poetic narrative text is accompanied by captioned illustration in the register of an information text. Nicola Davies's *Ice Bear* (2006), evocatively illustrated with paintings by Gary Blythe, is a fine example. The book opens, 'Our people, the Inuit, call it Nanuk. White bear, ice bear, sea bear, others say. It's a bear alright, but not like any other! A POLAR BEAR, made for our frozen world!' (2005n.p.). Blythe's impressionistic illustrations capture the feeling of size with a page devoted to an icy paw print and an image of a blood-stained muzzle presents a truthful rather than cosy image of the natural world.

Some commentators have called these books transitional texts, highlighting the bridging role that narrative plays as children gain confidence to tackle more unfamiliar non-fiction genres. Clearly they are supportive, but should they be seen as 'transitional' when more popular forms of non-fiction writing for adults are increasingly using narrative to communicate to readers? This is the case in the sciences as well as subjects that might more traditionally be associated with narrative techniques. A more positive stance would be to regard this as part of expanding young readers' repertoires as they embrace wider genres. Certainly narrative and non-fiction continue to work as partners in books that older children will read for pleasure. Stephen and Lucy Hawking's novel *George's Secret Key to the Universe* (2007) presents quantum mechanics through the vehicle of story; Paul Kieve's *Hocus Pocus* (2007) uses a framing narrative as a means of writing about the history of magic and the great magicians of the nineteenth century and Thomas Brezina's Museum of Adventures series (2005a; 2005b; 2006) draws children into the world of art history through a mystery narrative interspersed with code-breaking puzzles.

Speaking to the audience

Audience is important in any artistic endeavour consequently some understanding of the reader's potential use for the book as well as gauging existing knowledge is important. A book that will be used for researching facts, like an encyclopedia, will employ a different tone to one that is intended to be read primarily for pleasure. In 1975, Peter Usborne founded Usborne Books with the aim of making finding out fun. He says: 'The remarkable success of Usborne Books derives from the simple idea that it is possible, without any sacrifice of quality, to produce non-fiction books as interesting and entertaining as television, magazines and comics – media that most children instinctively prefer.' Any discussion about audience-pleasing, entertaining non-fiction must mention Terry Deary's phenomenally successful 'Horrible Histories'. The formula has sold over 10 million copies in the UK alone and has been translated into 31 languages. Undoubtedly popular with children, the series has not always been well received by the gatekeepers, who fear an undermining of serious history, although Terry Deary is clear that his intention is to appeal to the 9-year-old boy he once was. The history is well researched, the voice distinctive and the comic timing impeccable. However, no matter how well written these books may be, emphasis on humour and gore provides a limited perspective and there are many routes into history and science for children, who do not always need to be appealed to through the comic or the violent.

What is the truth?

Truth and reality are concepts that we need to think about when discussing non-fiction. There may be a tendency to believe that something presented as fact has veracity. Concepts of 'truth' and 'reality' are notoriously tricky and non-fiction texts are not necessarily 'true'. For instance, religious texts may be taken as true but perhaps not factual by some readers yet their truth may be contested by others. Mythologies arise from reli-gious belief: the Old Testament is the mythology of Judaeo-Christian reli-gion and the *Ramayana* is Hindu mythology. Sometimes these mythologies are written as non-fiction and you will find them shelved with divinity or theology, but in other instances they are fictionalized. The extent to which we judge a book to be 'true' is subject to changing values as well as increased knowledge. Revisionist histories attempt to redress the imbal-ances in historical accounts that are largely written by representatives of the dominant culture. New histories have emerged that are concerned with the lives of ordinary people or the disenfranchised. In science it is especially evident that truth is provisional: theories wait to be toppled by new theories. This is always most evident when looking back at books from the past. The difference between fiction and non-fiction is that the latter is judged to be true in the light of contemporaneous knowledge.

Validity and accuracy are, of course, important in non-fiction writing, and there are interesting issues here when thinking about the relationship of book and Internet publishing. It has been suggested that a book is more reliable than Internet sources for research. This arises from the belief that a book's validity is assured because the editorial process guarantees the quality. This seems to me to be wishful thinking rather than the expression of truth. Certainly, there is a lot of suspect material on the Internet but there is also a wealth of highly trusted primary and secondary source mate-rial. Furthermore, the accuracy of material in books can be no more guar-anteed than the accuracy of web-based material. The relationship between the Internet and printed material seems to me to be more symbiotic, with writers increasingly using online reference sources and books providing source material for web publishers. A recent development in non-fiction publishing is the explicit use of the Internet to extend the book, as with Dorling Kindersley's 'Google' series and Wayland's 'Weblinks'. What is important is that children are taught how, in the context of research and study skills, to make judgements about the reliability of texts whether they are web or print based and that they are explicitly taught to check facts using a range of sources. However, one of the advantages of the book relates to the previous discussion about voice. Much of web-based material will not engage young readers or provide the necessary context that a book written specifically for a younger audience will.

Extending from the concept of 'truth' is the question of the objectivity of non-fiction texts. The popular notion that the ideal non-fiction book pres-ents its subject objectively is erroneous. Early biographies were written to glorify leaders and focused on heroic accounts and good acts. By the 1800s with a growing awareness of subjectivity, biographers were beginning to address the weaknesses as well as the strengths of those leaders. Nevertheless, even those books claiming to be written objectively will, in subtle ways, encompass the values of their authors, whether this is through the selection of material for inclusion or indeed omission, the amount of space given to a particular topic, the structure and organization or the tone and selection of vocabulary.

So while writers may aim to represent their subjects in a balanced way, this does not mean that their books will be completely neutral or objective. Children in school learn to distinguish between fact and opinion and to detect subtle bias in texts and while it is important for them to able to do this, there is a further lesson in recognizing that subjectivity is not necessarily negative. Al Gore's *An Inconvenient Truth* has a subjective viewpoint, which he acknowledges in his introduction, but it is the personal perspective which engages the reader and makes this such a powerful and compelling read.

One test of the quality of non-fiction is the extent to which it refuses to condescend to its young readers, making the complex accessible without resorting to half truths. This respect for children can be found in books like Stefan and Beverley Buczacki's *Young Gardener* (2006), which implicitly asserts the position that children can be serious gardeners.

The best writers make their subject exciting and immediately relevant, and they understand that the language of non-fiction can create barriers to understanding. Complex ideas are often expressed using complex language, but good children's non-fiction writers are able to convey complex ideas in simple ways. For example, David J. Smith's *If the World Were a Village* (2004) explains facts about the world's population in a simple but fascinating way. Instead of unimaginable billions, it presents the whole world as a village of just 100 people. We discover that, of those 100, 22 speak a Chinese dialect, nine speak English, eight speak Hindi and seven speak Spanish. Using this book in the classroom it is interesting to pose the question what happens to minority groups when the numbers are rounded up in this way. Rochelle Strauss uses a similar idea reducing the scale from global to manageable for her book *One Well*, which invites the reader to: 'Imagine for a moment that all the water on Earth came from just one well. This is not as strange as it sounds. All water on Earth is connected so there really is just one source of water – one global well –from which we all draw our water' (2007: 3).

Production and design

One of the greatest changes that have occurred in the past 20 years is in the area of organization and layout. The organization of non-fiction texts, and consequently the way in which they require readers to engage with them, will vary. Some books invite the non-linear reading that young readers find familiar from their encounters with the Internet. However, others may build a story or argument that progresses in stages from cover to cover and demand more conventional linear reading in order to gain a complete understanding. This is perhaps more prevalent with historical and biographical subjects which are concerned with time rather then scientific concepts.

Changes made possible by the arrival of new technologies, design packages, desktop publishing and cheap overseas printing led to innovations in book production. Dorling Kindersely was a leader in the 'non-fiction' revolution of the 1980s. The clean look was visually striking and the emphasis on photographs drew attention to visual media as a vehicle for learning about the world. One of the strengths is the quality of scaffolded talk that is stimulated when supportive adults are on hand to draw attention to the salient features of images. As critics note however, the brief and partial information of the accompanying captions meant that the depth of learning that could be gained from more extended prose was missing. Emphasis on design at the expense of content is an issue raised by Stewart Ross, author of *Pirates, Plants and Plunder*:

> Too many non-fiction books are over-designed, trying to be something they are not and compete with screen media. There is too much going on for children to navigate. The emphasis is on browsing, flickability, endless lists. There are not enough non-fiction books with quality texts that children can lose themselves in. So it's hard for them to learn to write continuous non-fiction prose and they reach the sixth form unable to read heavy books or write essays.

In spite of these reservations about design over substance, high-quality visual material is both engaging and informative. A well-chosen picture can instantly convey information that may take several hundred words to explain. Photographs can dramatically communicate ideas that might be difficult to express in words alone. Yann Arthus-Bertrand's *The Future of the Earth* (2004) presents a collection of breathtaking aerial views, zooming out to enable children to see the world from a new point of view. As well as taking the macro view, the camera can present life in close-up. Wildlife photographer Steve Bloom's stunning photographic documentary *Elephants* (2007) allows readers to discover everything about elephants from trunks, tails, tusks to the soles of their feet. Photographs are also particularly suited to bringing places to life, providing an eye-witness to daily life in far flung places, but a good photograph is more than a record, as Prodeepta Das's photographs in the World Alphabet series (*P is for Pakistan*, 2007) clearly show. Das's humanistic photographs encourage reflection and the composition invites the viewer to ask questions about the subjects that are presented.

Drawn illustrations, on the other hand, have the potential to be analytical and focus attention on the salient parts of an image. David Macauley's detailed architectural books, *Cathedral* (1973) and *Castle* (sadly no longer in print but worth sourcing) are excellent examples, as are Stephen Biesty's amazing cross-sections. Charlotte Voake and Kate Petty's delightful *A Little Guide to Wild Flowers* (2007), is reminiscent of an Edwardian sketchbook. Delicate watercolour illustrations are arranged by colour for easy identification. Drawn illustrations have the added benefit here of suggesting that children might also draw what they see and in doing so come to achieve new understandings of plant structures. Instant photography would not engage with the subject in the same way.

A full range of media can be employed in the non-fiction book; drawing and impressionistic painting might most successfully convey movement which would suit a book about dance. While in Jeannie Baker's wordless picture-book *Window* (1993), a sequence of double-page spreads made from a collage of natural and artificial materials illustrates the point that the medium can be used to add to the message. A companion book, *Belonging* (2004) is recommended for its positive message about regeneration through community action.

Recent advancement in production processes has led to innovative techniques in presentation. Computer graphics interface (CGI) that has been used to create special effects in film is also being put to use in the production of books. Anne Rooney's *Volcano* (2006), one title in a series by Dorling Kindersley, has gone to great expense to show the inner workings of a volcano using this application. The photo-realistic effect enables the reader to experience a zone where it would be humanly impossible to travel.

Cheap printing costs using overseas markets has led to a burgeoning of novelty texts with intricate pull outs and other features all imaginatively used in non-fiction texts. Templar's *Egyptology* and *Mythology* bring the ancient world alive. Kingfisher *Voyages* is an imaginative science series. One title, *Space* (Goldsmith, 2005), for example, makes very good use of acetate inserts to illustrate both sides of the moon and throw-out leaves to show the stages of a shuttle launch and the astronauts' preparation for spaceflight. Combined with an authoritative and engaging text with quotations from consultant astronaut Sally Ride – 'outside the windows, the Shuttle in a fiery orange glow as we blazed through the air' – these features are more than novelties, being thoughtfully selected to enhance the text.

Non-fiction continues to change as knowledge evolves and technology and new media develop. It is vital that these vibrant, innovative texts are made available to young readers and that non-fiction is not merely regarded as a source of information in the service of research and study but also a source of pleasure and an aesthetic experience.

Further reading

Books to start an exploration of non-fiction for children

Two examples of picturebook non-fiction at its best: Jeannie Baker's *Window* and *Belonging* (Walker Books).

If the World Were a Village by David J. Smith and Shelagh Armstrong (A. & C. Black) explains facts about the world's population in a simple but fascinating way.

The delightful *A Little Guide to Wild Flowers* by Charlottte Voake and Kate Petty (Random House) is reminiscent of an Edwardian sketchbook with delicate watercolour illustrations and drawings which may inspire young readers also to draw and in doing so achieve new understandings of plants.

Young Gardener by Stefan and Beverley Buczacki (Frances Lincoln) includes projects such as growing cress in an egg shell as well as guidance on real gardening tasks.

Chocolate: The Bean That Conquered the World by Vivian French (Walker Books) is shaped like a bar of chocolate complete with gold foil and looks good enough to eat.

Poetry for Children

Michael Lockwood

> This chapter looks at:
>
> > What is 'good' poetry for children?
>
> > How poetry aimed at children has evolved
>
> > Ways of sharing poetry

Current opinions

Most adults would agree that poetry is a good thing for children to read. However, there is much less agreement about exactly what makes a good poem for children. These disagreements were vividly illustrated by an exchange of views in the journal *Carousel* in 1998. Anne Harvey, a well-known compiler of poetry anthologies for children, tried to separate what she considered 'real' poetry from the 'rubbish'. She identified 'the real' with 'classic' poems, whether written for an adult or child readership, remembering being 'set alight' by some lines of Alexander Pope's at the age of 3. 'The rubbish' consisted of 'smutty condescending verse', often about custard or snot, and often written 'in accents I can't understand', in the words of a poem Harvey quoted (Harvey, 1998). In the next issue of *Carousel*, the children's poet and anthologist, Brian Moses, replied in an article entitled 'Children's poetry: not just an exclusive club'. Moses recounted a rather different reading autobiography: 'The poetry that was read to me at school ["improving" texts] had the effect of closing doors and I left school at 18 with totally negative feelings towards poetry' (1998: 19). The doors were opened again by the 'fun', 'colloquial', non-establishment poems of the Mersey poets, Roger McGough, Brian Patten and Adrian Henri he encountered as a young man. For Moses, poetry should be 'for everybody', including those readers, often reluctant boys, it traditionally does not reach (Moses, 1998).

This debate, often characterized as being between supporters of 'poems for children' on the one hand and 'verse for kids' on the other, has rumbled on over recent decades and attracted some distinguished contributors over the years. For example, poets such as Roy Fuller and Vernon Scannell have weighed in with comments like: 'those who write poetry for children perforce enter the field of light verse' (Fuller, in Scannell, 1987: 205) and 'I believe that quite a lot of poetry written especially for children would be better jettisoned in favour of poems … written for people of any age' (Scannell, 1987: 207). The critic Peter Hunt agreed, stating: 'The bulk of original verse for children published today is scarcely competent even on its own terms' (Hunt, 1991: 198).

On the other hand, Peter and Iona Opie, researchers into children's playground rhymes, felt that: 'the more pure the poetry, the more difficult it can be to say for whom the poet is writing' (Opie and Opie, 1973: ix). But probably the most helpful intervention in the debate came from the poet W.H. Auden, who famously wrote: 'While there are some good poems which are only for adults, because they presuppose adult experience in their readers, there are no good poems which are only for children' (Auden, 1963: 18). This shifts the focus away from the age of the audience towards the quality of the poems. If a poem written for children is a good poem, it is suitable for any audience. This is partly due to the nature of poetry, which operates through images, rhythms and sounds as well as ideas, and can be enjoyed sensuously and affectively, as well as intellectually. Readers of different ages can enjoy the same poem but in different ways. Also, as the Opies' comment suggests, the simpler the poem the more effective it often is: *less* in poetry can be *more*.

A brief history of poetry for children

The history of British poetry written for children is a relatively short one: just over 300 years. Before this time, of course, there was a thriving oral tradition of songs and rhymes which children enjoyed, and there were poems written about children or for adults to read to children. However, it was only in the late seventeenth and early eighteenth centuries that poets and publishers began directly to address child readers. The first collection of nursery rhymes for British children, for example, *Tommy Thumb's Pretty Song Book*, was not published until 1744. The fact that publishers were willing to produce such material implies an audience of literate children and interested parents of sufficient size by this time to make the venture worthwhile. Three main poetic voices can be heard in British poetry for children from these beginnings up until the 1950s: the didactic, the lyric and the nonsense (Benton and Fox, 1985). I look briefly at these three voices which historically poets writing for children have used and ask what ideas about childhood and what ideas about poetry lie behind them.

The didactic voice

The first voice poets used when writing for children was a teaching voice, unsurprisingly, and the teaching was about religion. John Bunyan, better known for *The Pilgrim's Progress* (1678–84), published *A Book for Boys and Girls or Country Rhimes for Children* in 1686. Isaac Watts, famous as a hymnwriter, followed with *Divine Songs Attempted in Easy Language for the Use of Children* in 1715. Their poetry was a Puritan response to the oral and chapbook tradition of ballads and popular songs which they thought was a corrupting influence on children. Bunyan and Watts were quite deliberately using the devil's own tunes: using the popular forms of 'rhymes' and 'songs' to win children's hearts and minds. Bunyan saw himself as 'playing the fool', but for a serious purpose:

> Wherefore good Reader, that I save them may,
> I now with them the very Dottrel [simpleton] play.
> And since at Gravity they make a Tush,
> My very Beard I cast behind the Bush. (Bunyan, 1686: 3)

No doubt today Bunyan and Watts would be using rap and hip-hop to put their message across!

For these two nonconformists, children were naturally sinful and it was their duty to save children's souls. Poetry for them was therefore a way of sugaring the pill of the moral and religious lesson: an early form of 'edutainment'. The impulse to educate children through verse remains strong in the centuries after Bunyan and Watts. The didactic tradition they initiated carries on through the nineteenth century in great swathes of improving and edifying poems for children. By this time, though, the teaching is less about eternal salvation and more about table manners and bad behaviour. By the end of the century, explicitly didactic verse has shrunk in importance so much that Hilaire Belloc is able to satirize the earlier 'cautionary tales' with his own spoof versions.

The lyric voice

With the rise of Romanticism from the late eighteenth century onwards came a very different view of childhood. For Romantic poets, the child was innocent not sinful, and was nearer to God than adults: 'Heaven lies about us in our infancy' as Wordsworth put it ('Ode: Intimations of Immortality', 1807, st.5). Rather than children needing to be saved from original sin, it was the adults who needed to get back in touch with their inner child. Are William Blake's *Songs of Innocence* (1789) children's poems? Blake is certainly writing for the child in all of us, at the very least. Physically, the original text resembles a children's book, with its small size and coloured illustrations, and in the introductory poem to the collection, Blake seems to suggest he is writing for children:

> And I made a rural pen
> And I stained the water clear,
> And I wrote my happy songs
> Every child may joy to hear. (Blake 1789: plate 4)

Along with a radically different view of childhood came a different conception of poetry or 'song', which valued the imagination for its own sake and had less of a utilitarian purpose than the earlier didactic verse. The simplicity of language and form of Blake's songs recalls the Opies' comment that 'the more pure the poetry, the more difficult it is to say for whom the poet is writing'. Unlike Bunyan, Blake does not feel the need to play the fool and 'write down' to a child audience, even if it is the 'child-in man'. The lyric tradition which begins with him continues in the nineteenth century with poets such as Robert Louis Stevenson and Christina Rossetti, and into the twentieth century with Walter de la Mare and James Reeves.

The nonsense voice
With Edward Lear's *A Book of Nonsense* (1846) a different voice is heard in children's poetry:

> There was an old man with a beard,
> Who said, 'It's just as I feared!—
> Two owls and a hen,
> Four larks and a wren,
> Have all built their nests in my beard!' (Lear, 1846: 9)

The intensity and moral seriousness of Romantic poetry and the overt moralizing of didactic verse have been replaced by a view of poetry for children as playful, in particular a play with words and meanings. But like all children's play, this can be anarchic and subversive too. Nonsense poetry inhabits a world of misrule, albeit a safe one, where adult reason and language can be stood on their heads. Children are the natural audience for this debunking of the established order of things and the poet is a fellow conspirator with them against the adult world of sense and propriety. In the work of Lewis Carroll, the subversion of adult attitudes and pretensions in his nonsense poetry is extended to satirizing adult views of children's poetry and parodying improving poems such as those of Isaac Watts. It is no coincidence that Lear and Carroll were both more at home in the company of children than adults. They both also reveal a darker and more disturbing side to their nonsense worlds in longer narrative poems such as Lear's 'The Pobble who has no Toes' and Carroll's 'The Hunting of the Snark'.

Many voices: the contemporary scene

Since the 1950s, poetry written for children has become more diverse. As the poet Michael Rosen has put it, we can now hear 'many voices' (Rosen, 1992). The explicitly didactic, moralizing voice is heard far less (an exception might be some of Roald Dahl's poetry), though it can be argued that teaching children through poetry has not disappeared but become more indirect, as, say, in poems about environmental issues or bullying. As Peter Hunt has said: 'Didacticism is far from dead in modern children's literature ... it tends to disguise itself in modes of telling and controlling' (Hunt, 1991: 117). The lyric voice is still present, for example, in their very different ways, in the work of Ted Hughes and Charles Causley, who both made no rigid distinction between their poems for adults and for children. The nonsense voice certainly continues strongly in the work of many children's poets but particularly Spike Milligan's, regularly voted the most popular children's poet.

With the appearance of Michael Rosen's *Mind Your Own Business*, though, in 1974, a different voice is heard. Rosen tries to present the voice of the contemporary, urban state-school child previously not represented in British poetry for children. Using the speech and thought patterns of the child, usually a boy, Rosen seeks to avoid writing down to children, or using a special poetry voice for them, by using their own language to speak about their experience, usually in anecdotes. At its best, it is an artful representation of the child's voice, not a transcript:

Once my friend Harrybo
came to school crying.

We said:
What's the matter?
What's the matter?
And he said
his granddad had died.

So we didn't know what to say. (Rosen, 1988: 122–3)

Rosen's view of poetry is that it is 'memorable speech' and he is one of the first poets to use free verse for children to convey speech rhythms and thought patterns in memorable ways. This 'urchin verse', which represented 'the move from the poetic to the demotic' (Townsend, 1990: 300), opened the door for many other new voices to enter British poetry for children. Other quite different, 'demotic' voices, which also tried to represent children's own language and experience, such as those of the Mersey poets Roger McGough and Brian Patten, Gareth Owen and Allan Ahlberg, entered children's poetry. In the 1980s, the rise of this pluralism in children's poetry saw the emergence of black voices for the first time, such as those of John Agard, Grace Nichols and James Berry, speaking of Caribbean childhoods not just in non-standard dialects and accents but in West Indian creoles. In the 1990s, black British poets such as Benjamin Zephaniah and Jackie Kay have added their voices to an increasingly diverse poetry scene and developed the performance aspect of children's poetry in exciting and energizing ways.

What qualities to look for in anthologies and collections

The key words to apply to children's poetry books are quality and variety. To enjoy the full range of the broad church that is now British poetry for children, readers need to experience both good quality collections of poems by single authors and good quality edited anthologies presenting the work of many poets. Too often in poetry, children only encounter anthologies, often with a narrow range of poets and poems, and do not engage with an individual author's work. As with fiction, they need to be able to develop tastes and preferences by reading widely. It is disappointing, then, to read that there has been a sharp reduction in the number of single poet collections as part of a general decrease in poetry book publication in recent years (Carter, 2007: 14), but the appointment of Michael Rosen as Children's Laureate for two years from 2007, with an agenda of promoting poetry, may change that decline.

Anthologies need to offer a range of poems which reflect the richness of children's poetry as it has developed over time. This means:

> contemporary as well as classic poems
> funny as well as reflective poems
> urchin verse as well as didactic, lyric and nonsense
> the oral as well as the written tradition
> poems by writers from other cultures as well as British
> by women as well as men
> about boys and girls
> by children as well as adults
> from popular culture as well as literary

> written for adults as well as for children
> unrhyming as well as rhyming
> unpublished as well as published
> in non-standard Englishes as well as standard.

As W.H. Auden commented, a good children's poem is a good poem for anybody. What represents good quality poetry (or even poetry itself) will always vary with individual readers, but Dr Johnson's often quoted dictum that good literature should help us better to enjoy or endure life is still a useful measure. Good quality poems ask to be read again as soon as we have finished them, and not just because we did not understand them. Either through form or content, or usually both working together, good poems excite or comfort, startle or calm, and can engage all types of emotions and thoughts in between these poles. They have an impact which is remembered and can be conjured up again, slightly differently, in each rereading. Lines from good poems pop into our heads in all sorts of situations life throws at us.

Sharing poetry with young readers

Because good poems are usually a 'fresh listen' as well as a 'fresh look', to use Robert Frost's terms, they need to be read aloud, for all readers but particularly younger ones. James Carter points out that many contemporary children's poets such as himself make their livings as performers and so write for the stage as well as the page (Carter, 2007: 15), but most older poems also benefit from being heard as well as seen. Going further and encouraging children to perform and present poems using drama techniques allows them to get inside poems and explore them actively and collaboratively. Regular poetry performances for a variety of audiences help spread the word that poetry is for enjoyment by performers as well as audience.

There needs to be time too for individual reading of poems on the page and the right environment for this. Children need the opportunity to browse through a variety of poetry books in a comfortable and relaxed setting. The rights of the reader of poetry books, to adapt Daniel Pennac's charter (Pennac, 2006), include: the right not to read from beginning to the end but to dip in; the right to read and reread favourite poems; the right to read them aloud; the right to learn them by heart; the right to read anything you consider poetry; and, the right not to finish a poetry book if you don't like it.

Making their own personal anthology of poems, in a format which is continually expandable, is a way in which children can take ownership of poetry and be aware of their own development as readers. Poems can be written or typed out in appropriate fonts and styles and accompanied by illustrations. Children's own anthologies can be shelved with published ones to build or expand a poetry library.

Children experience much of their entertainment through information and communication technology (ICT) today, whether digital audio or video on computers, mobile phones or MP3 players. There is no reason why they should not experience poems in this way too. An iPod can just as easily store podcasts of poems and a computer download videos of poetry performances. One of Michael Rosen's first ideas as Children's Laureate, inspired by his son, was to set up a YouTube-style website for poetry performance.

Poems can be taken apart from time to time, like any well-made objects, but it is important to remember to put them back together properly at the end and check that they still work. Looking at how a poet has built up sound patterns through rhythm, rhyme, alliteration, assonance, ono-matopoeia and other devices, or how word pictures have been built up through images, or meanings made through puns and wordplay, can add a different sort of enjoyment as well as understanding of poems. But poems should not be used just as excuses for feature-spotting, for example hunting down metaphors and similes for the sake of a naming of the parts. Poems are often left in pieces after this kind of activity as the lesson moves on to ransacking another text for the same feature or topic. It should be a rule to read the poem aloud again after any form of analysis, relishing its sounds and images anew after the insight into how they fit together.

Research suggests that those teachers and other professionals who read widely in children's literature, who enjoy what they read and, most importantly, can communicate this enjoyment to children, are the most effective teachers of literacy. This is particularly true of children's poetry. But engaging with children's poems offers more than just acquiring useful professional knowledge and skills. For many adults for whom poetry remains, literally, a closed book, reading children's poems offers a way back into enjoying poetry, maybe for the first time since they were children themselves.

Further reading

Ten 'must-read' poets and anthologies

Everyone should have their own 'top ten' list, including children, and this will change constantly as books are read or reread and new ones published. Sadly, poetry books tend not to stay in print for very long and therefore school and public libraries become important sources for out-of-print favourites. The following list reflects my tastes as a reader and teacher and is put forward in the spirit of 'try these and see if you'd add them to your list'. Many are inevitably old favourites, along with some newer arrivals:

Single poet collections

Please Mrs Butler by Allan Ahlberg and illustrated by Fritz Wegner (Puffin, 1983). This favourite of teachers and pupils alike has to be on any list. Ahlberg uses songs, rhyming and non-rhyming poems to record the highs and lows of the primary school day. *Heard it in the Playground* (Puffin, 1989) continues the theme.

Collected Poems for Children by Charles Causley and illustrated by John Lawrence (Macmillan, 1996). Causley is the master of traditional rhyming forms, such as the ballad, and uses them to write about his own childhood and those of the children he taught in Cornwall. Local folklore, nursery and playground rhymes inform many of his poems, but his range includes nonsense verse and non-rhyming forms too. He perfected the art of making language sing and dance, but asks difficult questions too.

Collected Poems for Children by Ted Hughes and illustrated by Raymond Briggs (Faber, 2005). Hughes wrote poetry for children throughout his career and the full range is collected here, from his early conventionally rhyming, humorous poetry to later free verse poems closer to his adult work, often dealing with the natural world, where close observation combines with use of myth and metaphor.

Mustard, Custard, Grumble Belly and Gravy by Michael Rosen and illustrated by Quentin Blake (Bloomsbury, 2006). This recent silver anniversary edition combines two previous favourite collections by Rosen along with new artwork by his long-time collaborator and predecessor as Children's Laureate, Blake. It also includes a CD of Rosen reading aloud all 45 poems in the book.

All the Best: Selected Poems by Roger McGough (Puffin, 2004). This selection of over 100 poems shows how McGough has perfected the art of being seriously flippant. His poems for children work through sharp wit, clever rhyme and wordplay, but the laughter they evoke often leads to moments of insight and reflection.

Plum by Tony Mitton and illustrated by Peter Bailey (Scholastic, 1998). A beautifully produced book of deceptively simple poems for primary age readers. Mitton has a real gift for using rhyme and rhythm, both in short lyrics and narrative ballads, which makes him Causley's natural heir. Read also *Pip* (Scholastic, 2001) and *Fluff and other stuff* (Orchard, 2001).

Songs and Verse by Roald Dahl (Cape, 2005). This selection, with pictures by no less than 26 leading illustrators, brings together poems from Dahl's novels with others from his themed collections such as *Dirty Beasts* and *Revolting Rhymes*. Dahl is the master of the comic rhyme, but his poems usually teach a lesson too, often a painful one!

Come on into my Tropical Garden by Grace Nichols and illustrated by Caroline Binch (A & C Black, 1988). This collection was one of the first to open a window onto a Caribbean childhood and many of the poems have become classics. Nichols uses the rhythms and language of Guyanese Creole to conjure up a tropical world at once exotic and familiar.

Let Me Touch the Sky by Valerie Bloom (Macmillan, 2000). This selection shows Bloom writing with gentle, ironic humour about life both in Jamaica and Britain in vigorous rhymes and rhythms. Bloom's poetry begs to be read aloud and performed.

Picture a Poem by Gina Douthwaite (Red Fox, 1999). Douthwaite has made the art of the shape or concrete poem her own in this and other collections. Not only is she wildly inventive in the design of her poems on the page, her poems also use rhyme and rhythm with great skill so that they work when read aloud as well as looked at.

Anthologies

John Agard and Grace Nichols (eds), *Under the Moon and Over the Sea* (Walker, 2002). Over 30 poets, five different illustrators and 50 poems are included in this evocation of the land and sea, the food and folk tales of the Caribbean. The poems also deal with the experience of leaving as well as living there.

Brian Patten (ed.), *The Puffin Book of Utterly Brilliant Poetry* (Viking, 1998). Ten leading poets, each with his or her own illustrator, are included in this sampler of contemporary British poetry for children, along with brief interviews with each poet.

Gerard Benson, *This Poem Doesn't Rhyme* (Viking, 1990). A wide-ranging and influential anthology which demonstrates, using non-rhyming forms of all kinds from Shakespeare to Anon., that poems for children don't have to rhyme to be poetry.

John Foster, *101 Favourite Poems: Poets pick their favourite poem* (Collins, 2002). Foster, one of the most prolific and influential of anthologists, asked a hundred and one leading children's poets, including himself, to choose their favourite poem from their own work and to say why they chose it.

Roger McGough, *Sensational* (Macmillan, 2005). A well-chosen mixture of classic and contemporary poems, ranging from Wordsworth to Carol Ann Duffy, all inspired by at least one of the five senses.

Guides for adults

Edgardo Zaghini and Deborah Hallford, *Universal Verse: Poetry for Children* (Barn Owl Books, 2006). An extensive guide for parents, teachers, librarians and other professionals to poetry books for children currently available.

Paul B. Janeczko, *A Kick in the Head: an Everyday Guide to Poetic Forms* illustrated by Paul Raschka (Walker, 2005). A lively and imaginative text that can be enjoyed in many ways: as a superbly illustrated anthology, a comprehensive reference guide and a stimulus for writing in a wide range of formats.

Morag Styles, *From the Garden to the Street: Three Hundred Years of Poetry for Children* (Cassell, 1998). An authoritative but very readable overview of poetry for children by an academic author who has done more than any other to promote the subject.

Useful websites

The Internet is a rich resource for children to use to find poems, post reviews or to share their own work. There are far too many sites to mention, but some particularly worth visiting by both children and adults are:

www.poetryzone.ndirect.co.uk

www.poetrylibrary.org.uk

www.childrenspoetrybookshelf.co.uk

www.poetryarchive.org
www.poetryclass.net

10

Picturebooks: Looking Closely

Judith Graham

This chapter looks at:

> Why picturebooks are so important for young readers

> Visual terminology

> Different sorts of picturebooks

Illustration is everywhere, not only in children's books but in books for all ages, in comics, magazines, advertisements, on posters, food, packaging, the television and computer screen. Though many of these outlets for illustration seem utterly contemporary, illustration has been around for a long time, perhaps over 3000 years if we think of Egyptian papyrus rolls, and it pre-dates printing by 1,500 years. Put simply, illustration is a series of pictures connected to a text and 'illuminating' it in every sense of that word. Illustration in children's books may be simply decorative, but more often it aims to interpret or supply narrative meaning that is not present or accessible in written text alone. Two succinct definitions of picture-books (rather than illustrated books) are useful to hold in mind:

> A picturebook is a text, illustrations, total design; an item of manufacture and a commercial product; a social, cultural, historical document; and fore-most an experience for a child. As an art form, it hinges on the interde-pendence of pictures and words, on the simultaneous display of two facing pages, and on the drama of the turning page. (Bader, 1976: 1)

> Picturebooks – books intended for young children which communicate information or tell stories through a series of many pictures combined with relatively slight text or no text at all – are unlike any other form of verbal or visual art. (Nodelman, 1988: vii)

Bader and Nodelman define the picturebook. The illustrated book, as opposed to the picturebook, usually has a written text that, while it may be enhanced by the illustrations, can survive without them and indeed may have existed without them for a great many years. Very few picturebooks are republished with a different set of illustrations; illustrated texts frequently reappear with new illustrations, with *Alice's Adventures in Wonderland* perhaps topping the charts as the most frequently re-illustrated children's book. Though both are equally valid art forms and both have contributed significantly to children's literature, this chapter is primarily concerned with the picturebook rather than the illustrated book.

It would be wrong to imagine that reading a picturebook is a simple operation. When John Burningham's *Come Away from the Water, Shirley* was first published in 1977 (see the further reading section for all children's books cited), it was apparent that many adults, expecting pictures to duplicate the written text, were bemused by the apparent mismatch and failed to see the more subtle interaction going on between word and picture. In this book, as in many picturebooks, the words are few and can be read in a short space of time, but the pictures need more time and scrutiny if their detail and meaning are to be perceived. Becoming alert to the way in which a written text constantly pushes the reader on while a picture stops us in our tracks and slows down the reading is the first requirement for students in their appreciation of picturebooks. As Nodelman puts it: '[The] sort of ironic relationship between the sequential storytelling of words and the series of stopped moments we see in a sequence of pictures is, I believe, the essence of picturebook storytelling' (1988: 239).

It is also important to appreciate how very varied the picturebook can be. Pictures in reading schemes may intentionally show what the written text indicates ('here is a dog'; 'here is a ball') but most illustrators are more ambitious than that and will aim for the unusual or unexpected, a secondary story, a running gag, a surreal embroidering, incongruity, ambiguity and irony, even in books aimed at the youngest audience. Writers will also want to focus on what words can do best (such as what things and people are called, what people say and think, when things happen, what happened earlier or later – off-stage as it were) and eliminate language made superfluous by the illustration. Illustration is better suited to creating mood and atmosphere, using colour, tone, light and dark; showing characters' clothes, faces and expressions of feeling; or representing their spatial relationship to one another and what places look like.

Picturebooks may appear to be produced for the youngest children, but it should not be forgotten how much readers know and need to know if they are to enjoy books. At six months, babies tend to chew their books, explaining why 'rag' books have come into being. They may hold their books the 'wrong' way round, they may turn the pages from back to front and possibly turn several pages at a time. This is not only a question of manual dexterity; the appreciation that stories have a logical sequence, requiring readers to start at the beginning and look from top to bottom and from left to right (though not in all scripts), is a necessary aspect of a child's learning. Many children's books tell their stories through double-page spreads, which may not obviously be organized on the principles of left and right, so learning how to read these has to be mastered too. Before we look in detail at categories of picturebooks, we need to consider what some of the 'rules', codes and conventions for reading words and pictures are. (Technical terms are found in Figure 10.1.)

Bleed
A picture in a picturebook 'bleeds' or is 'bled' to the very edge of the paper when it has no frame and leaves no margin. The effect is to pull the reader more actively into the picture (cf. 'frame').

Closure
Of particular relevance to comic strips, this refers to the way in which readers must make sense of (interpret) the gaps in information left between one frame and the next (McCloud, 1994: 60–93).

Double-page spread
An opening in a picturebook where the image spreads over the two facing pages (cf. 'page opening').

Endpapers
The pages that are immediately inside the front and back covers. The story in a picturebook often starts or ends here, though the illustrator may use the endpapers decoratively or symbolically. Paperback picturebooks are sometimes, regrettably, published without the original endpapers.

Format
The physical size and shape of the book. 'Portrait' format is taller than it is wide; 'landscape' is wider than it is tall. The choice should be influenced by the nature of the illustration, with portrait more commonly used when a focus on character is required and landscape for when the setting is more important.

Frame
The border around an illustration, which may simply be the white margin of the page or can be a printed line, a drawn free-hand line or a decorated band. Often the separate illustrations on a page are called separate frames. When a picture bursts through a frame ('breaks the frame'), extra momentum and significance is added. (In *Handa's Surprise*, by Eileen Browne, a very important mound of tangerines breaks through the picture's frame to draw the reader's attention to the happy outcome of the story.) 'Frame' is also used occasionally in a very different to sense to indicate everything about a book that is not the text; in other words, those elements, such as author's and illustrator's names, title, blurb, typographic

continued over

Figure 10.1 *Visual Terminology*

aspects, publishing details, etc. which surround the book and package it (cf: 'peritext').

Gutter
The grooved space at the centre of a book, created by the binding, where pages abut. It is also the space between frames in a comic strip or between different frames on one page of a picturebook.

Page opening
Where the picture on the left is distinct from the picture on the right.

Page turn
Turning the page in a picturebook is a different experience from turning over the page in an unillustrated text; it requires the reader to pause and peruse the picture. At the same time, the written text (if there is one) – especially if the turn comes in the middle of a sentence as in Maurice Sendak's *Where the Wild Things Are* – impels the reader to turn over. The text may sometimes foreshadow the next picture so that the reader is in a state of high anticipation as the page is turned. Turning the page may also reveal surprising information or effects. All of this creates a typical picturebook rhythm for the reader, whether reading aloud or silently.

Peritext
All the material that is not the text itself (cf. 'frame' above). In a picturebook where the illustrations and written text together count as text, the peritext does not include the illustrations, though a case could be made for the peritext to include the cover illustration. Typically, the peritext is not in the author's nor in the illustrator's control and is the domain of designers, typographers, publishers, publicity and marketing people.

Pictorial/iconic sequence
Of particular relevance to comic strips, this refers to pictorial or iconic frames placed in a narrative sequence (as opposed to the self-contained frames you might find in illustrations).

Recto
The right-hand page of a book.

Speech bubble
Typically found in comic strips and graphic texts, this refers to dialogue contained within a stylized 'bubble' and which is usually superimposed onto pictorial images. Speech bubbles frequently break frames (see 'frames') and can be used to indicate who is speaking, or to convey sound.

Tone
The level of brightness, lightness or darkness used in coloured images.

Verso
The left-hand page of a book.

Viewpoint
The position from which the reader views the illustrations. There may be a static viewpoint, where the illustrations are seen from the same point throughout, or the illustrator may change the viewpoint from, perhaps, a high position where the scene is surveyed from above, to a low viewpoint, where the image dominates.

Many other intellectual and perceptual challenges face the young child. If I look out of a window, the view I see could be considered to make a picture. Yet it is utterly different from a printed image, particularly because everything is moving. How do we come to accept static representations? How do we learn that objects shown in two dimensions, sometimes far too small, occasionally too big, stand for those objects in real life? Why do we accept heavy lines drawn around items, the incompleteness of some items, the fact that backgrounds may be absent so that the characters appear to float in space?

A further challenge is that the child is asked to accept things that are never normally encountered in life. Perhaps more than half the output of children's books features animals or toys as characters, often in clothing, usually speaking, living in recognizable human houses and behaving rather as humans do. And then there is a whole cast of witches, monsters, dragons, goblins and others who are pictured for us but which have parallels, if at all, only in our heads. Even when children are the main characters, they may seem to exist without adults to care for them, and they often do impossible things. Of course, such books appeal to children for a variety of reasons to do with their inner lives and their delight in topsy-turvydom; nevertheless, the taking on board of these facets of picturebooks has to be learned.

If newcomers to the field are to have any chance of finding a way through the wealth of picture and illustrated books available, it is necessary to try to impose an order. I have chosen to divide the field into four categories and within those categories to discuss a few representative titles.

Books of pictures

Into this category come those books with minimal written text, which are designed particularly for the inspection and enjoyment of the pictures. The written text is not only minimal; it is frequently, a 'given', with little or no variation possible, as in the case of most alphabet and counting books. The organizing principle of the alphabet is probably lost on most of the children who are looking at these books, though naming the pictured items will certainly be a game that develops. Concept books, designed to teach colours, shapes, materials, animals and much else, also come into this category. While there are obvious restrictions in terms of what may be done with the written text in such books, the very constraint seems to attract and inspire illustrators. There are ABCs dating from the mid-eighteenth century (which is when we can say children's books began), and several of those created in the nineteenth century (those of Edward Lear and Kate Greenaway, for instance) are still obtainable. Currently, there are thousands of alphabet books and thousands of counting books and probably tens of thousands of concept books. Many of these are extraordinarily inventive and even approach being works of art. Many of the most talented illustrators are drawn to create books of pictures at some point in their careers and the originality on show is impressive.

Helen Oxenbury is a narrative illustrator, and so, in every simple image in her *ABC of Things*, there is the germ of a story. So for 'B', Oxenbury is guiding the child to see cause and effect: four demanding creatures – baby, badger, bear and bird – clamber over an exhausted baker. This skill will be necessary in reading written texts in the future. Every now and again the image covers the two pages of an opening, changing the rhythm of the book agreeably. Making narrative links between the openings is not required of the young reader but the book goes beyond the average ABC book in terms of the narrative interest within each picture, in the surprising combinations, the humour and the careful draughtsmanship.

Counting is something children do even before they learn the alphabet; inviting a child into the world of numbers and counting interests illustrators. In *Anno's Counting Book*, Mitsumaso Anno makes sophisticated demands on his readers. Each picture, neatly framed and drawn and read from a fixed position, shows a landscape bisected by a river, but, as the numbers increase, so do the numbers of children, adults, birds, buildings, trees, animals and much else. Child beholders need to bring what they have counted, sorted, classified or grouped from one picture to the next. So, on page 1, the reader identifies a single sun, a single house, a single boy and a single girl, but for the number two, the memory of what has happened on the previous page needs to be evoked so that when the picture shows that a church has been built, it is now necessary to talk about two buildings. Similarly, the boy and the girl now count as two children, and Anno has helpfully grouped them together. Frequently, as the numbers mount, the image shows, for example, two cats facing three cats, so that there is an opportunity not only to count but also to add.

An intriguing concept book, which could also be discussed in the category of wordless picturebooks below since the title is the only written text, is *The Colours* by the Swiss illustrator Monique Felix. A small mouse nibbles his way into the book (the hard cover has a missing piece and teeth marks) to find he is alongside the art materials of a young girl whom we can see leaving the room. Colours, first the three primary colours, are introduced to the reader by the small mouse, who squeezes oils from the tubes of paint and then runs over to the empty left-hand page with his loaded paintbrush. With great effort, he squeezes two tubes together to make green, then orange and then purple.

In addition to the understanding about how pictures and books work, which children need to have acquired in order to enter a text, they must also realize that, although the mouse is shown several times in a single picture, this does not mean that there are several mice in the story. Moreover, there are gaps between the pictures: not every race across the page is shown; children must fill in the unpictured events.

Novelty books

Into this category come those books where the reader lifts flaps, pulls tabs, spins discs, reveals three-dimensional panoramas on the turn of the page, removes items from integrated pockets or envelopes, unfolds hinged pages, looks through holes, turns over half-pages and engages with the book in many another active way. 'Movable' is the more accurate term for those books where the reader physically manipulates a device in the book. Such books come closer to toys than other books, though they are often more fragile than toys, and the best of such books are those in which the paper engineering is not merely clever, but closely linked to the story.

Some of the most successful novelty books are designed for very small children and have simple flaps, holes or half-pages. Rod Campbell's *Dear Zoo*, Jan Ormerod's *Peek-a-boo!* and Lucy Cousins's *Where Does Maisy Live?* are all small masterpieces, principally because the folded paper flap is integral to the story. So, each animal that is sent to the narrator in *Dear Zoo* arrives in its own crate/box/basket, and the reader must reveal its occupant before sending it back. Jan Ormerod's babies are playing the timeless game of peep-bo and so, to see their faces, the reader must peel back the towel, the dress, the quilt, the teddy, the gloved hands or the bib. Looking for Maisy involves opening up the henhouse, pigsty, kennel, and stable before she is found in her house.

One problem with novelty books is that a tension can be created between the narrative, which wants to go forward, and the need to lift flaps and explore other effects. Certainly, Janet and Allan Ahlberg's *The Jolly Postman* and Cressida Cowell's *Little Bo Peep's Library Book* require readers to interrupt the narrative to read the letters and the little books that are inserted into the body of the texts. But because, as with all picturebooks, which by their very nature require pausing to inspect images, these books are usually revisited frequently by their readers, the disturbance to the narrative flow may only be a problem on the first reading. In addition, it may be that the very interruptions build a facility in the reader for putting narrative on hold and then picking up the threads again. For these reasons, such books are read rather differently from other books; the insertions may be read later – or even before a straight run-through of the book. We do not know enough about how these books are read by their child readers to be categorical about their impact on the reading process. We do know that the books are treasured and that their 'loose parts' are not lost, as was initially feared, indicating both care for the books and a recognition that such parts are integral to the narrative.

Wordless books

Picturebooks with no words other than the title form a small fraction of the sum total of picturebooks, but they are a sub-genre that repays attention. Many illustrators are drawn to the wordless book, perhaps because they rise to the challenge to tell a story using only images, and perhaps because they enjoy the prospect that their books will be bought and read by those who respect and enjoy close examining of pictures. Because there are no words to alert readers to what is significant or absent in the pictures, the reading of wordless books is not as straightforward as is often assumed. Until children are experienced with story structures, they may perceive the task of recounting the story of a wordless book as detailing everything that is taking place, which is both confusing and exhausting. Work that I have done (Graham, in Evans, 1998) with books such as Quentin Blake's *Clown* suggests that narrative inexperience rather than visual literacy is the problem for children when they try to reconstruct the narratives they see in words. The inexperienced reader–viewer cannot always perceive significance and sequence and does not, for instance, when reading *Clown*, group various pictured activities that show household chores being done and say, 'the woman is spring-cleaning'. With experience comes the ability to recognize both the general point being made and its place in the narrative. That said, visual literacy is certainly important; illustrators of wordless books frequently employ a language that owes much to comic strip, film and animated cartoons that use a pictorial sequence. Thus a wordless picturebook may use many more frames than a book with words in order to close narrative gaps. Use may also be made of a variety of 'shots' – long, medium and close-up – in order to focus the reader on the wider scene, the significant element and then the key emotions or transactions. The viewpoint will also change frequently, according to what needs to be emphasized, and colour may be used more deliberately than in a book with words in order to mark mood and atmosphere.

The wordless book *Sunshine* by Jan Ormerod contains 70 different pictures. Eighteen small frames alone go to showing a young girl, whose parents are finding it difficult to get up, dressing herself in the morning. That such a sequence enchants the reader is a tribute to Ormerod's accurate observation and shrewd decisions of how to keep the images lively; for instance, many of the child's garments spill into an adjacent frame. To indicate movement, Ormerod shows her characters against a frame rather than in one, so that they seem to be forever leaving or entering the stage. In order to keep variety in the text, the illustrator also has several full-page pictures, usually of something relatively static, such as the parents asleep in bed. Other wordless picturebook creators who proceed through the use both of many small frames and intermittent much larger scenes, as if the camera has pulled back, are Peter Collington, Philippe Dupasquier, Shirley Hughes and Raymond Briggs. Monique Felix in her wordless books about mice trapped in books uses the whole (admittedly small) page, not the frame, to convey the wordless story.

Australian illustrator Jeannie Baker creates wordless books for older readers as does the American David Wiesner. In *Window*, Jeannie Baker has the reader looking both at and through the same window, but the years are passing and gradual changes are recorded; the cumulative effect is sobering as nature gives way to an urbanized world. Baker's photographed collage constructions use several visual devices to indicate the passage of time – a child growing up (birthday cards on the window ledge, toys deteriorating and changing) as well as the changes beyond the window, where are shown, among other environmental destruction, the trees felled followed by a sign advertising firewood for sale. David Wiesner's *Tuesday* is typical of his work and is a book likely to be appreciated by older readers. The story begins before the title page (illustrators often need to exploit every one of the 32 pages a standard picturebook allows) as frogs begin to rise from the surface of a lake, each on its own lily-pad magic carpet. The frogs increase in number, become a flying flotilla, and have a wild night on the town. Two endings are offered. The book repays study not only in its full range of cinematic techniques (a frog's encounter with a dog is told in three horizontal strips which lend momentum and movement to the incident) but also in its understated, humorous detail (one of the frogs uses his prehensile tongue to change channels on the remote control), magical use of night-time colour and witty references to science fiction, animated cartoons, silent movies and super-hero literature.

Picture storybooks

Maurice Sendak's title *Where the Wild Things Are*, published in 1963, was regarded by Sendak as his first picturebook. His earlier books were well liked and finely illustrated but, like many books up to this point in time, they were counted as books with pictures rather than picturebooks. The arrival of *Where the Wild Things Are* in the USA and then in the UK was nothing short of sensational. Critics feared it would frighten children and some wished it to be banned. However, the book was, and is, well liked by children because, through the story of Max sent to bed without any supper for behaving in a wild fashion, the book speaks to them directly of their strong feelings (of anger, desire for power and control, longing for love) and because it recognizes that they live in worlds of fantasy as much as in worlds of fact. It is nowadays seen as a landmark title that brings so much together: an unforgettable story with sentences rhythmically bounding over several pages and painterly illustrations that pull us into Max's world, whether it be his bedroom or the land of the wild things to which he travels.

Some children's picturebooks can engender real tension and be profoundly moving; some can be created principally for humour and pleasure; some picturebooks leave readers reflecting on a sober message; some work well with no message at all. Some picturebooks form a composite text, with words and pictures sharing the telling; others retain a written text that is self-sufficient and use the illustrated text to add extra effects. Some picturebooks include painterly illustrations that could be framed and hung on a wall; some illustrators make skilful use of digital means to add photographic and other textures to the line drawing. Since Sendak, the picturebook has developed into a versatile medium capable of conveying narrative at a variety of levels and to different effect.

Beegu is the story of a forlorn little yellow three-eyed alien who crash lands on Earth and finds herself rejected or ignored by all save a playground of children. Ultimately her parents arrive from space to rescue her, and Beegu reports that any hope for Earth creatures lies with the small ones. In a story of fewer than 150 words, and without reverting to sentimentality, the author/illustrator, Alexis Deacon, uses his illustrations to achieve three (at least) critical effects. First, he creates interest and concern in his reader for his main character by making her stand out on every page in her glowing yellowness; the mostly dark and sinister backgrounds increase our sympathy. Second, Deacon creates the desired mood with a palette of dark turquoise and navy blue, textured backgrounds in grey and brown, line drawing that is also soft and textured, lots of space around the lonely creature. The pace is calm and measured, with page after page underlining, through repeated incidents, the themes of search and despair. Finally, the author–illustrator uses his illustrations to extend the minimal written text. Where the text simply says that the children 'want to say goodbye', the pictures show her playmates squeezing through the school railings, and offering her their hoop. Beegu's ears stand up straight, as they do in all the illustrations when she is happy, and later the hoop intrigues Beegu's father aboard the rescue spacecraft.

The themes of this story are not uncommon in children's literature: abandonment, loneliness, rejection and separation. Placing a child character (or equivalent) alone in an alien environment enables an author to present the isolation from a viewpoint familiar to young readers who know what vulnerability feels like. In addition, in this story, there is the theme of isolation through not being able to communicate – Beegu's language is not understood by the adults on Earth. This story functions on several levels, including as a metaphor for the condition of refugee children.

Who's Afraid of the Big, Bad Book? constructs the picturebook in an entirely different way. Those familiar with Lauren Child's work will know how much fun she has with the words, pictures, layout, fonts and the whole physical object that is the book. The collage effect in her pictures – there is much inspired sticking and pasting and use of photography – complements the cartoon style of her line drawing, and though the pages may strike readers initially as crowded, messy and rather difficult to read, familiarity allows her skill and wit to be appreciated. In any case, child readers probably have the edge on adults here as their reading of such pages is finely honed by contact with screen pages. Kress usefully discusses multimodal texts and the different 'reading paths' taken through a text such as this, and the demands made on readers by the screen-organized 'display' genre that he believes is replacing traditional text: 'Reliance on simple linearity is certainly not a useful approach to the reading (of such texts)' (in Styles and Bearne, 2003: 146).

Lauren Child's playful bending and breaking of literary rules and conventions puts her work firmly in the postmodern camp, where effects are achieved by challenge to and parody of traditional forms of storytelling, and by highlighting the very form of the book. Perhaps surprisingly, her written text stands independently of the pictures, but this does not detract from *Who's Afraid of the Big, Bad Book?*; indeed the book has so much going on that it is probably a wise decision.

Complex though Child's book sounds, it is still a picturebook for young children. Since Sendak, there have been a surprising number of story picturebooks that have much older people as their implied readers. The Australian writer, Gary Crew, has supplied the written text for several picturebooks aimed at teenagers. *The Watertower*, illustrated by Steven Woolman, is a horror story that leaves plenty of work for the reader to do. Two friends take a trip to cool off in a local watertower; something (what?) happens to Bubba, the more nervous boy, but he appears cheerful by the end. The black surrounds of the illustrations, the patterning on the watertower which is echoed everywhere, including on the hats of the adults and in the water, an ominous pitchfork whose shadow falls on and traps Bubba, the huge double-page close-up of his terrified face – all contribute to the impact of this unnerving, composite text. A thoughtful 12-year-old resolved the mystery to his own satisfaction by claiming that the adults who are seen approaching the watertower chuck Bubba in and thus enable him to overcome his fear. For this reader, the story became a, rather extreme, rite of passage story.

There are tens of thousands of picture storybooks; those discussed above are all extremely different from each other and suggest the range and complexity available. How to choose? Undoubtedly, age and personal taste guide choice. The 3-year-old who introduced me to *Beegu* is left perplexed by *Who's Afraid of the Big, Bad Book?* Six-year-old twins spent an hour giggling over the Lauren Child book and long to own all her equally inventive books. They, in turn, would be perplexed, not to say frightened, by *The Watertower*. *Where the Wild Things Are*, now that we are over its initial shock, seems to work its magic on most age groups.

Picturebooks are invariably the first books that children in the developed world encounter. They shape aesthetic tastes, they introduce principles and conventions of narrative. They are part of artistic and literary culture but they are also entertaining, moving, thought-provoking and witty. Adults studying children's picturebooks will find themselves learning to be alert to different elements from those associated with novels or conventional illustrated books. The best picturebooks are usually complete designs, incorporating covers, endpapers, layout, typography, format, size and, of course, colour. Great thought is given to the rhythm of the words, the balance of picture and word, the drama of the page turn. The best picturebooks enthral us; perhaps some will leave us indifferent. But all picturebooks do need to be given time; their qualities are revealed by repeated, patient and close looking. If we can share our readings and responses with others and keep an open mind, we should enter a most rewarding world.

There are so many excellent picturebooks available that it is impossible to provide a meaningful list here. Other works by the writers and illustrators discussed in this chapter are worth exploring, as are those discussed in the critical reading titles listed below.

Further reading

Children's books mentioned in this chapter
Many high-quality picturebooks are mentioned throughout this book, especially those for the very young. Seek out the following small selection of fascinating and thought-provoking picturebooks to get a taste of the how authors and artists have taken the genre beyond the 'childish' concerns. These books, and many others, make profound meanings, and occasionally discomforting themes, accessible to young readers. (Editor)

Ahlberg, A. and Ahlberg, J. (1986)*The Jolly Postman, or Other People's Letters.* London: Heinemann.

Anno, M. (1977) *Anno's Counting Book.* London: Bodley Head.

Baker, J. (1991) *Window.* London: Julia MacCrae.

Blake, Q. (1995) *Clown.* London: Jonathan Cape.

Browne, E. (1994) *Handa's Surprise.* London: Walker Books.

Burningham, J. (1977) *Come Away from the Water, Shirley.* London: Jonathan Cape.

Campbell, R. (1982) *Dear Zoo.* London: Abelard-Schuman.

Carle, E. (1970) *The Very Hungry Caterpillar.* London: Hamish Hamilton.

Child, L. (2002) *Who's Afraid of the Big, Bad Book?* London: Hodder Children's Books.

Cousins, L. (2000) *Where Does Maisy Live?* London: Walker Books.

Cowell, C. (1999) *Little Bo Peep's Library Book.* London: Hodder Children's Books.

Crew, G. and Woolman, S. (1994) *The Watertower.* Flinders Park, Australia: Era Publications.

Deacon, A. (2003) *Beegu.* London: Hutchinson.

Felix, M. (1991) *The Colours.* New York: Stewart, Tabori and Chang.

Ormerod, J. (1981) *Sunshine.* London: Kestrel Books.

Ormerod, J. (1997) *Peek-a-boo!* London: Bodley Head.

Oxenbury, H. (1967) *ABC of Things.* London: Heinemann.

Sendak, M. (1963) *Where the Wild Things Are.* New York: Harper and Row.

Wiesner, D. (1991) *Tuesday.* New York: Clarion Books.

Additional picturebooks for older readers

Chris Van Allsburg, *The Mysteries of Harris Burdick*, Houghton Mifflin Company

Martin Auer and Simone Klages, *The Blue Boy*, Gollanz

Raymond Briggs, *When the Wind Blows*, Penguin

Anthony Browne, *Zoo*, Red Fox

Gary Crew and Jeremy Geddes, *The Mystery of Eilean Mor*, Lothian Books

Michael Foreman, *War Game*, Pavilion Children's Books

Neil Gaiman and Dave McKean, *The Wolves in the Walls*, Bloomsbury

John Marsden and Shaun Tan, *The Rabbits*, Lothian Books

Ntozake Shange and Kadir Nelson, *Ellington was Not a Street*, Simon and Schuster

Shaun Tan, *The Arrival*, Lothian Books

A version of this chapter was first published in *Modern Children's Literature – an Introduction*, edited by Kimberley Reynolds and published in 2005 by Palgrave Macmillan. We are grateful for their permission to reproduce much of the chapter here.

11

The Powerful World of Graphic Texts

Mel Gibson

> This chapter looks at:
> > The different types of graphic texts
> > Ways to share them with young readers
> > How to evaluate graphic texts

Comics, graphic novels and manga (the Japanese word for comics) are a wonderful set of groups of texts that offer much to explore for readers of all ages, ranging from the simplest short humour story to multi-volume epics. Spanning a huge range of genres, they contain profound and powerful texts, as well as pleasurable, reassuring and stimulating reads. In addition, they can play a part in encouraging enthusiastic reading amongst teenage (or young adult) readers.

What are graphic texts?

Although comics have often been typified in Britain as humourous texts for much younger children, it is important to keep in mind that the majority of what is published today that takes the form of the comic is aimed at older readers. Indeed, in Britain, the history of the comic has always included material specifically for adults, from *Ally Sloper's Half Holiday* onwards, but the focus throughout most of the twentieth century was on material for children, in an increasingly segmented market that offered titles for specific ages and separately for boys and girls. For instance, in relation to girls, titles like *Twinkle* were produced for the youngest girls, *Bunty* for older readers and *Jackie* for teenagers. Some comics, like *Beano* and *Dandy* (two of the very few weekly British comics still in existence), were seen as for all readers and titles specifically aimed at boys included *Victor*. This is a model that also appears in the Japanese manga industry, which is currently increasing in popularity among young adults from Britain, and means that the texts produced can be divided, like the British industry, along lines of gender and age.

Graphic novels, in contrast, really begin to appear in the 1980s. The majority of these texts are aimed at adults or young adults, although there are titles that also appeal to younger readers, such as *Bone* by Jeff Smith (see the further reading list for full details of this and subsequent graphic texts cited). While the comic in Britain tended to have one- to three-page stories that were either self-contained or ran for around 14 weeks in a single narrative, the graphic novel format allows for more detailed and complex narratives to be developed. It may be a single volume, or several (*Bone*, for instance, is in nine volumes), will contain a complete narrative and could be on any subject or genre. Manga also operates in a similar way, with multi-volume single narratives being the format which British readers are most familiar with, including the very popular girls' manga (the genre is called shojo) *Fruits Basket* by Natsuki Takaya. While collections of short stories may also be called graphic novels (for instance Matt Groening's *The Simpsons* and *Futurama*) this is more about them being published in a bound volume than about what they contain.

The key to understanding these texts is to focus on the flexibility of the comic medium. At one extreme, it can be used to tell stories in a simple way. However, this same flexibility means that the comic can also tell phenomenally complex stories or explain difficult ideas. The central point is that this is a medium, rather than a genre (so thinking of comics simply as genres such as 'humour', or 'superhero' is counterproductive), and can be used to create demanding texts across a range of genres.

Further, the medium, while often associated with fiction, is also used to create non-fiction, including biographies and autobiographies, such as Art Speigelman's *Maus* (now used in schools alongside *The Diary of a Young Girl* (Frank, 1997) and Marjane Satrapi's *Persepolis: The Story of a Childhood* (the first volume works very well with teenagers, although the second is much more for an adult audience) or *Ethel & Ernest* (1998) by Raymond Briggs.

Briggs's work is a useful way into understanding comics as a medium, not a genre, in that he has created books that are factual and even biographical, alongside works that are located within fantasy. In addition, the medium allows the creator to address a wide age range. Briggs exemplifies this in that he has created works for all ages of reader, from the wide appeal of *The Snowman* (1978) to the politicized and adult or young adult *When the Wind Blows* (1982).

Further, graphic texts can be 'text heavy' or 'text light' (terms referring to the way that comics may combine a large number of words along with the images, or none at all). Again, Briggs's work functions as a useful reference point, with texts ranging from the wordless *The Snowman* through to the text-heavy *Fungus the Bogeyman* (1977).

Given the increasing complexity of the medium, if it is a long time since you have read any of these texts yourself, it will take some practice to get back into reading them. This is an absolute necessity when the aim is to share books with younger readers. Reading widely within the medium will help you to familiarize yourself with what has changed, but, particularly for female readers, I would recommend starting with Bryan Talbot's *The Tale of One Bad Rat*, which was designed to draw readers back into an engagement with the medium, as well as simply being a terrific book. It is also a powerful read for young adults.

The growth of the manga market is also an element that adds to the importance, and to the challenge, of becoming familiar with graphic texts, necessitating, as it does, reading in what may be an unfamiliar way. Generally, a younger reader new to manga will ask one simple question, 'Why do they start at the back?' Most of the Tokyopop and Viz titles sold in Britain are published in the original format, something which adds to their cachet. For those starting off with this type of graphic text, the publishers often include instructions on how to read them. There are variations, in that manga created by American and British writers is published in a more familiar format, such as Craig Conlon's *Hairy Mary* books. In addition, Korean comics (manhwa), also included in the collections of both of the publishers above, also read from left to right. I would suggest trying *Fruits Basket*, or something like *Jing: King of Bandits* as ways in to understanding titles for girls and boys.

The flexibility of the medium means that when looking for titles, it is perhaps best to think about how you would wish to use them (for instance, *The Simpsons* as leisure reading, using *Ethel & Ernest* as a history text in a classroom, using manga to start a discussion on diversity with a youth group) and who you wish to use them with. Do not think of them as texts for less able readers aimed at encouraging them towards 'real' reading (that is, of text-based novels). It is worth noting, however, that emergent readers tend to be most enthusiastic about humour titles. Instead, think of graphic texts as a parallel world to the world of the novel, with the same range of genres and where some texts are better written and illustrated, more engaging and more demanding than others. It is entirely possible to build comic collections that offer challenges to the good reader and support to the less enthusiastic, whether they are located at home, at school or in libraries.

Views of graphic texts

Comics have often been dismissed as a medium in Britain, something that reflects their history here, a situation very unlike that of much of Europe, where comics are a respected and honoured art form.

This is why, even today, in Britain, they are usually approached with caution by both libraries and schools, as their content has often been seen as controversial, and the medium as somehow undermining literacy and morality. Most recently, manga have been seen in this way. The enthusiasm of younger readers for the medium has resulted in some British media offering alarmist portrayals of manga, for example Owen (2004). The assumptions about manga typically include that only one style of art exists (with 'big eyes') that only one genre exists (science fiction) and one audience (older males interested only in sex and violence). To counter such assumptions I urge older non-readers to try some titles for younger readers (the major publishers put age suggestions on the covers) as a way of becoming familiar with manga.

In summary, seeing comics in a negative light starts from the premise that comics are bad for readers, thus making such views part of the debates around 'media effects' and 'moral panics'. In addition, this negative view often, inaccurately but firmly, positions comics as suitable only for children, making material aimed at adults seem more shocking.

In contrast, comics are also seen by some in a very positive way. One great champion of the medium, for readers of all ages, is Paul Gravett, who has written extensively about manga (2004), graphic novels (2005) and comics (2006). In effect, those seeing the comic in this light may accord comics the status of an art, taking a more typically European approach, while the former group sees them in the light of notions of a historical construction, that being as 'bad' mass culture. In addition, spaces are emerging for professionals to discuss comics, most notably the Graphic Novels in Libraries UK discussion list (http://groups.google.co.uk/group/GNLIBUK?hl=en).

Comics are also seen in a third way, solely as a way of drawing poorer readers into literacy. Clearly, developing new readers is a good thing, but it does reveal a telling set of assumptions about comics. Here the comic is a 'bad thing', but a useful tool, a perspective that reflects a limited enthusiasm for the medium, something which younger readers pick up on. This can have the result that comics are read by younger readers in an act of reading as rebellion, to antagonize those who disapprove. This in turn leads, as Styles and Watson (1996: 179) suggest, to a cycle being established in that 'the fact that children take such pleasure from these texts is enough to convince some commentators that they must be harmful'. Finding even a single title that you, as an older reader, can be enthusiastic about rather than simply feeling that you do not like the medium, or understand it, but can see that it appeals to others (a view I often come across) avoids the possibility of alienating the younger readers you wish to engage with, even if they do not like the titles that you do.

Another way of viewing graphic texts is to classify them as an altogether different kind of text from books, even though they typically are books. This is reflected in the way that comics appear as part of the media studies GCSE rather than elsewhere.

A final way of approaching graphic texts is to look at them from an academic point of view, as objects that reward study in various disciplines. The works created also show a range of underlying assumptions about comics, often in relation to issues around gender, and may reflect the key perspectives held above, or may explore them. A key text by Martin Barker (1989), *Comics: Ideology, Power and the Critics*, intended for adult readers, offers a series of case studies which take a range of theoretical positions that can, and have, been used in relation to comics (including feminism) and interrogates them.

To conclude, while there are a range of ways of thinking about graphic texts in Britain, most of these exist in tension with one another, whether in classrooms or elsewhere. As Morag Styles and Victor Watson asserted, 'Many teachers are aware that the comic is one of the best and most motivating genres for teaching reading' (1996: 179). However, they also said, 'this is too unsettling for those with fixed views of what children should read and how they should learn to do it' (Styles and Watson, 1996: 179) indicating, as I suggested, the problematic cultural position of the comic.

Sharing graphic texts

When sharing these texts with young adult readers, it is possible to include them in a general 'book talking' session with a group, but, unlike a traditional novel, you cannot read graphic texts aloud effectively. It is more likely that you will give a plot summary, or, if possible, show a key page on screen using a visualizer or other means, and talk about where it fits into the overall narrative. That kind of talk is best followed by giving readers an opportunity to just look through the books and ask questions. Just adding one graphic novel, or manga to the texts you discuss will flag up that these are books too, and enjoyable reads.

With this kind of text, you will often find groups of readers looking at them together, and their discussion is as likely to be about the artwork as the narrative, often analysing the text in very complex ways, demonstrating mastery and passion for their subject. Another response is an intense silent and individual contemplation. It is also quite common to share these books with pencils and paper in hand. For many readers a major response is to start to want to copy the artwork, create new narratives about the same characters or use the comic as inspiration for original work. Many current comic creators started as fans, copying the work of those they admired.

Another good way into sharing these texts is to talk through how the page is laid out, the grammar of the comic, as well as what the images depict and the narrative. A good text to help familiarise you with how comics work is the excellent *Understanding Comics* by Scott McCloud (1993), which is also a comic. It is also worth looking at some of the texts that play with the basic rules. For instance, while most British and American comics have around six to nine panels on a page, Raymond Briggs, in *When the Wind Blows*, sometimes uses 25 or more.

You may also want to talk about the overall layout of the book, thinking about the number of panels per page, the use of full-page images, and so on. Again drawing on Briggs, he makes use of single image double-page spreads in *The Snowman* to signify freedom. When the snowman and boy go flying the number of panels drops, while, at the end the number increases again as the boy returns to home and bed. Further, the use of the specific medium has an impact on how the story might be told. The use of soft pastel crayons in *The Snowman* contributes to the expansive feel of that book, as do the rounded panel shapes.

In contrast to young adults, it is much more challenging to share comics with very young readers. This can be shown with reference to *The Snowman*, a text seen as addressing precisely this group. To make sense of this text, the reader needs to understand the grammar of the comic book, for instance, how panels work. In an example located towards the end of the book, a page containing 12 panels showing the boy turning in his sleep over the remainder of the night and then waking up in the morning, demands that the reader understands that these are not 12 separate images of different boys (as someone unfamiliar with this kind of text might well assume) but a series of images of the same boy that should be read from left to right, and from top to bottom, as a sequence unfolding in time. That, even without the addition of speech bubbles, makes a lot of demands upon the reader.

Being aware of the way that one reads a comic, however, makes it easier to share that skill. Picturebooks that draw on the grammar of the comic, such as those by Colin McNaughton, with their use of panels and speech balloons, and comics like the *Beano* and *Dandy*, with their shorter stories can also open up this space for discussion with much younger readers. In addition, the challenging experience of starting to read manga, until one becomes familiar with that form, is a useful reminder of the challenges that reading in general presents to the emergent reader.

Talking about who the audience might be for any given book is also a useful way of sharing these texts. Age, gender, class, ethnicity, location and what knowledge readers have to bring to the book to make sense of it, can make for interesting discussion. For instance, one could argue that *Ethel & Ernest* could be seen as primarily addressing an older adult, British, white, middle-class reader. Such connotations could be read from a number of aspects of the book, including the cover, which looks like a traditional 'quality' novel.

Another important consideration with sharing these texts, picking up on an earlier theme, is that of the gender of the reader. Male readers form the majority for most comics and graphic novels. The readers already involved with the medium are often very enthusiastic and enjoy the opportunity to share their knowledge. They may have a passion for a specific genre, or read more generally, and will talk about both image and text (offering the older reader a model of sharing these texts to use with other, less knowledgeable readers). Be prepared to learn a lot if talking with an enthusiastic younger reader of graphic texts. You will quite possibly end up with a list of what you should be reading.

What has changed in relation to gender and reading of graphic texts in very recent years is the introduction of manga to Britain. Typically, 60 per cent of sales are to female readers. This means that for the first time since the collapse of the girls' comic in Britain (which came to pass largely in the 1980s, although it finally ended in 2001 when *Bunty*, the last of over 50 titles for girls, was retired) girls are reading comics. As with boys, they too will be expert, enthusiastic and, quite possibly, creating their own artwork.

Another important aspect of sharing these texts is to be prepared for surprises. One example of this is the way that the recently published manga Shakespeare books are being actively chosen by some younger readers for leisure reading. The series is also being picked up on in schools as a way of making the texts more accessible to younger readers. I have had similar experiences with Hunt Emerson's version of *Rime of the Ancient Mariner* (which is full text) receiving several requests as to whether the writer and artist had 'done any other books'.

Having made these general points about sharing graphic texts, it is important to remember that each book you choose will offer a unique set of possibilities for sharing. For instance, *Ethel & Ernest* by Raymond Briggs offers a decade in each chapter and contains references to shifts in education and culture in Britain, personalizing cultural changes and so is full of rich possibilities for discussion. Key pages include one in which Briggs gets a place at grammar school, which shows his working-class parents' responses to what they see as their son's achievement. In particular, the father's comment that he hopes his son will not get too posh for the family articulates a great deal about shifting class and educational structures.

Evaluating graphic texts

In thinking about what qualities to look for in graphic texts, it may be useful to think about the following questions, which will help in relation to assessing any given text.

Audience
Who do you think the intended audience is in terms of age and gender? Is the language accessible for the audience you want to share it with? Are there several potential audiences? Is it a satisfying read for you? If this book were going to be put into a library, would it be located in the children's, teen or adult collections? How, if at all, could the book be used in a classroom?

Appearance
Is it physically well produced and attractive? Does the cover art do justice to what is contained within (and vice versa)? Is the printing of high quality?

Layout
Is the text legible or is it obscured by illustration? Is the text hard to follow? Think about whether this is because of a lack of familiarity with the medium, or because of the layout. Does the graphic novel or manga make full and creative use of the full range of comic strip grammar and conventions? Are techniques from the language of film used (such as flashbacks, establishing shots, tracking shots, close-ups, high and low angle shots, and so on)?

Type

Is it fiction or non-fiction? If it is the latter, what is the subject area and how well is it covered?

Narrative

If the text is fiction, what, if any genre does it belong to? Is the storyline imaginative, coherent and interesting? What kinds of issues does it flag up and how does it handle them?

Colour/black and white

Is it printed in colour or black and white? If the images are black and white will they appeal to the target audience? Keep in mind that manga is typically black and white and that this has changed audience expectations (in that colour is no longer typically seen as the 'preferred norm' for younger readers).

Illustrations

Are the illustrations of a high technical and artistic standard? Do the illustrations merely adhere to the narrative sequence or do they provide a commentary/counterpoint/expansion on the written word? Do the illustrations move the story forward? Are the words and pictures interdependent?

Further reading

Some great graphic texts to look out for
The books on the list below are principally suitable for older children and young adult readers:

Briggs, R. (1998) *Ethel & Ernest.* London: Cape. Will predominantly appeal to older children readers, but can be shared with 9+ and be very useful in discussing history and memory across generations.

Coleridge, S.T. and Hunt E. (1989) *Rime of the Ancient Mariner.* London: Knockabout Comics.

Conlon, C. (1998) *Hairy Mary.* London: Slab-O-Concrete. Several titles published.

Groening, M. (1996) *The Simpsons: Simpsorama.* London: Titan Books. All ages, many titles published, of which this is one example.

Groening, M. (2004) *Futurama.* London: HarperCollins Entertainment. All ages, many titles published, of which this is one example.

Kumakura, Y. (2006) *Jing: King of Bandits.* London: Tokyopop. Recommended for 13+ readers. Five volumes forming a single coherent ongoing narrative.

Manga Shakespeare (adaptations: for information see www.selfmadehero.com/manga_shakespeare/manga_shakespeare.html).

McCloud, S. (1994) *Understanding Comics: The Invisible Art.* New York: HarperCollins.

Satrapi, M. (2003) *Persepolis: The Story of a Childhood.* London: Jonathan Cape.

Smith, J. (2005) *Bone: Vol 1: Out From Boneville.* New York: Graphix. All ages. Nine volumes forming a single coherent narrative.

Spiegelman, A. (1987) *Maus I: A Survivor's Tale.* London: Penguin; *Maus II: And Here My Troubles Began.* (1992) London: Penguin. Initially published as a series in *Raw* (Raw Books & Graphics) from 1980 to 1991.

Takaya, N. (1999–2006) *Fruits Basket.* London: Tokyopop. Recommended for 13+ readers. Fifteen volumes forming a single coherent ongoing narrative.

Talbot, B. (1996) *The Tale of One Bad Rat.* London: Titan Books.

References

Chapter 1

Appleyard, J.A. (1990) *Becoming a Reader.* Cambridge: Cambridge University Press.

Burgess, M. (2003) *Doing It.* London: Andersen Press.

Chambers, A. (1993) 'The difference of literature: writing now for the future of young readers', *Children's Literature in Education*, 24(1): 1–18.

Department for Education and Skills and the Primary National Strategy (DfES and PNS) (2006) *Framework for Teaching Literacy and Mathematics.* London: DfES.

Graham, J. (2005) 'Mr Magnolia met the Literacy Mark: Did he Survive?' in P. Goodwin (ed.) *The Literate Classroom.* London: David Fulton.

Jennings, P. (2003) *The Reading Bug.* London: Penguin.

Medwell, J., Wray, D., Poulson, L. and Fox, R. (1998) *Effective Teachers of Literacy.* Report commissioned by the Teacher Training Agency. London: Falmer.

Meek, M. (1991) *On Being Literate.* London: Bodley Head.

Munro, R. and O'Donnell, M. (1961) *Janet and John: Here we go.* London: James Nisbit & Co Ltd.

Perera, K. (1984) *Children's Writing and Reading.* Oxford: Basil Blackwell.

Williams, M. (2005) *The Velveteen Rabbit.* London: Egmont.

Chapter 2

Butler, D. (1980) *Babies Need Books.* London: Bodley Head (out of print).

Carle, E. (1969) *The Very Hungry Caterpillar.* World Publishing Co.; 1970 London: Hamish Hamilton Children's Books.

Collins, F., Svensson, C. and Mahony, P. (2005) *Bookstart: Planting a Seed for Life.* Roehampton: Roehampton University.

Crowther, R. (1977) *The Most Amazing Hide-and-Seek Alphabet Book.* London: Kestrel Books/Viking Press.

Hill, E. (1980) *Where's Spot?* London: William Heinemann.

Rose, J. (2006) *Independent Review of the Teaching of Early Reading.* London: DfES.

Chapter 3

Blake, Q. (1995) *Clown*. London: Red Fox.
Department for Education and Skills (DfES) (2003) *Excellence and Enjoyment: A Strategy for Primary Schools*. London: DfES.
French, F. (1998) *Jamil's Clever Cat*. London: Frances Lincoln.
Garland, S. (1985) *Going Shopping*. London: Puffin.
Gough, P.B. and Tumner, W.E. (1986) 'Decoding, reading and reading disability', *Remedial and Special Education*, 7, 6–10.
Hru, D. (2002) *Tickle Tickle*. London: Bloomsbury.
Hughes, S. (1997) *Alfie Gives a Hand*. London: Red Fox.
Hughes, S. (2002) *Alfie's Weather*. London: Red Fox.
Inkpen, M. (1993) *Lullabyhullaballoo*. London: Hodder.
Murphy, J. (1980) *Peace at Last*. London: Macmillan.
Rosen, M. (1989) *We're going on a Bear Hunt*. London: Walker Books.
Scieszka, J. (1991) *The True Story of the 3 Little Pigs*. London: Puffin.
Vygotsky, L. (1986) *Thought and Language*. Cambridge, MA: MIT Press.
Waddell, M. (1992) *Owl Babies*. London: London: Walker Books.
Webb, S. (2003) *Tanka Tanka Skunk*. London: Red Fox.

Chapter 4

Ahlberg, J. and Ahlberg, A. (1978) *Each Peach Pear Plum*. London: Kestrel Books.
Atkins, J. and McNicholas, S. (1997) *Lost in the Mist*. Oxford: Heinemann: Storyworlds.
Chambers, A. (1992) *Tell Me*. Stroud: Thimble Press.
Child, L. (2000) *My Uncle is a Hunkle, Says Clarice Bean*. London: Orchard.
Cope, W. (1986) 'Reading scheme' in *Making Cocoa for Kingsley Amis*. London: Faber and Faber.
Eliot, G. (1859) *Adam Bede*. Edinburgh and London: William Blackwood.
Gregory, E. (1992) 'Learning codes and contexts: a psychosemiotic approach to beginning reading in school', in K. Kimberley, M. Meek and J. Miller (eds), *New Readings. Contributions to an Understanding of Literacy*. London: A. & C.Black.
Hutchins, P. (1968) *Rosie's Walk*. London: Bodley Head.
Meek, M. (1982) *Learning to Read*. London: Bodley Head.
Meek, M. (1988) *How Texts Teach What Readers Learn*. Stroud: Thimble Press.
Rowling, J.K. (1997) *Harry Potter and the Philosopher's Stone*. London: Bloomsbury.
Serraillier, I. (1960) *The Silver Sword*. London: Puffin.
Styles, M. and Arizpe, E. (2006) *Reading Lessons from the Eighteenth Century*. Shenstone: Pied Piper.
Waterland, L. (1988) *Read With Me*. Stroud: Thimble Press.
Williams, S (2001) 'A bridge too far? How Biff, Chip, Kipper and Floppy fail the Apprentice Reader', in *English in Education*, 35(2): 12–24.

Chapter 5

Bettelheim, B. (1991) *The Uses of Enchantment: The Meaning and Importance of Fairy Tales*. London: Penguin.
Booker, C. (2005) *The Seven Basic Plots: Why We Tell Stories*. London: Continuum.

Hallford, D. and Zaghini, E. (eds) (2004) *Folk and Fairy Tales: A Book Guide.* London: Booktrust.

Jones, S. Swann (2002) *The Fairy Tale. The Magic Mirror of the Imagination.* London: Routledge.

Opie, I. and Opie, P. (1974) *The Classic Fairy Tales.* Oxford: Oxford University Press.

Tatar, M. (2002) *The Annotated Classic Fairy Tales.* New York and London: W. W. Norton.

Warner, M. (1994) *From the Beast to the Blonde: On Fairy Tales and Their Tellers.* London: Chatto and Windus.

Yolen, J. (2000) *Touch Magic. Fantasy, Faerie and Folklore in the Literature of Childhood.* 2nd edition. Little Rock, AR: August House.

Zipes, J. (2000) *The Oxford Companion to Fairy Tales.* Oxford: Oxford University Press.

Zipes, J. (2006a) *Fairy Tales and the Art of Subversion: The Classical Genre for Children and the Process of Civilisation.* 2nd edition. Abingdon: Routledge.

Zipes, J. (2006b) *Why Fairy Tales Stick: The Evolution and Relevance of a Genre.* Abingdon: Routledge.

Chapter 6

Bawden, N. (1980) 'Emotional realism in books for young people', *The Horn Book Magazine*, 56(1): 17–33.

Carpenter, H. (1987) *Secret Gardens.* London: Unwin Paperbacks.

Chambers, A. (2001) *Tell Me: Children, Reading and Talk.* Stroud: Thimble Press.

Craig, A. (2003) 'Unforgettable, that's what you are', *Times*, (Weekend Section) 9 August, p. 6.

Craig, A. (2007a) 'Harry's place in history is secured', *Times*, (Books Section) 28 July, p.15.

Craig, A. (2007b) 'Two reasons to celebrate', *Times*, 22 April.

Crossley-Holland, K. (2007) 'Race for the prize', *Times*, (Edinburgh International Book Fair Supplement) 8 August, p. 4.

Frye, N. (1957) quoted by Lavender, R. (1978) 'Living fact or fiction', in E. Grugeon and P. Waldon (eds) *Literature and Learning.* London: Ward Lock Educational and OU Press.

Hunt, P. (1994) *An Introduction to Children's Literature.* Oxford: Oxford University Press.

Kellaway, K. (2006) 'The stuff of nightmares', *Observer*, 8 January.

Mark, J. (1993) *The Oxford Book of Children's Stories.* Oxford: Oxford University Press.

Morpurgo, M. (1997) *Times*, 27 November, p. 4.

Paterson, K. (1989) *The Spying Heart.* New York: Lodestar Books.

Pearce, P. (1969) 'The writer's view of childhood', in E. Whitney (ed.), *The Horn Book Reflections: On Children's Books and Reading*, Boston, MA: The Horn Book.

Pullman, P. (2007) 'Pullman writes a book that will shed light on darkness of his beliefs', *Times*, 1 August, p. 9.

Reynolds, K. (1994) *Children's Literature in the 1880s and 1990s.* Tavistock: Northcote House, in association with the British Council.

Watson, V. (2003) in M. Meek and V. Watson, *Coming of Age in Children's Literature.* London: Continuum.

Chapter 7

Almond, D. (2003) 'Moving through borders: the Marsh Award for Children's Literature in Translation', *School Librarian* 51(1) 12–13.

Berna, P. (1957) *A Hundred Million Francs*, tran. John Buchanan-Brown, illus. Richard Kennedy. London: Bodley Head.

Breslin, T. (2004) *Dream Master: Arabian Nights.* London: Doubleday.

Dasent, G.W. and Lynch, P.J. (2004) *East o' the Sun and West o' the Moon.* London: Walker Books.

Enzensberger, H.M. (2001) *Where Were You, Robert?* Trans. Anthea Bell. London: Puffin.

Frank, A. (1997) *The Diary of a Young Girl: The Definitive Edition.* Eds O.M. Frank and M. Pressle. Trans. S. Massotty. London: Penguin.

Funke, C. (2002) *The Thief Lord.* Trans. O. Latsch. Frome: Chicken House.

Funke, C. (2003) *Inkheart.* Trans. A. Bell. Frome: Chicken House.

Gaarder, J. (1995) *Sophie's World.* Trans. P. Møller. London: Orion Children's Books.

Hallford, D. and Zaghini, E. (2005) *Outside In: Children's Books in Translation.* London: Milet.

Holm, A. (2000) *I Am David.* Trans. L.W. Kingsland. London: Egmont Children's Books.

Holzwarth, W. and Erlbruch, W. (1994) *The Story of the Little Mole Who Knew It Was None of His Business.* Trans. unacknowledged. London: Chrysalis Children's Books.

Innocenti, R. (1985) *Rose Blanche.* English text by I. McEwan. London: Jonathan Cape.

Jansson, T. (2001) *The Book about Moomin, Mymble and Little My.* Text by S. Hannah from a literal translation by S. Mazzarella. London: Sort of Books.

Jansson, T. (2003) *Who Will Comfort Toffle?* Text by S. Hannah from a literal translation by S. Mazzarella. London: Sort of Books.

Kästner, E. (2001) *Emil and the Detectives.* Illus. W. Trier. Trans. E. Hall. London: Red Fox.

Kuijer, G. (2006) *The Book of Everything.* Trans. J. Nieuwenhuizen. London: Young Picador.

Leeson, R. (2001) *My Sister Shahrazad: Tales from the Arabian Nights.* Illus. C. Balit, London: Frances Lincoln.

Lindgren, A. (2002) *Pippi Longstocking.* Trans. E. Hurup. Illus. T. Ross. Oxford: Oxford University Press.

Mankell, H. (2000) *Secrets in the Fire.* Trans. A.C. Stuksrud. London: Allen and Unwin.

Mankell, H. (2002) *Playing with Fire.* Trans. A. Paterson. London: Allen and Unwin.

Mankell, H. (2005) *A Bridge to the Stars.* Trans. L. Thompson. London: Andersen Press.

Mankell, H. (2007) *Shadows in the Twilight.* Trans. L. Thompson. London: Andersen Press.

McCaughrean, G. (1982) *One Thousand and One Arabian Nights.* Oxford: Oxford University Press.

Pausewang, G. (2004) *Traitor.* Trans. R. Ward. London: Andersen Press.

Pennac, D. (2002) *Eye of the Wolf.* Illus. M. Grafe. Trans. S. Adams. London: Walker Books.

Peters, A.F. (1999) *Sheep Don't Go to School.* Illus. M. Prachatická. Trans. various. Tarset: Bloodaxe Books.

Prøysen, A. (2000) *Mrs. Pepperpot Stories.* Trans. M. Helweg. London: Red Fox.

Reuter, B. (2004) *The Ring of the Slave Prince.* Trans. T. Nunnally. London: Andersen Press.

Richter, H.P. (1987) *Friedrich.* Trans. E. Kroll. London: Puffin.

Satrapi, M. (2003) *Persepolis: The Story of a Childhood.* Trans. A. Singh. London: Jonathan Cape.

Satrapi, M. (2004) *Persepolis 2: The Story of a Return.* Trans. A. Singh, London: Jonathan Cape.

Chapter 8

Ackroyd, P. (2001) *London: The Biography.* London: Vintage.

Arnold, H. (1992) 'Do the Blackbirds Sing?' in M. Styles, E. Bearne and V. Watson *After Alice: Exploring Children's Literature.* London: Cassell.

Arthus-Bertrand, Y. (2004) *The Future of the Earth.* New York: Harry Abrams.
Baker, J. (1993) *Window.* London: Walker.
Baker, J. (2004) *Belonging.* London: Walker.
Bloom, S. (2007) *Elephants: A Book for Children.* London: Thames and Hudson.
Brezina, T. (2005a) *Who Can Crack the Leonardo Code?* London: Prestel.
Brezina, T. (2005b) *Who Can Save Vincent's Hidden Treasure?* London: Prestel.
Brezina, T. (2006) *Who Can Open Michelangelo's Seven Seals?* London: Prestel.
Bryson, B. (2004) *A Short History of Nearly Everything.* London: Black Swan.
Buczacki, S. and Buczacki, B. (2006) *Young Gardener.* London: Frances Lincoln.
Das, P. (2007) *P is for Pakistan.* London: Frances Lincoln.
Davies, N. and Blythe, G. (2005) *Ice Bear.* London: Walker.
Dickens, C. (2007) *Hard Times.* London: Longman.
French, V. (2007) *Chocolate: The Bean That Conquered the World.* London: Walker.
Geras, A. and Robertson, M.P. (2007) *Cleopatra.* London: Kingfisher.
Goldsmith, M. (2005) *Voyages: Space.* London: Kingfisher.
Gore, A. (2007) *An Inconvenient Truth.* London: Bloomsbury.
Hawking, S. and Hawking, L. (2007) *George's Secret Key to the Universe.* London: Random House.
Hornby, G. (2006) *Wolfgang Amadeus Mozart: The Boy Who Made Music.* London: Short Books.
Hutton, C. (2007) *A Picture History of Britain.* Oxford: Oxford University Press.
Kieve, P. (2007) *Hocus Pocus.* London: Bloomsbury.
Macauley, D. (1973) *Cathedral.* Boston, MA: Houghton Mifflin.
Mallett, M. (1999) *Young Researchers.* London: Routledge.
Meek, M. (1996) *Information and Book Learning.* Stroud: Thimble Press.
Rooney, A. (2006) *Volcano.* London: Dorling Kindersely.
Ross, S. and Roberts, D. (2005) *Pirates, Plants and Plunder.* London: Random House.
Sands, E., Steer, D., Harris, N. and Ward, H. (2004) *Egyptology.* Dorking: Templar.
Sebag Montefiore, S. (2007) *Young Stalin.* London: Orion.
Steer, D.A. Harris, N., Wyatt, D. and Palin, N. (2007) *Mythology.* Dorking: Templar.
Smith, D.J. and Armstrong, S. (2002) *If the World Were a Village.* London: A. & C. Black.
Steer, D. (2004) *Egyptology.* Dorking: Templar.
Steer, D., Harris, N., Wyatt, D. and Palin, N. (2007) *Mythology.* Dorking: Templar.
Strauss, R. (2007) *One Well.* London: A. & C. Black.
Usborne, P. (2007) http://www.thebookseller.com/books/author-profiles/46850-the-usborne-identity.html. 18 February.
Voake, C. and Petty, K. (2007) *A Little Guide to Wild Flowers.* London: Random House.

Chapter 9

Auden, W.H. (1963) Introduction to *A Choice of de la Mare's Verse.* London: Faber.
Benton, M. and Fox, G. (1985) *Teaching Literature 9–14.* Oxford: Oxford University Press.
Blake, W. (1789) *Songs of Innocence and of Experience.* Edition used, 1970. Oxford: Oxford University Press.
Bunyan, J. (1686) *A Book for Boys and Girls.* Edition used,1987. Wells: Ina Books.
Carter, J. (2007) 'Whatever happened to children's poetry?' *Carousel*, 35 (:14–15, March).
Harvey, A. (1998) 'Children's poetry: the real or the rubbish?' *Carousel*, 8 (:10–11, Spring).
Hunt, P. (1991) *Criticism, Theory and Children's Literature.* Oxford: Blackwell

Lear, E. (1846) *A Book of Nonsense.* Edition used, 1996. London: Penguin.

Moses, B. (1998) 'Children's poetry: not just an exclusive club', *Carousel*, 9 (:19, Summer).

Opie, I. and Opie, P. (1973) *The Oxford Book of Children's Verse.* Oxford: Oxford University Press.

Pennac, D. (2006) *The Rights of the Reader.* London: Walker Books.

Rosen, M. (1974) *Mind Your Own Business.* London: André Deutsch.

Rosen, M. (1988) 'Harrybo' in *The Hypnotiser.* London: André Deutsch.

Rosen, M. (1992) 'Poetry in all its voices', in M. Styles, E. Bearne and V. Watson (eds), *After Alice.* London: Cassell.

Scannell, V. (1987) 'Poetry for Children', *Children's Literature in Education*, 18(4): 202–9.

Townsend, J.R. (1990) *Written for Children.* 5th edition. London: Bodley Head.

Watts, I. (1715) *Divine Songs Attempted in Easy Language for the Use of Children.* Edition used, 1971. Oxford: Oxford University Press.

Chapter 10

Bader, B. (1976) *American Picturebooks from Noah's Ark to the Beast Within.* New York: Macmillan.

Evans, J. (ed.) (1998) *What's in the Picture? Responding to Illustrations in Picturebooks.* London: Paul Chapman Publishing.

McCloud, S. (1994) *Understanding Comics.* New York: HarperCollins.

Nodelman, P. (1988) *Words about Pictures: The Narrative Art of Children's Picturebooks.* Athens, GA, and London: University of Georgia Press.

Sendak, M. (1989) *Caldecott & Co.* London: Reinhardt Books, in association with Viking.

Sipe, C. (1998) 'How picturebooks work: a semiotically framed theory of text–picture relationships', *Children's Literature in Education*, 29: 97–108.

Styles, M. and Bearne, E. (eds) (2003) *Art, Narrative and Childhood.* Stoke-on-Trent: Trentham Books.

Chapter 11

Ally Sloper's Half Holiday (1884–1914 and revived 1922–23). London: W.J. Sinkins/Dalziel/The Sloperies/Milford

Barker, M. (1989) *Comics: Ideology, Power and the Critics.* Manchester: Manchester University Press.

Beano (1938– to date). Dundee: D.C. Thomson.

Briggs, R. (1977) *Fungus the Bogeyman.* London: Hamish Hamilton.

Briggs, R. (1978) *The Snowman.* London: Hamish Hamilton.

Briggs, R. (1982) *When the Wind Blows.* London: Hamish Hamilton.

Briggs, R. (1998) *Ethel & Ernest.* London: Cape.

Bunty (1958–2001). Dundee: D.C. Thomson.

Dandy (1937– to date). Dundee: D.C. Thomson.

Frank, A. (1997) *The Diary of a Young Girl.* London: Penguin.

Graphic Novels in Libraries UK, discussion list. http://groups.google.co.uk/group/GNLIBUK?hl=en.

Gravett, P. (2004) *Manga: Sixty Years of Japanese Comics.* London: Laurence King.

Gravett, P. (2005) *Graphic Novels: Stories to Change Your Life.* London: CollinsDesign.

Gravett, P. (2006) *Great British Comics.* London: Aurum Press.

Jackie (1964–93). Dundee: D.C. Thomson.

McCloud, S. (1993) *Understanding Comics: The Invisible Art.* New York: Harper Perennial.

Owen, G. (2004) 'Child murder, incest and rape … is this really how our schools should be encouraging boys to read?', *Mail on Sunday*, 21 November, p. 49. Available at http://forums.animeuknews.net/album_page.php?pic_id=38.

Styles, M. and Watson, V. (1996). *Talking Pictures: Pictorial Texts and Young Readers.* London: Hodder & Stoughton.

Twinkle (1968–99). Dundee: D.C. Thomson.

Victor (1961–92/3). Dundee: D.C. Thomson.

Index

Ben S. Wasike

The Diffusion of GIS in Journalism

Ben S. Wasike

The Diffusion of GIS in Journalism

Examining the Diffusion and Adoption of Applied Media Technology

VDM Verlag Dr. Müller

Imprint

Bibliographic information by the German National Library: The German National Library lists this publication at the German National Bibliography; detailed bibliographic information is available on the Internet at http://dnb.d-nb.de.

   Any brand names and product names mentioned in this book are subject to trademark, brand or patent protection and are trademarks or registered trademarks of their respective holders. The use of brand names, product names, common names, trade names, product descriptions etc. even without a particular marking in this works is in no way to be construed to mean that such names may be regarded as unrestricted in respect of trademark and brand protection legislation and could thus be used by anyone.

Cover image: www.purestockx.com

Publisher:
VDM Verlag Dr. Müller Aktiengesellschaft & Co. KG
Dudweiler Landstr. 125 a, 66123 Saarbrücken, Germany
Phone +49 681 9100-698, Fax +49 681 9100-988, Email: info@vdm-verlag.de

Copyright © 2008 VDM Verlag Dr. Müller Aktiengesellschaft & Co. KG and licensors
All rights reserved. Saarbrücken 2008

Produced in USA and UK by:
Lightning Source Inc., La Vergne, Tennessee, USA
Lightning Source UK Ltd., Milton Keynes, UK

ISBN: 978-3-8364-3611-3

TABLE OF CONTENTS

ACKNOWLEDGEMENTS

I would like to extend my appreciation to my family and the Manship School of Mass Communication at Louisiana State University for making this book possible. I am most appreciative of Dr. Renita Coleman for her constant guidance and unrelenting support for my research and learning.

LIST OF TABLES

LIST OF FIGURES

CHAPTER 1: INTRODUCTION

Computer-assisted reporting has gained popularity among journalists in the last two decades with the use of spreadsheet and database software in news reporting. Recently, journalists have added GIS, short for Geographical Information Systems, to the array of computer-assisted-reporting tools they use in their work. GIS simply takes this process to the next level. GIS is "a system of hardware and software used for the storage, retrieval, mapping and analysis of geographical data" (Herzog, 2003, p.3).

Although GIS is not the only mapping system out there, it is unique in that it overcomes the limitations presented by the other systems. Electronic atlases only display images of geographical areas, but provide no tools for spatial analysis. Thematic mapping systems only allow users to create graphical visualizations based on data from spreadsheets and databases. Street mapping systems, though more sophisticated than the other two, only map geographical locations on maps. Some more sophisticated mapping systems allow for analysis of tabular data and the importation of database and spreadsheet information. GIS combines all these functions and more (Breslin, Frunzi, Napoleon, & Ormsby, 1999).

GIS allows users to access information from a map or vice versa. It also allows users to automatically update maps by simply updating the information linked to a particular map. This makes GIS a powerful system that can analyze maps based on layers of data, map out street and location data, analyze geographical locations, update this information easily, and finally create powerful visual presentations of such analysis (Breslin et al., 1999).

For decades, journalists have used maps to communicate information to readers. With GIS, they can now incorporate data onto these maps and look for patterns and interactions that would otherwise go unnoticed. For example, they can perform spatial analysis of these data to study the geographical proximity of elements. This way, a journalist can easily determine how close a school is to environmental hazards, for example (Herzog, 2003). It allows for the efficient simplification of complex data and the communication of these data visually (Goodchild, 2000).

This means that journalists can now incorporate database and spreadsheet software to produce powerful and unprecedented visualizations of news. Use of GIS in journalism ranges from analysis of national census data, to investigation of housing code violations. The *Miami Herald* used GIS to study damage patterns in the wake of Hurricane Andrew in 1992. The investigation led to discoveries of widespread housing code violations in Dade County. Reporters from the *Philadelphia Inquirer* used GIS to study the relationship between drunken driving and road fatalities. They found that most road accidents occurred within areas with high concentrations of liquor establishments (Herzog, 2003).

Using GIS, investigators from the *Columbus Dispatch* studied inequitable housing tax assessments based on race. The investigation found that minorities living in inner city areas were assessed higher property taxes than residents in suburban areas. Other uses of GIS in journalism include: linking race to spoilt ballots, investigations of environmental hazards, the effectiveness of desegregation in schools, etc.

The power of GIS lies in what it can do and the benefit thereof to reporters. It would have been very difficult for the *Miami Herald* to analyze and visualize the wind patterns against the property damage patterns without GIS. The *Inquirer's* investigation of the relationship between drunken driving and liquor establishments further exemplifies the uniqueness of GIS. Although it would be an over statement to say that such analysis is exclusively possible with GIS, still the visual capacity to display data is what makes GIS unique.

This means that reporters now have a tool to enhance the quality of news reporting in order to give the public a better product. Large amounts of data can now be summarized simply and quickly. The discreet patterns mentioned above can now be displayed visually with maps alongside other infographics. Using GIS maps, reporters can now visually depict crime statistics, census data, tax information, and even ballot information.

Some of these journalistic uses of GIS have gained national prominence, winning prestigious journalistic awards (Herzog, 2003). But more importantly, these are issues that are of extreme importance to the public in everyday life. Some of these investigations resulted in intense public debates leading to new legislation or changes in existing legislation. For example, the *Miami Herald* story on Hurricane Andrew led to tougher regulations on house constructions not only in Dade County, but also in Broward County. Contractors now had to use better quality materials to build houses. In Philadelphia, the *Inquirer* story led to heated public debate. Soon after the story ran in the paper, residents used the *Inquirer's* online bulletin to post their reactions. This soon resulted in the adoption of a new blood alcohol level of .08 (Herzog, 2003). Increased use of GIS in journalism has the power to create a more informed citizenry, contribute to increased public debate, and even lead to important changes in public policy and government leadership that may result in a better society.

GIS has been popular among media marketing agencies to map out the demographics and locations of viewers and subscribers. Similarly, circulation departments have used GIS to map out efficient delivery routes for newspapers. It is in the newsroom that GIS is still trying to gain a foothold, and thus the focus of this paper. The purposes of this paper are 1) to study the likelihood of journalists to adopt GIS for use in the newsroom and 2) to predict the future of GIS in journalism. The study looks at demographics and other factors like technology clusters as described in the literature, and their effect on the likelihood of journalists to adopt GIS. The study also aims at looking at the factors that will hinder or promote the future of GIS in journalism.

3

CHAPTER 2: LITERATURE REVIEW

Background

The history of journalism has been marked by important technological advances since Guttenberg's invention of moveable type in 1405. Friedrich Koenig's steam driven press (1814) introduced mass circulation of newspapers. Ottmar Mergenthaler's Linotype machine first used by the *New York Tribune* in 1886 would be an industry standard for the next 90 years. The mid-1930s saw the introduction of cold type and photocomposition technologies that later replaced the expensive and labor-intensive hot-metal typesetting (Moghdam, 1978).

Computers were first used by newspapers in order to replace routine tasks in newspaper production. Two such tasks were line justification and hyphenation, both which took about 40% of the human typesetter's time to perform. The *Los Angeles Times* was the first to use a linecasting machine in 1962 (Moghdam, 1978). With the introduction of time-sharing[1] computers, typewriters slowly disappeared from the newsroom. Reporters now worked on their stories on video display terminals linked to mainframe computers. It was not until the 1980s with the introduction of desktop computers that computer prices went down and the technology diffused quickly. With the desktop computers came a vigorous software industry ready to sell packages for word-processing, spreadsheet analysis, and database management (DeFleur, 1997).

Geographical Information Systems

GIS is "a system of hardware and software used for the storage, retrieval, mapping and analysis of geographical data" (Herzog, 2003, p. 3). It is a computer technology for "managing geographic feature location data and data related to those features" (Cox & Gifford, 1997, p. 449). GIS uses

---

[1] Simultaneous use of a central computer by multiple users.

spatial data that can be manipulated, queried, and analyzed. The use of GIS dates to the 1960s when need arose to integrate computation and map processing (Goodchild, 2000). It was the Canada Land Inventory that first used a GIS system called the Canada Geographical Information System. They justified the use of GIS on the premise that computational analysis of digital maps was a much faster and cheaper process than if humans did the analysis. The land inventory thought that GIS would do more accurate numeric determinations of land area than humans could.

In order to reduce human error in the analysis of census data, the U.S. Bureau of the Census constructed and used a simple GIS system in 1970. This simple GIS was used to tabulate and spatially analyze the census data. Back then, GIS required extensive training and knowledge of specialized programming languages, making it very difficult to use. However, the 1980s saw the advent of the PC revolution. Not only were desktop computers more affordable and accessible, but so was the GIS software. Currently there are about one million licensed users of different GIS applications that cost $10,000 or more, while users of cheaper GIS applications number almost at 10 million overall. Also, GIS is used in a myriad of fields including but not limited to telecommunications, resource management, urban and regional planning, and delivery services (Goodchild, 2000).

How GIS Works

GIS works with two primary kinds of data: geographic coordinate data and attribute data (Cox & Gifford, 1997). Geographical coordinate data, also called spatial data or shape files refers to map data that show features and locations on earth. These data may be presented in any of the three forms: points, lines, or areas/polygons. Points refer to features like cities or schools, lines may depict streets or highways, and polygons may depict parks, counties, or neighborhoods. Attribute data is the information linked to the features on the map and usually comes in the form of a database. The attribute may describe the parish, the school, the highway, or the area under study. For example attribute data for a county may contain the population, the area in square miles, names of cities, etc.

In a GIS application, a user may upload a shape file that contains certain features that are under study. Each feature contains an attribute table that contains both string and numerical data describing certain aspects of the feature. Different features and their attributes make up layers. For example, a city map might have layers that represent railroads, highways, schools, parks, buildings etc. Each layer may be linked to an attribute table that gives details about that particular layer. For example, an attribute table for the schools might have the names of the schools, the number of students, location of each school, etc. All these layers make up a GIS database that is used for analysis. In order to map out the best delivery routes for example, a user can compare highway and street layers against locations of customers layers.

Since GIS uses maps and symbols to depict data, it is an important tool for visual analysis. Perhaps the most important feature of GIS is its ability to visually display information. It allows users to simplify complex data efficiently and communicate large amounts of data visually and quickly (Goodchild, 2000). The final analysis display, also called the layout, may include color coded maps, legends, infographics, and even text. This makes GIS an unprecedented tool for research and analysis.

GIS And Journalism

Computer-assisted-reporting has gained popularity among journalists in the last two decades with the use of spreadsheet and database software in news reporting. Recently, some journalists have added GIS to the array of computer-reporting tools that they use in their work. GIS brings news to life with its capability to produce powerful visualizations of patterns and interactions of spatial data that would otherwise go unnoticed with traditional newsgathering techniques (Herzog, 2003). Several reasons have led to the adoption of this new technology in journalism:

> As mentioned earlier, computer-assisted-reporting enables journalists to analyze data and look for interesting relationships and relate these to news stories.

> With the advent of desktop computers, GIS applications are now widely available for office use. Initially, researchers had to use cumbersome mainframe computers and extensive network systems.

> Government agencies from the federal to the city level are using GIS more and more. Not only does this help the general diffusion of GIS, but most of these agencies provide relevant data either free or at a low cost.

> The Internet also provides a vast store of readily available data at no cost. This data comes from government agencies, GIS consortiums, universities, and commercial ventures (Herzog, 2003).

The Environmental Systems Research Institute (2000), commonly known as ESRI, and who are the developers of one of the most popular suite of GIS software,[2] report an extensive use of GIS by the *Associated Press* and *USA Today*. ESRI reports that the *AP* Graphics Department makes use of MapShop and ArcView to create its news maps. During the presidential elections of 2000, *AP* used GIS to update dynamic maps that showed the results from the presidential and congressional races about 11 times in one night.

In order to hasten data accessibility to its staff, *AP* has uploaded Census 2000 data into MapShop. The staff can then readily access this data and produce accurate census maps while reporting breaking news. This cuts the time needed to trace relevant map information.

---

[2] ArcGIS, ArcView, ArcIMS, MapShop, ArcSDE, and the Geography Network.

USA Today was the first to use ArcIMS on Census 2000 data, allowing its readers to interactively explore a spatial form of the data online. First, *USA Today* used ArcView and SAS to combine data templates into maps that were later processed through ArcIMS and posted on the web as Macromedia Flash objects. Web users could point on a national level Flash map that would lead them to a county level map and they could view demographic changes since 1990. Drop-down menus of counties and cities in each state led the viewers to ArcIMS. Here, they could view demographic changes at units as small as census tracts (ESRI, 2002).

Florida had long been known to have the most stringent building codes in the nation. Shortly after Hurricane Andrew hit Florida in August 1992, reporters from the *Miami Herald* started covering the extent of the damage. They wanted to investigate whether the damage to homes was entirely due to the hurricane or due to the lack of proper inspections by the authorities. They first obtained data on damaged homes from Dade County, then joined these data to an already existing database that the *Herald* kept on property assessment for the county (Herzog, 2003).

Using Atlas GIS, they combined the data with two maps: a map of the county showing every township and section, and a wind contour map of the hurricane winds. What the output indicated was that damage was not necessarily related to the wind patterns. Homes built after 1980 were more susceptible to wind damage. Further investigations indicated that the same houses were susceptible to the violation of building codes. As a result, and after extensive debate, Dade and Broward Counties tightened their building codes (Herzog, 2003).

With increased concern about road fatalities related to drunken driving, investigators from the *Philadelphia Inquirer* decided to use spatial analysis to study the related patterns. First, they obtained road accident data from the Pennsylvania Department of Transpiration. Next, they obtained data on liquor dispensing establishments from the Pennsylvania Liquor Control Board and geocoded it. Geocoding is a function in GIS where physical address information in the form of a database is plotted on a map. GIS processes each individual address and represents it on a map with a dot. Using maps downloaded from the Internet, investigators then mapped out the accident data to a shape file of the 5-county metro area that the *Inquirer* covered. For this they used Spatial Analyst (an ArcView extension program) that mapped out the densities of the liquor establishments (Herzog, 2003).

They then mapped out the accident crash area, showing streets shaded according to the rates of fatalities. What they came up with was a map that showed that most accidents happened around areas with a concentration of liquor establishments. In order to give the readers more details, the Inquirer developed an interactive online map using ArcIMS. Here, readers could zoom in and look at the statistics in their own neighborhood (Herzog, 2003). Figures1 through 4[3] illustrate this process.

Figure one shows how the investigators color-coded the streets based on the alcohol related accidents. Figure 2 shows how they geocoded the liquor license locations in the area. They then used Spatial Analyst to calculate and map out the density of liquor establishments (Figure 3). For this investigation they only used densities of areas that had more than two liquor establishments per square mile. Figure 4 shows the output when liquor establishment locations were compared with crash locations. The resultant visuals show clear patterns between the presence of liquor establishments and the occurrence of alcohol related car accidents.

However good the results looked, the *Inquirer* was yet to be satisfied. Other factors might have influenced the rate of road fatalities. The investigators wanted to make sure that the relationship between liquor establishments and road crashes was not spurious. They commissioned two external researchers who performed further analysis of the data and verified the results.

---

[3] All figures derived from: Herzog, D. (2003). *Mapping the news. Case studies in journalism.* ESRI Press: Redlands, CA.

Figure 1: Color Coded Streets Based on Alcohol Related Crashes

Theory: Diffusion of Innovations

The examples described above indicate that GIS is applicable in the field of journalism. Even with this potential usefulness, not many reporters have adopted this software. This study looks at the likelihood of reporters to adopt GIS in their work. The most appropriate theory to guide such a study is the diffusion of innovations theory. Hence, this study uses this theory to determine how likely journalists are to adopt GIS and to predict the diffusion of this technology in journalism.

Figure 2: Point Locations of Liquor Establishments

Figure 3: Density of Liquor Establishments

Figure 4: Comparison of Liquor Establishments and Alcohol Related Crashes

Diffusion is the "process by which an innovation is communicated through certain channels over time among the members of a social system" (Rogers, 1995, p. 5). An innovation refers to a new idea, object, or practice (Rogers & Shoemaker, 1971). The newness of an innovation is subjective and depends on the interpretation of the individual reacting to it. Although GIS has been around for quite some time in other fields, it is still a very new technology in journalism. The four elements that make up the process of diffusion are: a) the innovation, b) communication channels, c) the social system, and d) time (Rogers, 1995). The process starts out with an innovation that is communicated through a social system over a period of time (Rogers, 2004). This study looks at how much GIS, has diffused within the field of journalism at present, the factors that will affect its future adoption, and how long it will take to diffuse in journalism.

As defined earlier, an innovation is a new idea, object, or practice that is subjectively interpreted by an individual with the possibility of adoption. Even in the case of long time-lags after discovery or first use, if an idea seems new to an individual, that makes it an innovation to him/her

(Rogers & Shoemaker, 1971). Mostly, the word innovation is used interchangeably with technology. Technologies usually have two components: software components that are symbolic and hardware components that represent the material form of an idea. GIS is a software form of an innovation (Rogers, 1995).

Communication refers to the process by which a new idea is transmitted from one individual to another. In the diffusion process, an innovation is passed from the individual who is knowledgeable about it to that individual who is not (Rogers & Shoemaker, 1971). This study will attempt to determine how far GIS has diffused within the journalism industry.

A social system refers to the social confines within which the diffusion process occurs (Robertson, 1971). The social system also can be defined as a group of differentiated individuals engaged in problem-solving activities. Although the individuals are differentiated, they all work in unison to solve a common problem (Rogers & Shoemaker, 1971). In this study, the social system is the newspaper industry. The study was limited to the newspaper industry because GIS has mostly been used by newspaper reporters. David Herzog's *Mapping the News* (2003), the only comprehensive book published to look at GIS and journalism did not contain a single example of the use of GIS and broadcast journalism. Also, a review of literature did not find any examples of GIS use in the broadcast industry.

Time refers to the timeline for the adoption: from the point that an individual hears about an innovation to the time that he/she adopts it. The individual therefore goes through the five steps of the adoption process: "awareness, interest, evaluation, trial, and adoption" (Rogers & Shoemaker, 1971, p. 17). This study will use these steps to determine the present stage of the diffusion of GIS, and to help predict the future diffusion of GIS in journalism. These steps are discussed in more detail later in this paper.

The Characteristics of Innovations

Innovations have five main characteristics. These are relative advantage, compatibility, complexity, trialability, and communicability (Rogers, 1995).

Relative Advantage

This refers to the extent by which a new innovation has superiority over an older idea, and may be measured in terms of the resultant economic profit. Although GIS does not replace traditional news gathering methods, GIS will help journalists accomplish these tasks much faster, more efficiently, and more accurately. One way that relative advantage manifests is through heavy promotional efforts (Rogers, 1995). The makers of the most popular suite of GIS applications (ESRI) are marketing their products to journalists by holding an annual "Mapping the News" conference in conjunction with the Association of American Geographers, and the National Geographic Society. Apart from inviting specialists and guest speakers, the conference offers seminars and hands-on training on how to use GIS to improve news reporting.

Other organizations affiliated with ESRI also provide GIS workshops that are open to journalists. One such organization is Portland, Oregon-based GIS^3 (GIS Cubed) that offers GIS workshops nationwide.

Compatibility

Compatibility refers to the extent that an innovation is in line with pre-existing values and previous experiences of the adopters. The higher the compatibility, the higher is the likelihood of adoption. This gives the potential adopters some form of security and makes the innovation more meaningful to them. This means that low compatibility rates may in fact hinder the adoption of innovations (Rogers, 1995). Since GIS is a form of computer-assisted-reporting tool, journalists could easily incorporate it into their already existing tools for computer-assisted reporting. CAR refers to the use of computers and computer-related software in newsgathering and reporting.

Complexity

Complexity refers to the degree of difficulty related to the understanding and use of an innovation. Innovations can be ranked on a complexity-simplicity scale with those easier to understand on the simplicity end. The general suggestion has it that complexity affects the rate of adoption (Rogers, 1995). One factor that might hinder the diffusion of GIS into journalism is the relative complexity of the software as compared with other computer-assisted reporting software. However, ESRI has recently developed a newer version of GIS software (ArcGIS) that has a more user-friendly interface than the older version, ArcView3x.

Trialability

Trialability refers to the extent to which an innovation can be tried on a limited basis. Potential adopters are more comfortable with those innovations that they can try on a limited basis and make judgments based on initial results (Rogers, 1995). While early adopters do not have any past references, laggards can refer to the successes of early adopters before adoption. Herzog (2003) describes eight case studies that successfully used GIS to report news. Two of these are the *Miami Herald* and the *Philadelphia Inquirer* stories described earlier. These can be the reference points for the late adopters.

Observability

Observability refers to the extent that the results of an innovation are observable to others. Results that are obvious and those that are easy to communicate diffuse much quicker than those that are not. The more observable the results are, the more the chances are that laggards will adopt the innovation (Rogers, 1995). Some communication of this kind has already occurred in the journalism industry. ESRI's marketing of the benefits of adopting GIS to reporters is one such example. The successful use of GIS at different news organizations like the *Miami Herald* and the *Philadelphia Inquirer* are other examples of observability.

Adopting Innovations

It is important to state that adoption and diffusion are two very similar concepts with different definitional connotations. Rogers (1995) defines adoption as the "decision to make full use of an innovation as the best course of action available" (p. 20). On the other hand, diffusion is the spread of an innovation from its inventors to its adopters/users. This means that while diffusion is more of a group phenomenon, adoption is basically an individual process.

Rogers credits Ryan and Gross (1943)[4] as the first to recognize the stages in the adoption process. These stages are awareness, interest, evaluation, trial, and adoption. This study will use these steps to predict the diffusion of GIS into journalism. The following diagram illustrates the steps as described by Robertson (1971).

The Stages of Adoption

Stage One: Awareness

This is also called the knowledge stage. At this point, although the individual is exposed to the innovation, he/she neither has adequate information about it, nor possesses the motivation to

---

[4] Ryan, B. & Gross, N.C. (1943). The diffusion of hybrid seed corn in two Iowa communities. *Rural Sociology.* 8, 15-24.

gather more. However, this stage is very important as it initiates the sequence for the other four stages.

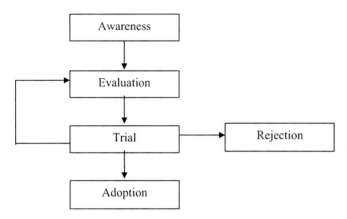

Figure 5: Simple Flow Diagram for the Adoption Process[5]

The assumption is that the individual accidentally becomes aware of the innovation and that the awareness occurs in a random fashion. Although the assumption is that awareness is a passive act, the individual might in fact actively seek information about the innovation. This means that people seek out innovations that help them solve their problems (Robertson, 1971; Rogers, 1962, 1995).

Stage Two: Interest

The interest stage is not included in Figure 5 but is still an important step in the diffusion process. It is also called the information or persuasion stage. Here, the individual seeks more information about the innovation. It is a cognitive stage where the individual looks at the innovation in a general

---

[5] Source: Robertson, Thomas. S. (1971). *Innovative behavior and communication.* Holt, Rinehart, and Winston, Inc.: NY

manner but is more involved than at the awareness stage. Therefore, the individual is psychologically more vigorous in seeking information about the innovation. His/her intentions now become more purposive and are guided by the norms of the social system. These norms also influence where the individual seeks information, and how he/she interprets this information (Rogers, 1962, 1995).

Stage Three: Evaluation

Here, the individual performs a mental trial by matching the use of the innovation to his/her present and future situation(s). The potential innovator then makes a decision based on the applicability of the innovation and whether the advantages outweigh the disadvantages. The individual may consult with others as a method of reinforcement for the eventual decision (Robertson, 1971; Rogers, 1962).

Stage Four: Trial

Also called the decision stage, here, the individual applies the innovation to his/her unique circumstances. The individual runs a validity test on the innovation before adoption. If the individual needs to seek more information at this stage, it is will be very specific to his/her needs. At this stage the innovation is susceptible to rejection in case the results of the trial stage are misinterpreted (Robertson, 1971; Rogers, 1962, 1995).

Demographic characteristics are among the unique circumstances that have been shown to affect the adoption of technologies. For example, younger religious broadcasters were more likely to adopt digital over analog television than their older counterparts (Shultz, 2002). Technology enthusiasts, also called "techthusiasts" have also been found to be younger people (Crispell, 1994). In a survey of medical doctors in Canada, younger doctors were more likely to have the Internet than older doctors (Martin, 2003).

Gender has often been associated with use of technology, with women being portrayed as passive users. For example, gender is a predictor of an individual's likelihood to engage in online shopping. Men have been found to be more likely to use the Web to buy goods and/or services than women (Van Slyke et al., 2002). Age also has a similar effect on the use of the Internet. Gender differences have also been noticed with the adoption of computers (Krendl, Brohier, & Fleetwood, 1989; Reismann, 1990).

Stage Five: Adoption

This is also called the implementation stage. Based on the results experienced at the trial stage, the individual then decides whether to continue using the innovation. Two important factors come into play before and after adoption -- rejection and discontinuance. Rejection refers to the decision to stop using the innovation before adoption. Discontinuance refers to the decision to stop using the innovation after adoption. Early adopters are less likely to discontinue than late adopters (Robertson, 1971; Rogers, 1962, 1995).

Factors that Affect Adoption at the Organizational Level

The success of an innovation depends on various factors. At the organizational level, the four factors that determine the success of an innovation are: benefits, costs, resources, and discounting factors (Agnew, 1980).

Benefits

Most benefits are grouped into three major categories. Programmatic benefits refer to benefits that come as a result of improved effectiveness and efficiencies. Prestige benefits accrue in the form of recognition as a result of early adoption. An example is when the *Miami Herald* won the 1993

Pulitzer Prize for the report on housing code violations and Hurricane Andrew. Structural benefits refer to greater satisfaction received as a result of using a certain innovation (Agnew, 1980). Research also shows that perceived benefits can affect the adoption of new technologies (Davis, Bagozzi, & Warshaw, 1992).

Studies have shown that digital imaging increases a photographer's flexibly, time management, and usability (Fahmy & Smith, 2003). Photojournalists said that the advantages of adopting this technology outweigh its disadvantages. Some of the benefits that resulted from use of digital imaging included increased flexibility, easier transfer of digital images from locations, and more information-sharing in the newsroom. Use of digital imaging also allowed photojournalists to be more aware of their images and this helps to pre-determine usable images before they are sent to the newsroom (Fahmy & Smith, 2003).

Costs

These are the costs that are accrued upon implementation of an innovation (Agnew, 1980). GIS is now sold in the form of licenses. A single-use license for the main GIS software ArcGIS costs $1,500. Another related GIS software 3D Analyst costs $2,500 for a single-license use. The expensive nature of this software might be a limiting factor for its adoption.

Resources

Resources are a central factor influencing the adoption of innovations especially at the organizational level. These resources include: wealth, manpower, equipment, information, and staff. Use of GIS in journalism requires trained staff and proper equipment (hardware and software). These are factors that determine whether an organization will make the extra investment in this new technology (Agnew, 1980). In order to improve the adoption of new technologies, organizations have to invest in the early adopters and make their activity more visible (Berwick, 2003).

Discounting Factors

Discounting factors include the four utility functions that organizational decision-makers put into consideration when faced with decisions on innovations. These decisions are driven by costs, benefits, and resources. The four utility factors are: risk considerations, the average cost of discontinuance of an innovation at some point before full adoption, uncertainty and doubts about the cost-benefit calculations based on adopting an innovation, and projections of instability as far as future benefit-cost ratios are concerned (Agnew, 1980). Venturesomeness, which refers to the likelihood of decision makers to ignore potential risks and uncertainties when adopting an innovation, is also a factor (Foxall & Bhate, 1991). Since GIS is still a new technology in journalism, these utility factors could as well prove to be obstacles as far as adoption is concerned.

Technology Clusters

"A technology cluster consists of one or more distinguishable elements of technology that are perceived as being closely interrelated" (Rogers, 1995, p. 15). What this means is that people will adopt technologies in bundles. For example, people who buy personal computers also are likely to own technological gadgets like VCRs, camcorders, cell phones, videotext etc. (Lin, 1998, 1994). People who use audiotext are also likely to use videotext and e-mail (Atkin, 1995; LaRose & Atkin, 1992). Since GIS cannot be used in a vacuum, it is assumed that prior knowledge of other technologies/software like CAR-related software might influence one to adopt GIS.

The Diffusion Process

People do not adopt innovations simultaneously (Brown, 1981). That is why diffusion can be viewed as the percentage of people within a social system who adopt certain innovations over time (Robertson, 1971). The diffusion process can be can be depicted either using the cumulative curve or the non-cumulative curve. The cumulative curve plots the cumulative proportion of users against time of adoption and takes an S-shape. The non-cumulative curve is segmented and is divided into five categories. The non-cumulative curve uses the standard deviations from the mean time of adoption to divide adopters into five categories: the innovators, early adopters, early majority, late majority, and laggards. These two curves are illustrated in figures 6 and 7. It is important to note that both curves assume a 100% adoption rate.

Cumulative Adoption

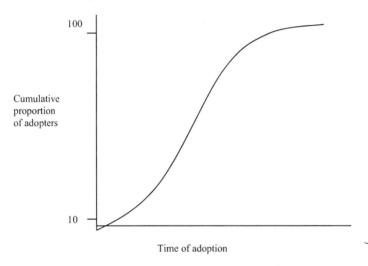

Figure 6: Cumulative Diffusion Using Time of Adoption[6]

---

[6] Source: Robertson, Thomas. S. (1971). *Innovative behavior and communication*. Holt, Rinehart, and Winston, Inc.: NY

The cumulative curve takes an S-shape, most common with the life-cycle of a marketing product and it goes through four stages (Robertson, 1971).

1. At first the innovation is introduced and experiences a slow adoption rate.

2. In the second phase the innovation experiences a rapid adoption rate.

3. In the third phase the adoption rate declines and hits a plateau.

4. Finally the adoption rates begin to drop.

Non-cumulative Adoption

The non-cumulative process divides adoption into five different categories: innovators, early adopters, early majority, late majority, and laggards. Innovators are the more venturesome people who first adopt an innovation; they do not have to be part of the social system. Early adopters are an integral part of the social system and mostly are opinion leaders in that system. They form a reference point for other potential adopters. Even though they are not opinion leaders, the early majority adopt innovations much faster than the average member of the social system. Late adopters usually are skeptical about innovations. It takes peer pressure for them to finally adopt the innovation. Laggards are the last people in the social system to adopt innovations. They are likely to be societal isolates and have deep suspicion of innovations and change agents (Rogers, 1995). When these categories of people are plotted against time, a normally distributed curve emerges as illustrated in figure 7.

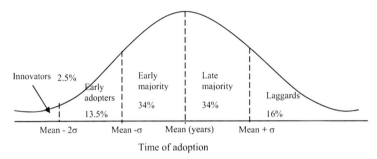

Figure 7: Non-Cumulative Diffusion Using Mean Time of Adoption[7]

This normal curve depicts the innovators being two standard deviations below the mean years of adoption, early adopters lie within one standard deviation below the mean while the late majority are within one standard deviation above the mean. Laggards fall more than one standard deviation above the mean (Robertson, 1971; Rogers, 1995)

The Diffusion of Other Technologies in Journalism

The use of new technologies is revolutionizing the newsroom. One area where this has occurred is computer-assisted reporting. Three decades ago, researchers like DeFleur and Ball-Rokeach (1975) predicted that computers would forever change the process of communication. The development of computer-assisted reporting dates back almost 30 years, coinciding with the introduction of *precision journalism* (Meyer, 1973). Precision journalism involved the use of social science methods applied to journalism. For example, surveys, data analysis, experiments, and use of computers and databases.

CAR is the "use of computers to gather information for a news presentation" (Garrison, 1995, p.4), and is made up of online research and database journalism. Online research refers to the

[7] Source: Robertson, Thomas. S. (1971). *Innovative behavior and communication*. Holt, Rinehart, and Winston, Inc.: NY

search and retrieval of information from the Internet; database journalism is the computerized use of information data banks for news stories (Garrison, 1995). For example, reporters can do online research by performing simple Internet searches. They also can use e-mail lists, news groups, and online encyclopedias to find information on various topics. One example of database journalism is the Pulitzer Prize winning investigation of the pork industry in North Carolina by the *News and Observer*.[8] Using a database of state telephone calls, reporters discovered a peculiar pattern of calls from powerful legislators to a prominent hog farm. The investigation later revealed that legislators who had connections with the hog industry had supported weak anti-pollution laws that favored the hog industry to the detriment of the environment.

Different CAR technologies have experienced different adoption rates in journalism. One rapidly adopted innovation is online research. Use of online research to supplement news reporting experienced a dramatic jump between 1994 and 1998; in 1994, use of online research in journalism stood at 57% and increased to 97% by 1998 (Garrison, 2001). Table 1 shows the projected demand for CAR-related software from 1995-1998 while table 2 shows the actual adoption rates for the same software by the year 2000 (Garrison, 2001). The projected demand for CAR-related software was based on responses from reporters when asked what they thought the demand for different software would be over the years. The projected demand for online research more than doubled in four years, while the demand for statistical software fluctuated while remaining relatively low. Even though the use of online research remained high, table 2 shows that the actual rates of adoption for other CAR-related software remained low (Maier, 2000).

---

[8] http://www.pulitzer.org/year/1996/public-service/works/about.html

Table 1: Percentage of the Projected Demand for CAR-Related Software in Journalism from 1995 to 1998

Category	1995	1996	1997	1998
Database software	15.8%	11.4%	15.4%	31.1%
Mapping software	9.9%	12.1%	12.5%	14.3%
Statistics software	1.8%	6.1%	2.2%	2.5%
Other new software	4.7%	6.8%	4.4%	4.2%

Source: Garrison, B. (2001). Computer assisted reporting near complete adoption. *Newspaper Research Journal. 22(1)*, 65-79.

Table 2: Adoption Rates for CAR-Related Software by the Year 2000.

Category	Use in the newsroom
Spreadsheet software	10%
Database software	4%
Mapping software	1%
Statistical software	1%

Source: Maier, S. (2000). Digital diffusion in the newsroom. The uneven advance of computer-assisted-reporting. *Newspaper Research Journal. 21(2)*, 95-110.

It has taken 30 years for CAR to enter the mainstream, with the most growth experienced in the last 15 years. One reason for this growth is the emergence of organizations that promote CAR such as the National Institute for Computer-Assisted Reporting. NICAR, based at the Missouri School of Journalism, was formed in 1989 as an endeavor to train journalists in the use of electronic information. Other factors that might have motivated newsrooms to adopt CAR-related technologies include:

➢ Improved productivity.

➢ Savings associated with better information gathering techniques such as the use of readily available online data.

➢ Improved accuracy of information.

➢ Efficient storage and retrieval systems (Garrison, 1995).

Technological innovations have not been limited to CAR. The field of journalism in general has experienced numerous innovations over the decades. These innovations have all had different adoption rates. One innovation notable for its lack of success is videotex. This is a computerized system that combines and transmits both text and graphics that can be displayed on a television set (Wikipedia, 2005[a]). Videotex was first adopted by the British Broadcasting Corporation in 1969 (Shedden, 2005), but was not introduced into the U.S. until 1980 by Knight Ridder (Finberg, 2003). However, videotex had a very short shelf life as its use died out with the introduction of PCs in the mid-'80s (Finberg, 2003).

The earliest use of an electronic database was by the *New York Times* in 1969 with the Infobank, a collection of news story abstracts. This would later develop into a full-fledged commercial database when Nexis bought the Infobank in 1983. This database is presently called LexisNexis and is popular with scholars, lawyers, and journalists. Other early electronic database systems include the Dialog database in 1971 and the ORBIT service started a year later. Dialog not only provides information to media practitioners, but also to people in many other disciplines. While Dialog is still in use, the ORBIT database service was closed in 1999 (Shedden, 2005).

In 1981, The *Columbus Dispatch* was the first newspaper to go online, with the help of CompuServe's dial-up system. CompuServe was one of the earliest Internet service providers. Soon other newspapers like the *Washington Post*, the *New York Times*, the *San Francisco Chronicle*, and the *Virginia Pilot* followed suit. This process of getting newspapers online was an endeavor between

CompuServe and *AP* member newspapers. By 2004 1,500 North American daily newspapers had gone online (Shedden, 2005).

By 1994 reporters were moderate users of the Internet. CompuServe Internet service was used by 35% of the reporters, while America Online was used by 21% of the reporters. Other Internet service providers were used by about 19% of the reporters (Shedden, 2005). Two years later, journalists were well versed in the use of online search engines. Yahoo was the most popular search engine with 29% of the reporters using it. This was followed closely by Netscape with 25% and Alta Vista with 18%. These numbers changed dramatically in 1997 when 43% of the reporters used Yahoo, with Alta Vista recording a distant second with 19% (Shedden, 2005).

Blogs are one of the latest developments in journalism. Blogs have probably experienced the highest rate of diffusion in journalism. While there were only a dozen blogs in 1999, blogs currently number in the millions (Columbia Journalism Review, 2003). The word blog comes from the term Weblog, coined by John Berger in 1997, an otherwise unknown avid Web surfer (Wikipedia, 2005[b]). Although blogs are not limited to news outlets, many news services have adopted blogs of their own. Examples include Spokane, Washington's *Spokesman Review* blog[9], The *HuffingtonPost.com*[10] run by *Yahoo News*, the *Washington Post*[11] blog etc.

The aforementioned factors might influence the diffusion of GIS in journalism. The purposes of this study are 1) to determine the likelihood of reporters to adopt GIS, and 2) to predict the future of the diffusion of GIS in the journalism industry. In order to meet these purposes, this study will answer the following research questions:

RQ1: What obstacles will the diffusion of GIS in journalism face?

---

[9] http://www.spokesmanreview.com/blogs/
[10] http://news.yahoo.com/i/2413
[11] http://blogs.washingtonpost.com/campaignforthecourt/

This research question deals with costs and cost-benefit analysis, factors that affect adoption at the organizational level (Agnew, 1980). GIS is now sold in the form of licenses. A single-use license for the main GIS software ArcGIS costs $1,500. Another related GIS software 3D Analyst costs $2,500 for a single-license use. The expensive nature of this software might be a limiting factor for its adoption. This will be answered with results from the in-depth interviews.

RQ2: What is the awareness level of GIS among reporters?

This is derived from the first stage in the adoption process where the individual is exposed to the innovation, but he/she neither has adequate information about it, nor possesses the motivation to gather more.

Table 3: Chronology of Key Technological Innovations in the Newspaper Industry

Year	Technology	Status
1969	Videotex in introduces in the U.K.	Use stops in 1986
1970	Infobank	Sold to Nexis in 1983; Nexis is currently called LexisNexis
1971	Dialog database System	Still in use
1972	ORBIT database system	Closed in 1999
1983	Knight Ridder launches videotex in the U.S.	Knight Ridder ends its videotext project in 1986. Use of videotex dies out around this time.
1981	First newspaper goes online *(The Columbus Dispatch)*	By 2003 1,500 North American newspapers go online
1983	NY Times adopts the Nexis database	Still in use
1997	Yahoo takes 43% of the search engine market among reporters	By 1998, 97% of reporters did online research using a variety of search engines.
2004	Blogs go mainstream	Current estimates list 14.2 million blogs (Technorati.com, 2005).[12]

This stage is important as it initiates the sequence for the other four stages (Robertson, 1971; Rogers, 1962, 1995). This will be answered using the percentage of reporters who said they had heard about GIS.

RQ3: How interested are journalists in learning more about GIS?

This measures the second stage of the diffusion process. In the interest stage, the individual seeks more information about the innovation. It is a cognitive stage where the individual looks at the innovation in a general manner but is more involved than at the awareness stage (Robertson, 1971;

---

[12] Technorati.com is a search engine that tracks blogs.

Rogers, 1962, 1995). This will be answered using the mean level of journalist interest in learning more about GIS.

RQ4a: What best predicts the likelihood of reporters to adopt GIS on a *trial/evaluation* basis using the variables of demographics, the use of other technologies, and organizational size?

RQ4b: What best predicts the likelihood of reporters to adopt GIS on a *permanent* basis using the variables of demographics, use of other technologies, and organizational size?

The difference between these two questions is adoption on a trial basis versus permanent adoption. Demographics have been shown to affect the adoption of technologies. Age has been shown to have such an affect (Shultz, 2002; Crispell, 1994; Martin, 2003), as has gender (Van Slyke et al., 2002; Krendl, Brohier, & Fleetwood, 1989; Reismann, 1990). Use of other technologies has also been shown to affect adoption. Technology clusters are those technologies that have functional similarities (Rogers, 1995). Use of certain technologies has led to the adoption of compatible technologies (Lin, 1988, 1994). At the organizational level, resources have been shown to influence the adoption of innovations (Agnew, 1980).

OLS regression will be used to determine the effect of the independent variables of demographics, use of other technologies and organizational size on the two dependent variables, likelihood to adopt GIS on a trial basis and likelihood to adopt GIS on a permanent basis.

RQ5: How much has GIS diffused in journalism?
This research question is based on the fact that people do not adopt innovations simultaneously (Brown, 1981). The diffusion process can be determined based on the cumulative proportion of adopters over time or the percentage of adopters in the five distinct time segments illustrated in figures 6 and 7. This will be answered using the percentage of reporters who currently use GIS in their work.

CHAPTER 3: METHODOLOGY

This study used two data collection methods: in-depth interviews and a Web survey.

Study 1: In-depth Interviews

There were three purposes for the in-depth interviews: one was to get a general understanding of the dynamics that are involved in the use of GIS in journalism. The second purpose was to have a guide to construct the survey instrument that was used in the Web survey. Thirdly, the results from the in-depth interviews were used to discuss research question 1, which deals with the obstacles that will affect the future of GIS in journalism.

In depth interviews are good when dealing with smaller samples. Unlike surveys, in depth-interviews give researchers a chance to obtain detailed information from respondents. Respondents get a chance to elaborate their opinions at length and recollect past events. Since the interview is done on a person-to-person basis, interviewers can customize the interview to suit each respondent (Wimmer & Dominick, 2000). This study lends itself to this method because it aimed at looking into the dynamics involved in the use of GIS in journalism. This required detailed responses from those reporters who had used this software before. In addition, since only 10 people were identified, this was the most appropriate method to use.

The 10 interviewees were purposively selected from David Herzog's book *Mapping the News* (2003). The snowballing technique was used in order to identify more reporters who have used GIS. An introductory e-mail explaining the nature and purpose of the study was sent to all the people listed in the book. Interviewees were then asked to choose an appropriate time for the interview. The interview was conducted over the phone and the responses were recorded on tape with consent. Both open and close ended questions were used for the in-depth interviews. The interview

32

started with an introduction and a brief discussion of the reporter's GIS project(s) as discussed in *Mapping the news*.

Some of the sample questions included (See appendix A for full version of questionnaire):

1. What factors motivated you to use GIS?

2. How did you learn about GIS?

3. What are some of the obstacles you faced when using GIS?

4. Do you still use GIS as a tool for newsgathering and reporting?

5. What other computer-assisted reporting tools do you use for news gathering and reporting?

6. What do you think is the future for GIS in the journalism industry?

Results from the in-depth interviews were analyzed and used to construct some of the questions for the Web survey. For example Web survey questions on the use of other technologies were derived from the results of the in-depth interviews. The Web survey asked respondents if they used any database, spreadsheet, or statistical software in their work. Web survey respondents were also asked about their use of online research to augment news reporting, as well as their use of other technological devices in their work.

Study 2: Web Survey

The Internet is changing the face of the survey research industry (Couper, 2000). The proliferation of the Internet and the increase in computerization both have led to the development of self-administered methods of data collection like Web surveys (Torangeau, Steiger, & Wilson, 2002). The Internet provides researchers with a quick and low-cost means by which to reach a vast number of respondents by using Web surveys as opposed to telephone and mail surveys (Dominelli, 2003). Research also shows that as far as response rates are concerned, Web surveys do not fare worse than other methods of data collection (McCabe, 2004). Unlike mail surveys Web surveys give instant responses and also offer automatic coding of the results. Web surveys are also easy to construct and administer. All one needs is access to the Internet and a Web server, both which are widely available (Dominelli, 2003).

Lately, administering Web surveys has become much easier as online research firms offer cheap and convenient services. For a small fee, one can easily construct and host complicated Web surveys and customized e-mail lists. One example is Surveyconsole.com which was used for this study. For $29 a monthly fee, one can construct surveys with skips patterns and multimedia with absolutely no prior programming knowledge. Surveyconsole also offers a dynamic contact list that automatically updates those respondents who have completed the survey. This way, e-mail reminders are only sent to those who have not yet completed the survey. Surveyconsole also allows for the exportation of data into spreadsheet files that are easily transferable to SPSS.

One important issue with Web survey methodology is coverage error. This occurs when all the units in a population lack a known non-zero chance of being selected in the sample (Dillman & Bowker, 2001). Even with the popularity of Web surveys, it is hard for researchers to come up with representative samples using e-mail. Not everyone has an e-mail, and even those who have e-mail do change the addresses often (Dominelli, 2003). This was not an issue with this study since all reporters in the sampling frame have standard e-mail addresses based on the newspapers they work for. Another issue that hinders the effectiveness of Web surveys is the fact that the respondent has to have computer access. It is unlikely that this could have been a problem with this study because a recent study showed 80% of the reporters access the Web at least once a week (Weaver, Beam, Brownlee, Voakes, & Wilhoit, 2003). Respondents may also worry about the security issues associated with Web surveys since it is hard to tell online, the legitimacy of a surveyor (Dominelli, 2003).

For the reasons mentioned above, a Web survey was deemed an appropriate method for this study. The survey was constructed using recommendations for effective Web survey design (Couper, Traugott, & Lamias, 2001; Dillman & Bowker, 2001; Dillman, Bowker, & Tortora, 1998; Dillman, 2000) in order to reduce measurement error. Measurement error occurs when respondents give wrong answers due to poor survey design. These guidelines include use of a progress bar, use of plain non-distracting backgrounds, use of single-screen questions, and avoidance of forced-response questions, among others. The Web survey was an adaptation of Garrison's (1995) "Computers and reporting 1994 questionnaire" and "Computer-assisted reporting study 1995 research questionnaire" (See appendix B for questionnaire).

Sampling Techniques

The population comprised of full-time reporters from the top 100 English language U.S. daily newspapers. The study was limited to newspaper reporters. As has been explained earlier, the review of literature revealed that the use of GIS has been limited to the newspaper industry. Also, the only comprehensive publication on GIS and journalism, *Mapping the News* (Herzog, 2003), exclusively reports the use of the software in the newspaper industry. The study was also limited to high circulation newspapers based on the reasoning that high circulation newspapers were more likely to afford an expensive software such as GIS since they had more resources, a limiting factor for lower circulation newspapers.

Sampling frame: The 2004 *Editor and Publisher International Yearbook* was used to generate the sampling frame for the top 100 U.S. daily newspapers. Contact information of all the reporters from these newspapers was obtained from Burrelles*Luce*, a leading media contact firm. The Burrelles*Luce*

Website[13] has an online searchable database. This service usually requires a paid subscription; however, offered a free subscription to students in journalism schools who are engaged in research. The search terms used for this study were: reporters, United States, daily newspapers, and circulation size more than 100, 000.

The initial spreadsheet contained about 6,000 reporters; after deleting duplicates the final number stood at 4,000. The initial spreadsheet also had other fields like the physical address of the newspaper, circulation size, and telephone and fax numbers. These were deleted and only the reporters' names, the newspaper title, circulation size, and e-mail addresses were used for the Web survey. Using SPSS, a 10% random sample was then selected for a sample size of 400.

The spreadsheet was then uploaded to the Web survey's hosting Website (www.surveyconsole.com). Using multiple contacts as described in Schaeffer and Dillman (1998) and Sheehan and McMillan (1999), each reporter in the sample was contacted through e-mail to inform them about the survey. A second e-mail was sent including a hyperlink to the web survey. The second e-mail was more detailed and included a description of the survey and privacy notices. Five e-mail reminders were sent to those who did not fill out the initial survey to help reduce non-response error, which occurs when the respondents who did not answer the survey happen to be demographically different from those who did (Dillman & Bowker, 2001). Survey Console has a function that identifies those who have completed the survey and those who have not, ensuring that reminders are sent only to those people in the sample who have not completed the survey.

---

[13] http://www.burrellesluce.com/

Dependent Variables

There were two dependent variables: Respondents were asked two questions about their likelihood to adopt GIS on a trial/evaluation and on a permanent basis. The variable was measured on a Likert scale 1-7 (where 1 = not at all likely, 7 = very likely to adopt GIS).

Independent Variables

- Age, measured on a continuous level.

- Gender, men were coded as 1 and women as 0.

- Education: this variable was measured on an ordinal scale where:

    1 = Less than high school
    2 = High school
    3 = Some college
    4 = Undergraduate degree
    5 = Graduate degree

- Organizational size: This variable was measured using the newspaper circulation size, included the database downloaded from the Burrelles*Luce* Website.

- Use of other technologies: this variable was measured as two questions then the two were summed together.

    o Prior use of computer-assisted reporting tools: Respondents were asked if they had ever used CAR tools (variations of spread sheet, database, or statistical software). For each software package used, the respondent received a point. The tally was then used to construct a composite score for CAR tools ranging from 0-10.

    o Use of other technological innovations: Respondents were asked about their use of technological devices in their work. For each device used, the respondent received a point. Apart from use of technological devices, respondents were asked how often they conduct online research to supplement reporting. Online research was used in a general sense to include use of search engines, online databases, e-mail etc. This was used to construct a composite score for use of other technological innovations ranging from 0-4. The overall range for the use of other technologies was 0-14.

CHAPTER 4: RESULTS

Study 1: In-depth Interviews

RQ1: What obstacles will the diffusion of GIS in journalism of face?

The main obstacles that will affect the diffusion of GIS are the technical nature of the software, the problematic nature of available data, and the effects of these data on map analysis. GIS needs a high level of skill to use effectively, and as one interviewee described, the software was "designed for people who have serious academic training in it, which journalists tend not to have." Even some of the self-taught GIS users have had to attend seminars to advance their skills. One respondent, well versed in GIS said that "my problems with GIS have been educational. Learning some of the more technical aspects of GIS, like statistical modeling and spatial analyst (a GIS extension software)…require a technical and sometimes a mathematical background." Spatial analyst is a GIS extension software that is used for advanced functions, for example to calculate and map out population densities. This extension usually needs extra training even for seasoned GIS users.

The nature of data available to users was also a problem. Although GIS data are becoming more and more available, some of these can be described as "dirty" data, as one respondent said: "journalists tend to be using databases that were gathered through bureaucratic means. Where…concern for spelling of addresses…or abbreviations of streets or avenues or things like that tend to be lost, and that makes GIS more difficult." Such inaccurate databases may pose a problem with the geocoding function of GIS.

Geocoding is a function in GIS where physical address information in the form of a database is plotted on a map. GIS processes each individual address and represents it on a map with a dot. The address information in the database must be exact or as similar as possible to the physical address in order to match. Only those addresses that match with real-life street information on a particular map are geocoded. This means that a simple spelling error or the omission of address information in the database may lead to geocoding errors. The problem with some of the data that users get from government agencies is that they are not accurate enough to geocode correctly.

Respondents said that it was easy to get help with GIS. Most of the interviewees knew sources that they could turn to in case they needed help with the use of GIS. One such source was the geography departments in various universities. Another source was the aforementioned NICAR Website. NICAR was formed in 1989 as an endeavor to train journalists in the use of electronic information. Based in the Missouri School of Journalism, it provides the aforementioned mailing list (NICAR-L), and a resource center that boasts contact lists and a database library. This library contains database information ranging from a listing of all aircraft registered in the USA to a listing of disaster assistance loans made to businesses and individuals.

NICAR membership is open to all media practitioners. Membership varies from professional, academic, associate, retiree, to student. Professional membership is limited to those actively involved in print, broadcast or online media. Academic membership is limited to those who are involved in research or teaching in the field of journalism. Associate membership is for those who used to work in the field of journalism and now work in a different field. Retiree membership is limited to those who are retired from the field of journalism. Membership is also open to journalism students (both U.S. and international).

The in-depth interview was also conducted to provide a general understanding of GIS and as a guide for the Web survey. Interest in GIS and how the respondents learnt the software was an example. Interviewees were asked how they first had heard about GIS, and how they came to learn it. The 1990 Census was one of the factors that introduced GIS to some of the reporters, as there was need to spatially analyze census data. Five out of the seven interviewees said that they found that GIS was already in use when they joined their newspapers. Three respondents were self-taught

GIS users. Three interviewees attended some form of seminar training for GIS, while only one interviewee took college classes in GIS.

Another area of interest was the types of software that the interviewees used in conjunction with GIS. The interviews revealed that other software used included database, statistical, and spreadsheet software like Access, SAS, SPSS, and Excel. All except one reporter said that they keep in touch with technological developments. One reporter said that most reporters who use computer-assisted reporting tools have to keep in touch with technological developments in general. This interviewee said that "the larger world of investigative reporters to varying degrees keeps up with technology. The sub status of people who do what we call computer-assisted-reporting, many of whom are involved in investigative reporting I would say yes...one of the primary ways they do that...is through the NICAR-L mail list." NICAR-L is a mailing list hosted by the National Institute for Computer-Assisted Reporting, a division of the trade organization of Investigative Reporters and Editors, and serves as a forum through which members can share discussion about computer-assisted reporting and new technologies.

Most interviewees painted a positive future for GIS in journalism. One respondent said "I think GIS has already proven its place and power. The number of stories that have been done that could not have been done any other way are growing every year." Another responded had this to say. "The future of GIS is very bright...mostly because maps are such a good tool to explain data (and) to present data to people. With a map...we can either read or visualize and make data simple."

The availability of map data is one important factor that might influence the future of GIS. "I don't generally have problems with data availability" said one respondent, who also added that "the Florida public record files are very good and the heavy GIS users in my area are very open and very generous." The fact that more and more government and private agencies are using GIS means that more data is becoming available to users.

Competition between media agencies was another factor that came up in the interview as one that could bolster the use of GIS in journalism. If one media organization successfully used GIS, other media organizations are likely to follow suit and adopt the use of GIS. This echoes what one respondent had to say. "As newsroom managers look around and see what their peers and competitors are doing with it (GIS) they realize that this is an important thing."

The interview also revealed that management is more likely to invest in this software once its functionality is demonstrated to them. "The ability (of GIS users) to sell to newsroom management that this is a good idea for doing even basic graphic work is increasing," explained one respondent. Another affirmed this notion by stating that "at first it is very difficult to get a newspaper to invest in it, precisely because it is expensive. Once an editor sees what can be produced with GIS all of those walls come crashing down, and the editors usually will buy it very quickly."

One respondent felt that although fewer people are likely to master the software, more people can still find use of its products. This means that even the reporters who do not know how to use the software can still make use of GIS maps to tell stories. The respondent described a project that he had undertaken where he downloaded map and census data onto a server and "different people on our staff were able to virtually just take the base map I had given them and populate variables on the server, so they could look at simple maps of all kinds of variables, and that led to other people other than me who really didn't understand the GIS being able to come up with some map ideas." Based on the fact that people are familiar with online travel map searches like MapQuest (which are in fact GIS products), the respondent went on to say that "there's a possibility of having more GIS that people would use but not necessarily GIS that people would do. If we served it up to them on a platter I think they would use it more."

Study 2: Web Survey

Of the 400 reporters who were sampled, 106 completed the survey for a 27% response rate. This kind of response rate is not unusual with Web and e-mail surveys (Porter & Whitcomb, 2003; Kaplowitz, Hadlock, & Levine, 2004). A basic tenet in survey research is high response rates because it can help reduce non-response error that occurs when those who do not respond to the survey systematically differ from the respondents (Curtis, Presser, & Singer, 2000). However, low response rates can still result in low non-response errors as long as the respondents and non-respondents do not differ greatly (Keeter, Miller, Kohut, Groves, & Presser, 2000). In fact it is very hard to tell the effect of increased response rates on non-response error. There is little evidence to show that a reduction in error occurs, for example, when response rates are increased from 30% to 50% or even from 50% to 70% (Keeter, et al., 2000).

In order to gauge non -response error, this study used a comparison of the respondents' demographics with known national demographics of reporters from all U.S. newspapers by Weaver and colleagues (2003), as shown in table 4. The table compares the 106 respondents with the sample of 400, the census of 4,000 journalists from the top 100 newspapers, and the Weaver study based on demographics of circulation size, gender, and education. Most of these demographics do not differ greatly. For example the median age in this study was 45 years; the national median age is 41 in the study by Weaver and others (2003). Gender in this study differed by no more than four percentage points from the initial sample of 400 from the 100 largest newspapers, and no more than seven percentage points from all newspaper reporters. The greatest difference was that this study oversampled in the 300,001 to 500,000 circulation category by roughly 16 to 20 percentage points. The other three circulation categories showed a difference of 10.5 percentage points or fewer between the sample of respondents and the census of reporters at the top 100 newspapers. This means that, with the exception of one circulation category out of four, the chances that non-respondents differed systematically from respondents are reduced.

Table 4: Comparison of the Demographics of the Respondents, the Sample, Population of Reporters in Top 100 Newspapers, and the Nationwide Weaver Study.

		Respondents N= 106	Sample N = 400	Population N = 4,000	Weaver* Study
Gender	Male	60%	56%	+	67%
	Female	40%	44%	+	33%
Circulation	100,000-300,000	41.5%	49.9%	52%	+
	300, 001-500,000	42.5%	25.6%	22.7%	+
	500,001-700,000	9.4%	4.6%	11.2%	+
	700,001- above	6.6%	19.9%	14.1%	
Education (college graduates)		92%	+	+	89%

*From Weaver et al., (2003)
+Statistics not yet available

As far as the use of CAR-related software is concerned, table 5 shows that Excel was the most popular while SPSS and SAS were the least used. Eighty-three percent of the respondents conducted online research at least once a day. Respondents were also asked about the technological devices they use in their daily work. By far the most popular device was the cell phone, followed by text messaging, instant messaging, and blogs.

Table 5: Frequencies and Percentages of CAR-Related Software in Use

Software	Frequency	Percentage
Online Research	102	96%
Spreadsheet Software	80	76 %
Database Software	59	56%
GIS	12	11%
Statistical Software	4	4 %

N = 106

Variable Transformations

Some variables were transformed due to skewness. Education had a moderate negative skew and was transformed using the square-root transformation SQRT (K-X). Use of other technologies and organizational size both had a substantial positive skews and were transformed using the log 10 transformation LG10 (K-X). Interest to learn more about GIS, likelihood to adopt GIS on a trial basis, and likelihood to adopt GIS at the permanent level all had moderate positive skews. These were also transformed using the square-root transformation SQRT (K-X). Non-transformed statistics were used in the interpretation for ease of understanding.

RQ2: What is the awareness level of GIS among reporters?

In order to measure the awareness level of GIS in journalism, respondents were asked if they had heard about GIS. Sixty-three percent stated that they had heard about GIS.

RQ3: How interested are journalists in learning more about GIS?

After a brief description of what GIS is, respondents were asked how interested they would be to learn more about the software. This was a Likert scale question that ranged from 1-7 (1 = not at all likely and 7 = very likely). The mean interest level was 2.64 (s.d. = 1.65).

RQ4a: What effect do demographics, the use of other technologies, and organizational size have on the likelihood of reporters to adopt GIS on a trial/evaluation basis?

Results of OLS regression analysis showed that three variables were significant predictors of likelihood of adopting GIS on a trial basis: being male, younger, and high use of other technologies. The model was significant at $p < .01$ and explained nearly 13% of the variance (See Table 6). Males were significantly more likely to adopt GIS on a trial basis than females (Male M = 2.59, s.d. = 1.67; Female M = 2.07 s.d. = 1.43). Age was significantly and negatively related to likelihood of adopting GIS; for every one year increase in age, there was a .074 decrease in likelihood of adopting GIS. Use of other technologies was significantly and positively related to the likelihood to adopt GIS on a trial basis; for every piece of technology that reporters said they used, likelihood of adopting GIS on a trial basis went up by .16 of a point. Education and organization size were not significant predictors of the likelihood to adopt GIS on a trial basis.

RQ4b: What effect do demographics, use of other technologies, and organizational size have on the likelihood of reporters to adopt GIS on a permanent basis?

The results showed that males were more likely to adopt GIS on a permanent basis. Men were more likely to adopt GIS than women (Male M = 2.57, s.d. = 1.61; Women M = 2.07, s.d. = 1.43). Age was significantly and negatively related to the likelihood to adopt GIS on a permanent basis. For every one year increase in age there was a .61-point decrease in the likelihood to adopt GIS on a permanent basis. Education, organization size, and the use of other technologies were not significantly related to the likelihood to adopt GIS on a permanent basis (See Table 7).

Table 6 : Standardized and Unstandardized Regression Coefficients for Demographics, Circulation, and Use of Technology on Likelihood to Adopt GIS on a Trial Basis.

Variable	B	S.E.	Beta
Constant	.416	.348	
Age	-.035*	.031	-.226
Gender	.76*	.052	-.243
Education	.304	.048	.120
Circulation	-2.23	.000	-.014
Use of other technologies	.22*	.074	.206
Df	5		
F	3.889**		
R²	.128		

*p<.05   **p<.01   ***p<.001   N = 106

RQ5: How much has GIS diffused in journalism?

The level of the diffusion of GIS in journalism was measured by the question: "do you currently use GIS?" Eight respondents indicated that they currently use GIS. These respondents were asked if they knew other people that use GIS at their respective newspapers. Four other people were listed for a total of 12 users.

This research question was also used to gauge the current level of the diffusion of GIS in journalism. This is illustrated in Figure 8 using the S-shaped cumulative adoption curve adopted from Robertson (1971). The curve shows that the diffusion of GIS is at the initial stage of diffusion and the diffusion is still at a very slow rate.

Table 7: *Standardized and Unstandardized Regression Coefficients for Demographics, Circulation, and Use of Technology on Likelihood to Adopt GIS on a Permanent Basis.*

Variable	B	S.E.	Beta
Constant	.393	.350	
Age	-.03*	.032	-.197
Gender	.76*	.052	-.241
Education	.30	.049	.117
Circulation	-3.84	.000	.026
Use of other technologies	.19	.074	.190
Df	5		
F	3.321**		
R²	.106		

*p<.05   **p<.01   ***p<.001   N = 106

This should explain the small number of reporters who currently use the software. This initial stage precludes the other stages where an innovation experiences rapid adoption, which later tapers off and starts to drop. The 12 GIS users make up about 11% of the sample. This qualifies them as early adopters according to the non-cumulative curve. Since the non-cumulative curve divides the time of adoption in segments representing the adopters, a determination of the current state of GIS diffusion in journalism can be made. Figure 9 shows that although GIS is past the innovators stage, it is still at the early adopters stage at best.

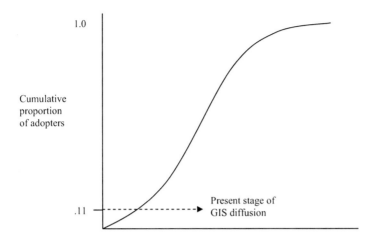

Figure 8: Estimate of the Cumulative Diffusion of GIS Using Time of Adoption

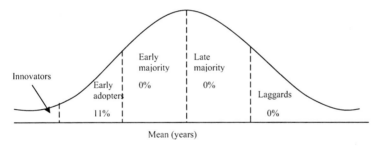

Figure 9: Estimate of the Non-Cumulative Diffusion of GIS Using Mean Time of Adoption

CHAPTER 5: DISCUSSION

The purposes of this study were to determine the likelihood of journalists to adopt GIS and to predict the future of the diffusion of GIS in journalism. The results show that a majority of journalists are aware of GIS but very few have adopted the software so far. Use of this software in journalism is still in its early stages. The awareness stage is an important step in the diffusion of innovations process as it is the trigger for the rest of the adoption process. Although awareness does not necessarily translate to action as far as the use of an innovation is concerned, the fact that 63% of the respondents know about GIS cannot be ignored. Since GIS is a relatively new development in journalism and is mainly confined to investigative reporting, such a high awareness level is bound to draw attention. More so, it is important to stress that this study looked at the general population of reporters and not just investigative reporters, who are more likely to use GIS.

Despite this high level of awareness, the results indicate that currently GIS has diffused very minimally in the field of journalism. This should not come as a surprise. By nature journalists are very slow in adopting new technologies. Garrison (1995) attributes this to the fact that journalists tend to be satisfied with the status quo as far as the use of technology is concerned. Another factor could be the technical nature of GIS. The complexity of an innovation or the relative difficulty to learn or use the innovation affects its diffusion. Complex innovations take longer to adopt (Rogers, 1995). This complexity has to do with the technical nature of GIS and the type of training needed to comfortably use the software.

Although it is also possible that some of the reporters did not see the applicability of GIS in their area since GIS has been restricted to investigative reporting, the software can be used more widely. Business reporters could use a combination of GIS and investigative reporting techniques to map out the relationship between the locations of high-interest predatory lenders and low-income areas. This way, they can visually demonstrate if high interest lenders are more likely to target low income people by situating in certain areas. Features reporters can map out the different types of community recreational facilities to see if there is inequitable distribution based on socio-economic factors. Similarly, they also could do similar analysis and map out the quality of the same facilities.

The two factors mentioned above also may explain why reporters were not very willing to learn more about the software. The mean for the interest to learn more about GIS (measured on a 1-7 scale) was 2.64. This is despite a 63% awareness level. Journalists are aware of the software but are not really interested in learning more about it.

This low interest rate among reporters may also be due to the aforementioned fact that GIS is a relatively new development in the field of journalism. The earliest report of GIS use by a reporter was in the early '90s (Herzog, 2003). This means that GIS has had a very slow adoption process than other software. For example, adoption of online research went from 57% in 1994 to 97% in 1998 – nearly doubling in four years (Garrison, 2001). However, GIS adoption has performed better than statistical software which has been in existence longer. Both software had an adoption rate of 1% in the year 2000 (Maier, 2000); but this study five years later has GIS with an adoption rate of 11% while statistical software remains at 1%.

However, the perceived demand for some CAR-related software followed a non-linear pattern from 1995- to 1998, as shown in table 1. While mapping software had a steady but modest increase over the four-year period, the perceived demand for database software dropped by more than four percentage points from 1995 to 1996, regained these points in 1997, and then rose sharply to 31% by 1998. Statistical software had a jump of four percentage points in 1996, but by 1998 its perceived demand had dropped to 2.5%. More research is necessary to understand why demand may increase, decrease, and even increase again.

Also, the nature of journalism might be a limiting factor for those reporters who might want to learn new software. Daily deadlines do not leave reporters with much time to attend seminars that require three eight-hour days such as those offered by ESRI training partner GIS[3] (Cubed). A reporter would have to take at least three days off from work specifically to learn GIS. This does not include the extra long hours needed to refine one's GIS skills. Coupled with the complex nature of the software, this makes it hard for reporters to learn GIS.

The results show that age and gender were predictors of the likelihood to adopt GIS both on a trial and long-term basis. This means that GIS might be a more attractive option to younger reporters than to older reporters, and that men are more likely to adopt GIS than women. These findings are in line with standard diffusions of innovations research (Shultz, 2002; Martin, 2003; Van Slyke et al., 2002).

The results indicated that the use of other technologies and CAR-related software increased the likelihood of adopting GIS on a trial basis. Use of GIS goes hand-in-hand with the use of CAR-related software like database, spreadsheet, and statistical packages. In fact, proper use of GIS requires a good understanding of these software packages. These findings are also in line with existing diffusions of innovations research. Rogers (1995) talks about the adoption cluster, a process by which people adopt different technologies that may have some form of functional similarity. GIS belongs in a cluster with use of innovations such as Access databases, Excel spreadsheets, and even statistical analysis using either SPSS or SAS. Rogers also talks about the compatibility of new innovations to pre-existing innovations. The in-depth interviews revealed that GIS users also have to master these CAR-related programs. This might increase the reluctance of reporters to learn GIS. Apart from learning GIS, they would now have to master database, spreadsheet, and statistical software too.

52

Even though organizational size was not a significant predictor for the likelihood to adopt GIS, this variable should not be dismissed. It should remain as an important factor related to the diffusion of GIS since the software is costly and requires extensive training and hardware. The results showed that there was not much variance in the circulation figures of the newspapers under study and this might explain why the variable did not turn out to be a predictor of adopting GIS. Literature also shows that resources are an important factor in the adoption of innovations at the organizational level (Agnew 1980). Management has to make decisions on whether to invest money in this software and the relevant training costs. This might be a tough decision given the minimal diffusion of GIS presently. It would still be reasonable to argue that larger newspapers with higher revenues would be more likely to invest in GIS than smaller operations. Although the results from the in-depth interviews indicate that it is easy to get management to invest in new software like GIS, one should note that these interviews were done with reporters who work at relatively large newspapers.

As far as other related software are concerned, fewer reporters use statistical packages than GIS or any other CAR-related tool. Even then, it is not good news for GIS. Only 11% of the respondents used GIS. This stands in stark contrast to the 96% that perform online research, the 76% that use spreadsheet software, or the 56% that use database software. To put these figures in context, the adoption rate for online research in 1994 was 57%. The adoption of spreadsheet software among spreadsheet software has been reported to be as low as 10% in 2000 and that of database software as low as 4% in the same year. Apart from online research, which seems to have reached its full capacity for adoption, database and spreadsheet software adoption are doing quite well, unlike GIS and statistical software.

Statistical software has been around much longer than GIS. However, statistical software has consistently scored low on adoption. In 2000 only 1% of investigative reporters had adopted statistical software (see Table 2). Demand for statistical software has not been very impressive since then either. In 1995 the demand was 1.8% and only 2.5% in 1998. This study showed that in 2005 only 4% of the reporters used statistical software. Like GIS, SAS and SPSS are very technical software. In fact to use SAS or SPSS one needs a good understanding of statistical methodology. One would have to take several statistics classes at the university level to grasp the wider concepts of research methodology. Just like is the case with GIS, journalists do not have the time to attend extra classes to learn statistics.

The indepth-interviews were conducted to get a better understanding of the dynamics involved in the use of GIS in journalism. The results revealed that while GIS is a "technical heavy" software that requires expertise to use, it should not necessarily be out of reach for reporters. Three out of the seven respondents who were interviewed were self-taught GIS users. In fact, only one out of the seven took college classes in GIS. Although this should be taken with guarded optimism, some respondents also painted a very bright future for GIS in journalism. Although GIS is costly, management is willing to invest in it once they get to see its functionality. This gets easier in the case of competing media agencies. If one agency successfully uses GIS, other competing agencies are likely to follow suit and buy the software.

The interviews also revealed that not everybody has to know GIS in order to use it. Some people can just use its products. Reporters can still use GIS maps and map analysis in their work, for example if they were to work in teams involving GIS experts. Some of the case studies described in this paper on GIS and journalism were done on team basis. Not all reporters knew how to use GIS. The easy availability of GIS (map and database) data also could bolster the diffusion of GIS in journalism. As more private and government agencies use GIS, it becomes easier to access relevant data. These are the key factors that will affect the diffusion of GIS in journalism.

Recommendations to Improve Adoption

These results bring about many important questions about how GIS stacks up in comparison to other innovations in journalism (see table 3). Will GIS be another promising technology to fizzle out like videotex? Will GIS ever enjoy such high adoption rates like online research and blogging? As more and more newspapers become more tech-savvy by going online, can any of this rub off on the adoption of GIS? Although GIS might not enjoy the kind of adoption rate that blogging currently enjoys, it will not die out as videotext did. Unlike videotex, GIS has had very humble beginnings. It has been confined to investigative journalism, where it has been used very successfully. Unlike videotex, GIS is not a commercial venture. It is a tool to tell news stories. While it does not revolutionize the newsroom, it enhances the news product. Also, GIS has already been in existence much longer than videotex did. Videotex lasted only three years in the U.S., giving credence to the fact that GIS is already time tested.

It is up to the manufacturers of the software, journalists who already use the software, media managers, and journalism schools to push for the use of GIS. One way manufacturers can help is by using well established marketing principles. One such principle is the use of product samples (O'Guinn, Allen, & Semenik, 1998; Bovee, Thill, & Wood, 1995). This can be done by providing free/sample software. ESRI, the makers of the most popular suite of GIS products, currently offers free evaluation software on its Website. The problem is that they only offer the software for a 30-day evaluation period. Granted that this is a kind gesture, it would be very hard for a novice to master GIS skills in 30 days. ESRI could extend the evaluation period for its sample software to six or eight months. These evaluation licenses should not be limited to potential GIS users; newer versions of GIS can also be extended to seasoned GIS users. This way, users can sample the improved functionality of newer GIS software and this might increase the likelihood to adopt.

Another marketing principle is the use of promotional price packages (O'Guinn, Allen, & Semenik, 1998). As mentioned earlier, GIS is expensive, with single use licenses running up to $1,500. Furthermore, some extension software cost upwards of $2,500. What a price-pack does is offer the software at a reduced price for a limited time. The price-pack also could be extended to certain segments of the industry. ESRI could offer special prices to smaller circulation newspapers. They also could offer reduced academic prices to encourage the use of GIS in journalism schools.

Training seminars oriented towards journalists could be another method to bolster the diffusion of GIS in journalism. The Mapping the News Conference aimed at journalists a positive step towards this goal. This seminar, sponsored jointly by the Association of American Geographers, The National Geographic Society, and ESRI, aims at bringing journalists, geographers, editors, and GIS experts together. It is hoped that the conference will help media organizations use maps in order to improve news reporting for the public. Prior conferences have dealt with a variety of topics on how to use maps when reporting election results, crime, and health stories, among other topics. Editors also get to discuss with geographers and government officials the role of maps in news reporting and how this shapes the meaning and context of news.[14]

Another way to improve the diffusion of GIS in journalism is to expand the curriculum at journalism schools to include GIS in CAR courses. This initiative has emerged in some schools already. NICAR is an endeavor between the University of Missouri School of Journalism and Investigative Reporters and Editors. David Herzog, whose book *Mapping the News (2003)* has been cited extensively in this study, teaches students how to incorporate GIS in news reporting[15] at the Missouri School of Journalism. Even in schools where GIS is not directly taught to journalism

---

[14] More information on the conference can found at:
http://www.esri.com/news/arcnews/summer04articles/mapping-the-news.html
http://www.aag.org/mapnews/

[15] http://journalism.missouri.edu/news/releases/2003/2003-09-10-herzog.html

56

students, journalism departments can organize ways for students to take classes in geography. In fact, the in-depth interviews revealed that some reporters actually get GIS help from the geography departments at different universities.

Advertising in specific publications is another marketing principle that the makers of GIS could use to push GIS into journalism schools (O'Guinn, Allen, & Semenik, 1998; Bovee, Thill, Dovel, & Wood, 1995). ESRI could advertise its GIS products in trade and research journals in order to attract journalism schools and professionals too. ESRI could also send pamphlets to the same schools touting the benefits of using GIS in news reporting. These pamphlets also could detail ways in which cheaper CAR-related tools like database and spreadsheet software could be incorporated with GIS to improve new reporting.

Those journalists who already use GIS can also encourage their colleagues to take an interest in GIS. One of the respondents in the in-depth interviews said that he once downloaded map and census data to his newsroom's server; other reporters who had no previous GIS knowledge where then able to perform simple spatial analysis with these data and produce simple maps. Most of the case studies discussed earlier in this paper indicate the successful use of GIS. It is important to note that most of these projects were done in teams and not everyone on the team knew how to use GIS. Those reporters who know GIS can easily team up with others to perform GIS related tasks.

The applicability of GIS also increases as the number of online newspapers increases. The key lies in the target audience of the online newspaper versus that of the print version. A local or regional newspaper will only reach a limited target audience in its circulation area while its online version will reach a limitless number of readers. This means that reporters could use GIS to do stories and analysis that surpass their local/regional bounds and focus on a national audience. Such analysis need not appear in the print version of the paper, but could appear online to interest a bigger and more varied audience. For example, a reporter could do a story on environmental justice by mapping out the proximity of chemical plants to poor neighbors. If such a relation existed locally, he could also expand this analysis to see if the trend is common in other parts of the country. This kind of story would interest not only the local audiences but also attract a national readership for the online version of the newspaper. This could even have an impact on readership numbers and eventually on revenue.

The fact that GIS would work better for some online stories does not mean that these stories are not suitable for the print version of the newspapers. It just means that online, the story could be more interactive and readers can access multimedia materials that supplement the story. They also get an opportunity to give instant feedback and even engage in public debate with readers from other parts of the country. The online story will also have more space in which to display different maps and map analysis. One map could concentrate just on the problem in one area of the locality, while another could display the problem on a regional and national basis.

GIS Benefits Journalism, Society

It is important to re-emphasize the importance of GIS in journalism. The power of GIS lies in what it can do, and how this can benefit a reporter in his/her work. The capability of GIS to analyze map data is unprecedented; its magic lies in the way it can produce these analyses visually in a way few other software can. The *Miami Herald* demonstrated this functionality when it used GIS to analyze the damage patterns from Hurricane Andrew. Without spatial analysis, it would have been very difficult to analyze and visualize the wind patterns against the property damage patterns. Similarly, the *Philadelphia Inquirer* investigated the relationship between drunken driving and liquor establishments. This is just another example showcasing the uniqueness of GIS in news reporting. These types of patterns and phenomena would be less discreet with other analysis tools.

This study also gives an insight into the potential effect of GIS on public debate and public policy. As described earlier, the two most successful uses of GIS in journalism at the *Miami Herald* and the *Philadelphia Inquirer* demonstrate that even with limited use, GIS can greatly affect public life. The *Inquirer* story led to heated public debate on the change of alcohol testing levels. People use the *Inquirer's* online forum to post their reaction to the story. This debate was not lost to the lawmakers as they finally adopted a new blood alcohol level of .08. In Dade County, authorities tightened housing codes for contractors after the *Herald* ran the story on Hurricane Andrew. One should picture the impact that these kind of stories even with a moderate use of GIS in journalism.

Summary

This study set out to predict the future of the diffusion of GIS in journalism. Figure 10 gives a good description of this future trend. GIS might not enjoy the adoption rates like those of online research, database software, or spreadsheet software. It will however diffuse much quicker than statistical software. In 1998 the demand for mapping software stood at 14% (see table 1). This study found that only 11% of the reporters sampled used GIS. In a period of seven (1998-2005) years, the 14% demand rate has resulted in an 11% adoption rate. In 2000 the adoption rate for GIS stood at 1% (see table 2). This means that in a five-year period adoption of GIS jumped tenfold. Assuming that all other factors remain constant, 20% of the reporters in the journalism industry will have adopted GIS by the year 2010. This will put the diffusion of GIS at least in the initial stages of the early majority stage (see figure 7).

The only way that this diffusion rate can be speeded up is if there are heavy promotional efforts by the manufactures and the introduction of GIS in the curriculum at the journalism schools. As mentioned earlier, the reporters who already use GIS could also become change agents at their respective newspapers. If these factors come into play then maybe the adoption of GIS will move from the early adopters' stage that it is in right now to the latter part of the early majority stage within the next decade. The early majority stage requires an adoption rate of at least 34%.

As stated earlier, this study may also inform those who are interested in the applied aspect of GIS and journalism. The in-depth interviews depict the use of GIS from the viewpoint of the journalists. These interviews reveal what it takes to be a GIS expert and what one has to learn and do to achieve this. The interviewees attended seminars, taught themselves to use the software, combined the use of CAR-related tools with GIS among other things. The interviews also tell us what it takes to improve the diffusion of GIS at the organizational level. Editors, who are the key decision-makers at the newspapers, have to be shown the functionality of this software in order for them to invest in it.

CHAPTER 6: CONCLUSIONS

The results send a mixed message about the diffusion of GIS in journalism. While a majority of reporters are aware of GIS, very few have taken up the use of this software. As stated earlier, the nature of GIS makes it a "hard" tool to learn and use. This alone is enough to discourage reporters from learning the software. They will have to attend lengthy seminars to learn the software and probably most reporters are not disposed to do this, given the nature of their work and the deadlines that they have to meet daily. GIS also comes with extensions. These are add-on programs that enhance its functionality. Even seasoned GIS users have to attend more seminars to learn these extensions.

The diffusion of GIS is still in its early stages. The adoption curves in figure 10 show that at best, GIS is still at the early adopters' stage, or at the very initial stage of the diffusion process. This stage is marked by a limited use of an innovation. Currently the awareness level of the software in journalism is high. This is positive indication but it should be viewed with guarded optimism. Probably most reporters are familiar with its unprecedented functionality in spatial analysis. Perhaps they just don't have the time to attend GIS seminars. Even with the cost factors, the in-depth interviews revealed that reluctant managers can be swayed into purchasing the software once its functionality is demonstrated to them. Competition among media agencies is another factor that will bolster the diffusion of GIS in journalism. Once one media agency successfully uses it, others will likely follow suit. Even for those reporters who don't know how to use the software, there is a high probability that they can still use GIS products. They can use GIS maps for news and analysis, or even perform simple spatial analysis under the guidance of veteran GIS users.

This study takes a pioneering look into the diffusion of GIS in journalism. Some of the findings in this study are fairly standard to the diffusions research. Demographics have been shown to dictate the adoption of innovations. However, the study also showed that the field of journalism might be unique in some ways. The study revealed that level of education might not be a determining factor in the field of journalism, since there is little variation as far as education is concerned. Most journalists have an undergraduate degree or better.

More importantly, this study advances the diffusion of innovations theory by comparing the diffusion of different innovations in the field of journalism. It starts by focusing on GIS and then expands to the diffusion of other innovations like CAR-related software, videotex, online research, etc. This simultaneous examination of myriad innovations in journalism offers new insights that result in theoretical additions to the model. Diffusions theory states that the adoption process of most innovations takes the form of a cumulative S-shaped curve. This study uses this cumulative curve to describe and predict the diffusion patterns of different innovations in the field of journalism. However, the findings regarding the diffusion of GIS and similar software, such as statistical packages, show a slower rate of adoption. Some innovations, such as online research and word processing take a much steeper curve with its rapid rate of adoption. This suggests that a multi-curve process offers a better explication of the theory than the single curve that currently exists. The multi-curve graph as illustrated in figure 10 gives a new depiction of the adoption of innovations in journalism.

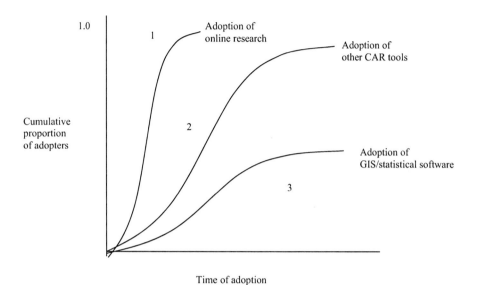

1.0

Cumulative
proportion
of adopters

1

2

3

Adoption of
online research

Adoption of
other CAR tools

Adoption of
GIS/statistical software

Time of adoption

Figure 10: Prediction of the Adoption of GIS, other CAR-related tools, Statistical Software, and Online Research in Journalism.

The figure shows that while the adoption of most innovations still may take an S-shape, the slopes for different innovations vary. This may be due to the complexity of different innovations. Diffusion of innovations theory postulates that complexity affects adoption (Rogers, 1995), but this contingent condition is not reflected in the normal S-curve. For example, the adoption of online research takes a steep curve while that of statistical software and GIS takes a much flatter curve. While it is easy for a reporter to conduct online research, it is much harder for him/her to do statistical analysis without having taken research methodology classes probably at the university level.

Another new construct this study adds to the diffusions theory is the idea of applicability of an innovation. Applicability refers to the extent and the ease with which different reporters can put a software to use in order to enhance their work. For example, online research has much more applicability than does GIS or statistical analysis. Almost every type of reporter, from business to sports to features, can make use of online searches. Online research requires little training – a colleague can show the novice how to do this a time or two and then the novice needs only a little bit of practice. It requires no time away from the office to master. Furthermore, online research can take as little as five minutes to complete; reporters can determine how much time they spend searching online, which fits well with a deadline-oriented job. With a 96% adoption rate, online research has almost reached its full adoption capacity. GIS and statistical software, on the other hand, have much less applicability. These two pieces of software are only likely to be used by an investigative reporter, thus limiting their utility to other kinds of reporters. GIS and statistical software require considerable training that cannot be accomplished in the newsroom; multi-day training seminars and possibly even semester-long college courses are needed to fully understand the applications and their use. Furthermore, a reporter must block out large chunks of time in order to conduct a statistical or GIS analysis – hours and hours over several days is common. This stands in stark contrast to the flexibility of online searches, which can take five minutes, or five hours, depending upon the reporter's needs and available time. What this means is that those innovations with wider applicability will have steeper S-curves. Also, the study shows that some software like GIS might not attain 100% adoption rates, but might never die out like videotex.

This theoretical process is posited to apply to the adoption of other kinds of innovations, not just GIS. The addition of steeper and slower curves to the normal S-curve, along with the explication of contingent conditions that will determine which curve an innovation takes, and the addition of the concept of applicability help enlarge the theoretical framework of diffusion theory. This gives us a better specified theory with greater ability to predict and explain the adoption of different kinds of innovations.

Recommendations for Future Research

Presently there is a paucity of literature that can guide researchers who examine the use and diffusion of GIS in journalism. In fact this study is a pioneer in that sense. The lessons learned while conducting this study will help related research in the future. Researchers should look at how the new cumulative S-curve described in this study can be applied to other technologies in journalism. Replication of these findings with other innovations will be necessary to test and expand this theoretical addition to diffusion of innovations models.

In addition, future studies can alleviate some of the difficulties encountered here. The nature of this study made it difficult to attain high response rates. The fact that respondents in the Web survey were asked in detail about the kinds of software they currently use and if they are likely to adopt GIS gave them the impression that it was a marketing ploy disguised as an academic study. The proliferation of junk and spam e-mail may be another contributing factor. This fact did not become apparent until the data collection process was well underway. This was deduced from the e-mail responses to reminders sent to those respondents who had not completed the surveys. Some of these responses are listed below:

Quotation 1:
"I did not think it was an attempt to sell me anything. I was questioning the purpose of information you are gathering. It looks more like a marketing survey than an academic survey of journalistic methods."

Quotation 2:
"Ben, this research seems more like a disguised sales pitch."

Quotation 3:
"I was more concerned that the survey appears to be geared toward information for marketing purposes than for the study of journalism. I have been advised not to participate in the survey."

Quotation 4:
"I took at face value your statement that this was not a marketing survey. You'll pardon me if I say it certainly read like one. What possible academic interest would anyone have in whether I'd be willing to try a certain kind of tool of very limited utility to a reporter on a trial basis? That sounds fairly close to a cold sales call to this reporter."

In the future, researchers should take extra steps in allaying these fears among the respondents. Another way of reducing this problem is to use a mixed-mode of data collection as described by Czaja and Blair (1996). This means that researchers could use mail surveys for those respondents who are not comfortable with online surveys. Telephone surveys can also be used to supplement online and mail surveys. Due to time and financial constraints, the mixed-mode method was not used in this study.

The study only looked at reporters in general. Future studies could focus mainly on the decision-makers like the management in different media houses. After all, it is their final decision when it comes to buying new software. Such a study would reveal if there is a disjunction between management and reporters as far as the adoption of GIS is concerned. Even though the diffusion of GIS is still at a very young stage it still has the potential of enhancing news reporting. As described earlier in the case studies, it would be very difficult to map out certain trends and interactions without map data. This, added to the power to visualize data, makes GIS an unprecedented tool to analyze trends and report news.

REFERENCES

Agnew, J. A. (1980). (ed.). *Innovation research and public policy.* Syracuse, NY: Department of Geography, University of Syracuse.

Atkin, D. (1995). Audio information services and the electronic media environment. *The Information Society. 11(1),* 75-83.

Berwick, Donald M. (2003). Disseminating innovations in healthcare. *Journal of the American Medical Association. 289 (15),* 1969-1975.

Breslin, P., Frunzi, N. Napoleon, E. & Ormsby, T. (1999). *Getting to know ArcView GIS. The geographic information system (GIS) for everyone.* Redlands, CA: ESRI Press.

Bovee, C.L., Thill, J.V., Dovel, G.P., & Wood, M.B. (1995). *Advertising excellence.* NY: McGraw Hill.

Brown, L. A. (1981). *Innovation diffusion: a new perspective.* NY: Methuen.

Cohen, J. & Cohen, P. (1983). *Applied multiple regression/correlation analysis for the behavioral sciences.* (2nd ed.). Hillsdale, NJ: Lawrence Erlbaum Associates.

Columbia Journalism Review. (2003). Emerging alternatives. A Brief History of Weblogs. Retrieved July, 29, 2005 from http://www.cjr.org/issues/2003/5/blog-jensen.asp

Couper, M.P. (2000). Web survey: A review of issues and approaches. *Public Opinion Quarterly. 64(4),* 464-494.

Couper, M.P., Traugott, M.W., & Lamias, M.J. (2001). Web survey design and administration. *Public Opinion Quarterly. 65(2),* 230-253.

Cox, A.B. & Gifford, F. (1997). An overview to geographical information systems. *Journal of Academic Librarianship. 23(6),* 449-461.

Crispell, D. (1994,February). Computers at home. *American Demographics. 16(2),* 59.

Curtin, R., Presser, S., & Singer, E. (2000). The effects of response rate changes on the index of consumer confidence. *Public Opinion Quarterly. 64(4),* 413-428.

Czaja, R. & Blair, J. (1996). Designing surveys. *A guide to decisions and procedures.* Thousand Oaks, CA: Pine Forge Press.

Davis, F.D., Bagozzi, R.P., & Warshaw, P.R. (1992). Extrinsic and intrinsic motivations to use computers in the workplace. *Journal of Applied Social Psychology. 22(14),* 1111-1132.

DeFleur, M.H. & Ball-Rokeach, S. (1975). *Theories of mass communication.* NY: McKay.

DeFleur, M.H. (1997). *Computer-assisted investigative reporting.* Mahwah, NJ: Lawrence Erlbaum Associates, Publishers.

Dillman, D.A. (2000). *Mail and Internet surveys: The tailored design method.* (2nd ed.). Wiley: NY

Dillman, D.A. & Bowker, D.K. (2001). The Web questionnaire challenge to survey methodologists. In U. Reips & M. Bosnjak.(Eds.), *Dimensions of Internet Science.* Lengerich, Germany: Pabst Science Publishers.

Dillman, D. A., Tortora, R. D., and Bowker, .D.K. (1998). Principles for constructing Web surveys. *(SESRC Technical Report, 98-50).* Pullman, Washington

Dominelli, A. (2003). Web surveys – benefits and considerations. *Clinical Research and Regulatory Affairs. 20(4),* 409-416

ESRI (2002). GIS and journalism: Serious tools for serious storytelling, Retrieved November, 30, 2004, from http://www.esri.com/library/brochures/pdfs/journalism_gis_bro.pdf

Fahmy, S. & Smith C. Z. (2003). Photographers note digital's advantages, disadvantages. *Newspaper Research Journal. 24(2),* 82-95.

Finberg H. I. (2003). Before the Web, there was viewtron. Retrieved July, 29, 2005 from http://www.poynter.org/content/content_print.asp?id=52769&custom=

Foxall, G. R., & Bhate, S. (1991). Psychology of computer use: XIX. Extent of computer use: Relationship with adaptive-innovative cognitive style and personal involvement in computing. *Perceptual and Motor Skills: 72 (1),* 195-202.

Garrison, B. (1995). *Computer-assisted reporting.* Hillsdale, NJ: Lawrence Erlbaum Associates.

Garrison, B. (2001). Computer assisted reporting near complete adoption. *Newspaper Research Journal. 22(1),* 65-79.

Goodchild, M.F. (2000). The current status of GIS and spatial analysis. *Journal of Geographical Systems. 2(10),* 5-10.

Herzog, D. (2003). *Mapping the news. Case studies in journalism.* Redlands, CA: ESRI Press.

Kaplowitz, M.D. & Hadlock, T.D & Levine, R. (2004). A comparison of Web and mail surveys responses rates. *Public Opinion Quarterly. 68(10),* 94-101.

Keeter, S., Miller, C., Kohut, A., Groves, M., & Presser, S. (2000). Consequences of reducing nonresponse in a national telephone survey. *Public opinion Quarterly, 64 (2),* 125-148.

Krendl, K. A., Brohier, M. C., & Fleetwood, C. (1989). Children and computers: Do sex-related differences persist? *Journal of Communication. 39(3),* 85-93.

LaRose, R. & Atkin, D. (1992). Audiotext and the re-invention of the telephone as a mass medium. *Journalism Quarterly. 69(2),* 413-421.

Lin, C.A. (1994). Exploring potential factors for home videotext adoption. In J. Hanson (Ed.), *Advances in Telematics.* Vol. 2 pp. 111-121.

Lin, C.A. (1998). Exploring personal computer adoption dynamics. *Journal of Broadcasting and Electronic Media. 42(1),* 95-111.

Maier, S. (2000). Digital diffusion in the newsroom. The uneven advance of computer-assisted-reporting. *Newspaper Research Journal. 21(2),* 95-110.

Martin, S. (2003). MDs office Internet use hits 57%. *Canadian Medical Association Journal. 164(4),* 475

McCabe, S. E. (2004). Comparison of Web and mail surveys in collecting illicit drug use data: a randomized experiment. *Journal of Drug Education. 34(1),* 61-72.

Meyer, P. (1973). *Precision journalism.* Bloomington, IN: Indiana University Press.

Moghdam, D. (1978). *Computers in newspaper publishing. User oriented systems.* NY: Marcel Dekker Inc.

O'Guinn, T.C., Allen, C.T, & Semenik, R.J. (1998). *Advertising.* Cincinnati, OH: South-Western College Publishing.

Porter, S.R. & Whitcomb, M.E. (2003). The impact of contact type on Web survey response rates. *Public Opinion Quarterly. 67(4),* 579-588.

Reissman, J. (1990). Gender inequality in computing. *Computer Literacy in Human Services Education: 3,* 45-63.

Robertson, T. S. (1971). *Innovative behavior and communication.* NY: Holt, Rinehart, and Winston, Inc.

Rogers, E. M. & F. Floyd Shoemaker,. (1971). *Communication of diffusions: a cross cultural approach.* (2nd ed.). NY: The Free Press.

Rogers, E.M. (2004). A prospective and retrospective look at the diffusion model. *Journal of Health Communication. 9 (supplement 1),* 13-19.

Rogers, E. M. (1962). *Diffusion of innovations.* NY: The Free Press.

Rogers, E. M. (1995). *Diffusion of innovations.* (4th ed.). NY: The Free Press.
Ryan, B. & Gross, N. C. (1943). "The diffusion of hybrid seed corn in two Iowa communities." *Rural Sociology. 8,* 15-24

Schaefer, D.R. & Dillman, D.A. (1998). Development of a standard e-mail methodology. Results of an experiment. *Public Opinion Quarterly. 62(3),* 378-397.

Shedden, D. (2005). New Media Timeline (1969-2004) Retrieved July, 29, 2005, from http://poynter.org/content/content_view.asp?id=75953

Schultz, B. E. (2002). The effect of age and background of religious broadcasting executives on digital television implementation. *Journal of Media and Religion. 1(4),* 217-229.

Scott, M. (2000). Digital diffusion in the newsrooms: The uneven advance of computer-assisted-reporting. *Newspaper Research Journal. 21(2),* 95-110.

Sheehan, K.B. & McMillan, S.J. (1999). Response variation in e-ail surveys: An explanation. *Journal of Advertising Research. 39(4),* 45-54.

Technorati.com (2005). About Technorati: Currently tracking 14.2 million sites and 1.3 billion links. Retrieved August, 2, 2005, from http://technorati.com/about/

Torangeau, R., Steiger, D.M., & Wilson, D. (2002). Self-administered questionnaires by telephone: Evaluating interactive voice response. *Public Opinion Quarterly. 66(2),* 265-278.

Vaughan, P. W. & Rogers, E. M.. (2000). A staged model of communication effects: evidence from an entertainment-education radio soap opera in Tanzania. *Journal of health communication. 5(3),* 203-227

Van Slyke, C. Comunale, C. L., & Belanger, F. (2002). Gender differences in perceptions of web-based shopping *Communications of the ACM. 45(8),* 82-86.

Weaver, D.H., Beam, R., Brownlee, B., Voakes, P.S., & Wilhoit, G.C. (2003). *The Face and Mind of the American Journalist.* Retrieved June 15, 2005, from www.poynter.org/content/content_view.asp?id=28778

Wikipedia. (2005)[a]. Videotex. Retrieved July, 29, 2005, from http://en.wikipedia.org/wiki/Videotext

Wikipedia. (2005) [b]. Weblog. Retrieved July, 29, 2005 from http://en.wikipedia.org/wiki/Blogs#Precursors

Wimmer, R.D. & Dominick, J.R. (2000). *Mass media research. An introduction.* (6th ed.). Belmont, CA: Wadsworth Publishing Company.

APPENDIX A: IN-DEPTH INTERVIEW QUESTIONNAIRE

Hi. My name is Ben Wasike from Louisiana State University. I sent you an e-mail earlier about a project I'm doing on the use of GIS in journalism. Is this a good time to talk?

It seems that not too many journalists are using GIS in their news gathering tasks, despite the fact that some (including you) have successfully used GIS in their work. As you are aware, GIS provides journalists with a powerful method by which to map out and visualize data in an unprecedented manner.

1. How did you first learn about GIS?

2. How did you learn GIS:

3. What encouraged you to use GIS in your work?

4. Do you still use GIS in your work?

5. Did your newspaper already use GIS when you started working there?

6. How many other people at your newspaper use GIS?

7. What GIS software do you use?

8. What version of GIS software is that?

    a. If using older version: when do you/your newspaper plan to upgrade

9. What GIS extensions do you use?

10. What other computer software do you use in conjunction with GIS?

    a. Do you use any statistical analysis software?

        i. Which one(s)

    b. Do you use any Spreadsheet software?

        i. Which one(s)?

11. In general do you keep up with technological development?

12. Do you use any of the following electronic gadgets?

    a. Cell phones

b. Text messaging

c. Instant messaging

d. Blogs

e. GPS equipment

f. Pagers

g. Any others?

13. In general, what are the problems you have encountered in the use of GIS:

a. Data availability

   i. Is it easy to get relevant maps?

b. Is it easy to get outside help when using extensions that you re not familiar with?

14. What is your view on the future of GIS in journalism?

a. How receptive are other journalists that you know to learning GIS?

b. Overall do you management at different newspapers are willing to invest in GIS?

c. In your opinion what would tale for more journalists to use GIS?

d. Do you think GIS will be a major instrument for investigative journalism in the future?

APPENDIX B: WEB SURVEY QUESTIONNAIRE

Hello:

Thank you for accessing this survey. This survey is in no way an attempt to sell anything. It is an academic survey about the diffusion and use of new technologies in journalism. The purpose of the research is to determine the types of tools/technologies that reporters use in the field of journalism.

The questions are very general in nature and query you on the types on technologies/devices you use in your reporting work. As stated earlier, this is purely academic research, and your responses are confidential. The survey should take an average of three minutes to complete.

In accordance to the Louisiana State University's IRB (Institutional Review Board) requirements, I have included a consent form (below). This form explains the names of the researchers, privacy and confidentiality issues, etc.

Investigators: The following investigators are available for questions about this study (M-F, 9:00 a.m. - 4:30 p.m.)

Ben S. Wasike, Ph.D. 956-544-6681/ ben.wasike@hotmail.com

Renita Coleman, Ph.D. rcoleman@lsu.edu

*Denotes Principal Investigator

Risks: No apparent risks are expected to occur.

Right to Refuse: Subjects may elect not to participate in the study or to withdraw from the study at any time without penalty or loss of any benefit to which they might otherwise be entitled.

Privacy: Results of the study may be published, but no names or identifying information will be included in the publication. Subject identity will remain confidential unless disclosure is required by law.

Signatures: The study has been described to me. I understand that additional questions regarding the study should be directed to investigators listed above. I understand that if I have questions about subjects' rights, or other concerns, I can contact Dr. Robert Mathews, Institutional Review Board, (225) 578-8692.

I agree to participate in the study described above and acknowledge the investigator's obligation to provide me with a signed copy of this consent form.

Does your newspaper use any of the following mapping software?

ArcGIS

ArcView

MapInfo

Atlas GIS

Map Publisher

None

Don't Know

Other _____

Do you use any of the following database software?

Access

Lotus Pro

None

Other _____

Do you use any of the following statistical packages?

SPSS

SAS

None

Other

Do you use any of the following spreadsheet software?

Excel

Lotus 1-2-3

Quattro Pro

None

Other

How often do you use online research to supplement reporting?

Daily

Weekly

Monthly

Less than monthly

Never

Do you use any of the following? (Check all that apply).

Cell phones

Text messaging

Instant messaging

Blogs

GPS equipment

Pagers

PDAs

Other

Have you ever heard of Geographical Information Systems (GIS)?

Yes

No

Have you used GIS in your work?

Yes

No

What is the main reason that you have not used GIS in your work?

Do you currently use GIS in your work

Yes

No

What is the main reason that you stopped using GIS in your work?

What specific tasks do you use GIS for

Do you know someone who can help you in the use of GIS?

Yes

No

Does anyone else at your newspaper use GIS?

Yes

No

If you answered yes above, please provide the names of the other people that use GIS at your newspaper:

Reporters use GIS software to digitally analyze maps and to produce graphical visualizations of news and other phenomena. Using a scale of 1 -7 where 1 means not at all likely and 7 mean very likely:

How likely would you be interested in learning more about GIS?

1   2   3   4   5   6   7

If you had the opportunity to learn this software how likely would you be willing to use this software on a trial/evaluation basis?

1   2   3   4   5   6   7

If you had the opportunity to learn this software how likely would you be willing to use this software on a permanent basis?

1   2   3   4   5   6   7

What newspaper do you work for?

In what year were you born?

What is your gender?

      Male

      Female

What is the highest level of education you have completed so far?

      Less than high school

      High school

      Some college

      Undergraduate degree

      Graduate degree

What most closely describes your job position?

Reporter

Editor

Graphic designer

Other _____

DATE DUE	RETURNED

LaVergne, TN USA
31 March 2010

177790LV00003B/12/A

9 783836 436113